American Hungarian
Relations 1918-1944

MARK IMRE MAJOR, Ph. D.

American Hungarian Relations 1918-1944

BY

Mark Imre Major, Ph. D.

Danubian Press, Inc. Astor, Florida, 32002, 1974

ISBN: 0—87934—036—3
Library of Congress Catalog Card No.: 74—80001

REPRINT BY HUNYADI M M K
HAMILTON, ONTARIO
1991

Printed in Canada by Patria Publishing Co. Ltd.
6 Alcina Avenue, Toronto, Ontario M6G 2E8

TABLE OF CONTENTS

PREFACE

The first Hungarian ever to set foot on the soil of the New World was a sixteenth century humanist and Protestant scholar, Stephanus Parmenius Budaeus. He accompanied Sir Humphrey Gilbert to Newfoundland in 1583 to acquire "any remote, barbarous and heathen lands" by the command of Queen Elizabeth of England. Parmenius was born in the fortified capital of Hungary, Buda, then in Turkish hands. Seeking education abroad, like many other Hungarian youths, he went to Oxford and to London, where the famous collector of autographs, Master Hakluyt, introduced him to Sir Humphrey. Upon his arrival in Newfoundland, Parmenius wrote to Hakluyt, but this was the last word heard from him, as he was shipwrecked on the return voyage. Among those who were lost, wrote Captain Haie, "was drowned a learned man, a Hungarian, born in the city of Buda, called thereof Budaeus, who in piety and zeal to good attempts, adventured in this action, minding to record in the Latin tongue, the **gesta** and things worthy of remembrance, happening in this discovery, to the honor of our nation.(1)

Stephanus Parmenius Budaeus wished to report to the European nations an unknown, new world, about which contemporary Hungarians knew hardly more than that it had been discovered "for the great glory of Christianity."(2) After the passage of

---

1 Quoted in Dominic G. Kosáry, **A History of Hungary** (Cleveland and New York: Benjamin Franklin Bibliophile Society, 1941), p. xvi.

2 Istvánffy (1583—1615), **Historia Regni Hungarici**, p. 16, quoted in Kosáry, **ibid.**

7

centuries, however, the situation of that unknown, new world has undergone a tremendous change. The United States of America embracing half of the North American continent from coast to coast, has become one of the great powers of the world and has become involved in the affairs of remote countries. This study, the result of the author's research in the Library of Congress and in the National Archives of the United States, is concerned with her involvement in Hungary's political, cultural, and economic life between the world wars.

Examining this period of Hungary's history, however, one comes across problems that were correlated with specific conditions pertaining to the whole of East Central Europe. Therefore it was necessary, for the sake of better understanding, to draw the reader's attention to the aspects not only of Hungary's problems, but also of those of East Central Europe, during the period mentioned above.

The key to the understanding of the Hungarian policy after World War I is Hungary's attitude toward the Treaty of Trianon. This treaty, imposed on Hungary at the close of World War I, in effect destroyed the historic Hungarian state. Although ethnically not homogeneous, for a thousand years Hungary had occupied the whole Carpathian Basin. In 1920, the North of this area was assigned to the state of Czechoslovakia, the South to the Serb-Croat-Slovene Kingdom, the East to Rumania, and a strip along the western frontier to the Republic of Austria. Even Poland and Italy received fragments of former Hungarian territory. This dismemberment of Hungary was carried out in the name of national self-determination, yet many concessions were made to the strategic and economic interests of the successor states. As a result, these states acquired no less than three and a half million persons, listed in the Hungarian census of 1910 as Hungarians by their mother tongue. As a result of this, the whole Hungarian nation was united in its conviction that the Trianon Treaty was unacceptable and the chief aspiration of Hungarian foreign policy was treaty revision. Therefore, Hungarian foreign policy followed with great attention how America and Americans —as well as the other nations—reacted to this desire, and neither cultural nor economic relations between the two countries were entirely free from the wish to gain American help for the purpose of treaty revision.

I owe my deepest thanks to each of the following persons: Professor John W. Bohon of Texas Christian University, for his numerous and valuable suggestions: Professors Nevin Neal and Maurice Boyd, both of Texas Christian University, for their helpful comments; Dr. Elemér Bakó and Dr. William Solyom-Fekete, Librarians of the Library of Congress, for their indispensable advice.

CHAPTER I

HUNGARY:
HISTORICAL INTRODUCTION

No state in European history has a beginning so precisely definable as that of Hungary. It was brought into being when the Magyars crossed the Carpathians in 896 and settled in the basin of the middle Danube. The chieftain Árpád led the first Magyars into the Carpathian basin, and he gave his name to the first great Hungarian dynasty, which ruled until 1301.

For the next half-century the Magyars were the scourge of Europe, which they raided far and wide. Their lithe, little horses outdistanced any news of their coming. Historians have counted thirty-three expeditions between 898 and 955, some of them to places as far afield as Bremen, Cambrai, Orleans, Nimes, Otranto, and Constantinople. Most of these raids were simply profitmaking expeditions, in which cities and churches were ransacked for gold and treasure.

In this half-century they inflicted dreadful damage on Europe, but this mode of life was not without risks. Arnulf of Bavaria almost annihilated one of their armies in 917 and in 933 Henry the Fowler gave them a frightful beating near Merseburg. Finally, in 955, Otto the Great inflicted a terrible defeat outside Augsburg. Their leaders were taken, hanged, and according to legend, only seven of the whole host escaped.

Duke Géza (972-997) broke with his father's policy and sent ambassadors to Otto's court. With the establishment of friendly relations the raids in the West ceased. Henry III consented to the marriage of his sister, Gisella, to Géza's son, Vajk, who had already been baptized under the name of Stephen. The marriage took place in 996. A year later Géza died.

St. Stephen (proclaimed a saint in 1083) was the real founder of the Hungarian Kingdom and perhaps the most important figure in Hungarian history. He ruled from 997 to 1038 and established direct contacts with Pope Sylvester II, who favored him with special temporal and spiritual privileges. The Pope sent him a crown and granted him the title of Apostle, presumably in recognition of his conversion of many souls to Christianity. The coronation took place on Christmas Day in 1000. Henceforth, Hungary became an outpost of the West against the East. The Pope gave Stephen and his successors the right to found episcopal sees, and Hungary was made independent of German ecclesiastical control. The Hungarian king appointed bishops, abbots, and other ecclesiastical dignitaries, simply informing the Pope of his choice. Thus, the bitter conflict over lay investiture which developed between the Pope and West European rulers was unknown in Hungary. When the Benedictines entered Hungary, their monasteries became not only centers of religion, but also centers of Western civilization. The monks cleared the lands, introduced Western methods of agriculture, and became the first teachers. St. Stephen's successors were known as Apostolic Kings of Hungary and the Holy Crown of St. Stephen became a symbol of the Hungarian nation.

St. Stephen also brought about internal reforms which shaped Hungarian history. Instead of organizing his kingdom on a feudal basis, he divided the realm into counties administrated by counts, after the fashion of Charlemagne's Empire. These counties became not only important units of administration, but also the foundations of local autonomy and self-government. The free men met in county assemblies, and eventually the counties sent deputies to the Diet. The counties continued to play an important role until very recent times, and the history of the development of Hungarian government is rooted in the county organization.

Three thirteenth century events deeply influenced Hungarian history. One was the granting of the Golden Bull of 1222 to the nation by the king. This was a charter of liberties, not unlike the Magna Charta of 1215 in England. Like the latter, the Golden Bull has been variously interpreted, but it has always been considered one of the cornerstones of the Hungarian Constitution.

The second development was that the kings welcomed immigrants and brought in large groups of Germans, who worked the gold mines of the Zips and settled in the border province of Transylvania. It was normal procedure to grant such foreign groups special privileges, and the thirteenth century brought a grant of extensive privileges to the "Saxons" of Transylvania (1224), who established an island of German culture and maintained their special position until the dislocations of World War II. They developed seven important municipal centers and were often referred to as the "Siebenburgen Saxons." At the time of the Reformation they became Lutherans and, along with some Slovak groups, were the chief representatives of that faith in Hungary.

The thirteenth century also saw the great Mongol invasion of 1241, which left the country devastated. Fortunately, the Mongols did not long remain.

The Árpád dynasty come to an end in 1301, and the nobles elected Charles I of Anjou (1301-1342) as their sovereign. He proved to be an able ruler and paved the way for the reign of Louis the Great (1342-1382), under whom Hungary came to the peak of its power. Louis the Great was an able administrator. He encouraged trade, granted many municipal charters, and founded the first Hungarian University at Pécs. Louis was also elected King of Poland and ruled over a vast empire which extended from the middle Vistula to the Adriatic and deep into the Balkans. The union of the Hungarian and Polish crowns was repeated again in the late Middle Ages, and at times there was also a union with the Bohemian crown.

When the Ottoman Turks began their march northward in the Balkan Peninsula, Hungary's location made her a natural leader in the attempt to block the expansion of the Turks to Western Europe. The popes encouraged the Hungarian kings to undertake a number of crusades. Sigismund I, who ruled Hungary from 1387 to 1437, and who also reigned as Holy Roman Emperor and King of Bohemia, for a time held off the Turks. His activity in the council of Constance, which ended the schism in the Church, as well as his attempt to suppress the Hussite heresy, were at least in part designed to unite Western Christendom in a common front against the new Eastern menace. Time and time again the Hungarians fought the battles of the West, and John Hunyadi won fame for his victories over the Turks.

The country enjoyed a period of prosperity and glory under Hunyadi's son, Mathias Corvinus, who ruled from 1458 to 1490. Mathias Corvinus was a patron of Renaissance learning and did much to advance the intellectual life of his kingdom. He founded a university at Pozsony (Pressburg) and revived the universities at Pécs and Buda. Corvins also organized a strong, efficient mercenary army. He stressed the light cavalry and thus originated the famous Hungarian hussars. He too was able to keep the Turks at bay: in addition he advanced to the west, winning control over parts of Austria and Bohemia.

On August 29, 1526, the Hungarians were defeated at Mohács by Suleiman the Magnificient. Louis Jagello, King of Hungary and Bohemia, perished with his whole army. The Sultan swept on to Buda, from which he returned to Constantinople, taking a tremendous booty and some 105,000 captives. This was the most tragic period of Hungarian history. The Turkish invasion devastated the country and led to one and a half centuries of partition. The Turks lorded over the heart of the country and reduced it to a near-desert. The Habsburgs held the western part of Hungary, while national independence survived only in Transylvania. These were also the years of the Reformation, and Protestant doctrines swept across Hungary. It was, however, the

Reformed doctrines of Calvinism that appealed to the Magyars, for Lutheranism was associated with German influence. The first legislative declaration in the world in favor of the free profession of religions was made in Hungary. The Declaration of the Diet of Torda (1557) read as follows: "Everyone may follow the faith he wishes, but he must not hurt those of other faiths."

Following their defeat at Vienna in 1683, the Turks had to abandon Hungary. To populate and defend the territories freed from the Turks, the Habsburgs started a vigorous policy of colonization. Immigrants and settlers came from all over Europe. Germans and Slovaks were settled in the southern regions. Many Serbs sought refuge from Turkish rule and were welcomed as settlers in the newly acquired southern territories.

The reconquest of Hungary also revived the old feuds with the Habsburg Empire. Francis Rákóczi headed a large armed movement of protest against Habsburg domination from Vienna. In order to obtain international recognition the Hungarian Diet proclaimed the dethronement of the House of Habsburg and elected Rákóczi Ruling Prince. Rákóczi's troops occupied most of Hungary. However, when the Habsburg army was released from the War of Spanish Succession, the long insurrection (1703-1711) was suppressed. A truce was arranged in 1711. Charles III persuaded the Hungarian Diet in 1723 to accept the Pragmatic Sanction which proclaimed that in default of male heirs, a female might inherit the throne. In return for this loyalty, the Habsburg agreed to preserve intact the Hungarian constitution with all its rights, laws, privileges, and customs.

The reforms of Joseph II (1780-1790) were a drastic effort to create uniformity in the administration of the Habsburg lands. But the Hungarians were able to maintain historic Hungarian customs, and Hungary retained its separateness. This continued even after the Habsburgs proclaimed themselves emperors of an Austrian Empire and the Holy Roman Empire was dissolved (1806). To the Hungarians, the emperor remained simply King of Hungary.

In the 1840's the rising revolutionary spirit swept across Europe, reaching Austria as well as Hungary. The leaders of the Hungarian reform movement, Stephen Széchenyi and Louis Kossuth, pressed Emperor Ferdinand I for substantially greater constitutional concessions. In 1848, the political tension erupted in the War of Independence, which was suppressed only with the intervention of Russia. The Habsburgs placed Hungary under martial law. Thirteen leading generals, Louis Batthyány, Prime Minister of independent Hungary, and many other patriots were either shot or hanged. Others took refuge abroad.

The new emperor, Francis Joseph I, attempted to rule Hungary from Vienna under a policy of centralization, known from its originator as the "Bach System." Alexander Bach, the Regent of the Emperor, staffed his administration with German and Czech officials from Bohemia, who did not know the language of the people, and German became the official language. The Magyars refused to cooperate.

The Compromise of 1867 established the Dual Monarchy of Austria-Hungary. Thus the Compromise recognized Hungary's constitutional status after a struggle of three centuries.

There were henceforth two entirely separate states: the Empire of Austria with its Parliament and the Kingdom of Hungary with its Parliament. In the first, Francis Joseph was to rule as emperor, in the second, as king. There were three common ministers, those of foreign affairs, war, and finance. Both Parliaments elected special committees, called Delegations, wich enacted legislation covering joint affairs. A common army was created, and after its quota was filled, recruits were assigned to serve in the state militias. The quota each state was to pay to the common budget was to be settled by treaty every ten years.

Under the Compromise, Austria and Hungary went their own ways in internal affairs, but Austrian and Hungarian troops fought side by side during World War I. The end of World War I brought the end of the Dual-Monarchy.

CHAPTER II

FROM KINGDOM TO SOVIET REPUBLIC:
HUNGARY AND THE PARIS PEACE CONFERENCE

In October, 1918, it became apparent that the Austro-Hungarian Empire had lost the war and its break-up was impending. During the last days of October, the Hungarian political parties agreed on the need for establishing a separate political entity, Hungary, and on a separate peace treaty. On October 30, 1918, the Habsburg King Charles IV was forced to make Count Michael Károlyi Prime Minister of Hungary (this was termed the "October revolution"). King Charles surrendered the reins of government but did not abdicate.

Count Michael Károlyi was the leader of the opposition in the Hungarian Parliament and a convinced "western" democrat. Károlyi believed that he was entitled to friendly treatment by the Allies because he had always been an advocate of Western European political Democracy. During the war a report spread that he was in secret but close contact with the leading statesmen of the Great Powers. Consequently, the opinion was held that he alone could secure the protection of the Hungarian nation.(1)

---

1 Károlyi went to Switzerland on November 25, 1917. He met with Hugh R. Wilson, United States Charge d'Affaires in Switzerland. He confidently predicted that he would soon come to power and would be in a position

As prime minister, Károlyi was obsessed with Hungary's boundaries. He and Dr. Oscar Jászi, Minister of Nationalities in the new Hungarian cabinet, attempted to save Hungary's territorial integrity by making the non-Magyar nationalities forget the past and reconcile themselves to the new Hungarian democracy. Oscar Jászi promised them true national equality in a "Danubian Confederation."(2) Even the English historian, R.W. Seton-Watson, who did not conceal his pro-Slavic and pro-Rumanian sympathies, wrote sympathetically about the proposals made by Jászi.(3)

The new Hungarian government faced staggering problems. The whole political and administrative organization of the country, as well as its economy, were in a state of collapse. Károlyi's government represented a coalition of his own small Independent Party (a bourgeois radical party), the Radical Party (the leftist intelligentsia), and the Social Democrats. The cabinet soon met with increasing pressure from within the country and from the Entente. The parties to the right of the government found it impossible to agree on common goals and methods in domestic affairs, such as land reform. They continued to go their separate ways and worked from the very beginning for Károlyi's over-

---

to dictate Austrian policy. In that case, the Allies should suggest a peace conference. He would send delegates to that conference and they would line up with the Allies against Germany. See U. S., **Foreign Relations**, 1917, Suppl. 2, 1, pp. 322ff.

A rumor also circulated among Czech and Slovak immigrants that Károlyi had come secretly to the United States in the hope of inducing President Wilson to preserve the integrity of Hungary. See Thomas G. Masaryk, **The Making of a State, Memories and Observations, 1914—1918** (London: Allen and Unwin, 1927), p. 209.

2 Wilhelm Böhm, **Im Kreuzfeuer zweier Revolutionen** (Munich: Verlag für Kulturpolitik, 1924), p. 109.

3 "He offered them independence and complete racial equality as the basis of a new Danubian Confederation of the free peoples. The Commune, and no longer the county, was to be the unit of political organization, and this unquestionably offered true democratic guarantees." **A History of the Roumanians** (Cambridge: University Press, 1934), p. 532.

throw. On the other hand, the left wing of the Social Democrat Party, which was by far the most powerful member of the government coalition, wanted more socialism. They were radical and sympathetic towards communism. The cabinet was divided and hopelessly paralyzed. Furthermore, tens of thousands of Magyars were seeking refuge in the country from the occupied territories, while the Entente continued to maintain its blockade against Hungary. These refugees only increased the number of the unemployed. Under these circumstances the government found the solution of its internal problems increasingly difficult.

The external problems were even more hopeless. Károlyi's primary objective was to secure a moderate peace by enlisting President Wilson and some European forces against the advocates of a harsh treaty. Therefore he favored a republican regime in order to convince Wilson that Hungary's transition to democracy was as thorough and sincere as that of Germany, Austria, and the successor states.(4) Hungary was proclaimed to be a "Peoples's Republic" on November 16, 1918, and the Hungarian National Council elected Károlyi President of the Republic in January, 1919. Even those who, in other circumstances, would have preferred a constitutional monarchy were satisfied in their belief that the republic was in the best national interest.

The government and the nation looked with both anxiety and hope toward the Paris Peace Conference, though none of the policy statements or acts of Western statesmen had given any grounds for hope.(5) Károlyi hoped to elicit a gesture of good will

---

4 Michael Károlyi, Memoirs: Faith without Illusion (New York: Dutton, 1957), pp. 125—142.

5 As Dr. Oscar Jászi said: "We had confidence in the democratic and pacifist quality of public opinion in the Entente states and especially in the policy of President Wilson. We were convinced that the conquering Allies would show the utmost good will to Hungary's pacifist and anti-militarist government. We were sure that they would apply the plebiscitary principle on which they had so often laid stress." Revolution and Counter-Revolution in Hungary (London: Grant Richards, 1924), p. 37.

and sympathy for himself and his regime, favorable occupation terms, and assurances for the integrity of Hungary's borders. To secure this and a modification of the Padua armistice, he himself headed a Hungarian delegation that traveled to Belgrade on November 8, 1918. (6)

But unlike Károlyi, the French• General Franchet D'Esperey, Allied Commander in Chief for the Southeastern theatre, was not disposed to forget that Hungary was a defeated enemy suing for terms at a time when French armies might still have to fight their way to Berlin. Treating the Hungarian delegation with rudeness and arrogance, he made it clear that the new Hungary was still the enemy. Károlyi pleaded for generosity toward the young Hungarian democracy, but Franchet D'Esperey, while paying homage to Károlyi personally, was determined to punish the Hungarians. He reminded them of France's support of the Hungarian rebels against the Habsburgs in the seventeenth and eighteenth centuries and reproached them bitterly for being accomplices of the Germans: "You marched with them, you will be punished with them. . . . You offended France and we will not forget." On being introduced to Baron Louis de Hatvany, a Jewish delegate, Franchet D'Esperey could not conceal his anti-Semitism. He took Baron Hatvany to a window in order to look him over closely and insolently remarked: "Ah, I see, you must be a Jew by your nose."(7)

To Hungary's political parties and the entire Hungarian nation Károlyi's meeting with General Franchet D'Esperey proved

---

6 The armistice at Padua, on November 3, 1918, which terminated hostilities between the Allies and the Austro-Hungarian Monarchy, was the last document which bore the latter's name. The armistice was signed by the representatives of the Italian Supreme Command and by the Supreme Command of the Dual Monarchy. The new Hungarian government, which had come into existence before this agreement, on October 30, 1918, was on principle opposed to the arrangement since it was signed by the Austro-Hungarian General Staff. See Károlyi, Memoirs, p. 130.

For the text of the Padua armistice, see U. S., For. Rel. Peace Conference, II, 175.

7 Károlyi, Memoirs, p. 134.

to be a bitter disappointment.(8) A new military convention was accepted and signed in Belgrade on November 13, 1918, by the delegates of the Károlyi government and representatives of General D'Esperey. This new Convention required the demobilization of all Hungarian forces except six infantry divisions and two cavalry divisions. In addition, it prescribed a line of demarcation which ran across the whole of south and east Hungary from Besztercze in Eastern Transylvania, southward to the Maros River, west along the Maros through Szabadka, Baja, and Pécs to the Mur River. Though Allied troops were to occupy the region south and east of this line, Hungarian administration was to continue to operate. After November 13, 1918, however, the region was occupied by Serbian and Rumanian troops (Hungary had expected this area to be occupied by troops of the Great Powers). This action greatly alarmed Hungary in view of the territorial claims of Serbia and Rumania to the area and the fact that the Hungarian administration was immediately deposed. (9)

Having failed in his first diplomatic foray, Károlyi appealed directly to President Wilson. In a message of November 16, 1918, he advised the President that his government relied on the generosity of the Western democracies, and that Wilson should support the Hungarian Republic in its crucial struggle against dissolution and against the menace of anarchy. Within ten days Károlyi sent a second note to the President asking for his support: "Mr. President, we appeal to your feeling . . . come to the assistance of the young Hungarian democracy."(10) Károlyi never received an answer.

---

8 Oscar Jászi wrote later: "The bright promise of Wilson's League of Nations, the just peace, the right of self-determination, and the plebiscite — in which the Hungarian people had placed their trust — burst like soap bubbles. They saw themselves not only defeated, broken and plundered, but, a much crueler wound to public feeling, bluffed and swindled." **Revolution and Counter-Revolution**, p. 56.

9 For the text of the Military Convention of Belgrade, see **U. S., For. Rel. Peace Conference, II,** 183.

10 Károlyi, **Memoirs,** p. 146.

When Czechoslovakia's territorial claims were presented to the Peace Conference by Eduard Benes on February 5, 1919, it became obvious that the Allies were taking the side of the successor states against Hungary. Benes asked for the Danube as a new frontier. He did not deny that the ethnic composition of the Hungarian districts north of the Danube was chiefly Magyar.(11) But he argued: "Slovakia must be a Danubian country, because the Danubian frontier is a geographic necessity and the new Czechoslovak state cannot survive without it."(12)

In early February, 1919, Rumania presented to the Supreme Council in Paris her claims to former Hungarian territories. On February 21, the Paris Peace Conference made a new decision about the Hungarian-Rumanian border. The new line of demarcation, behind which the Hungarians were to withdraw, was quite similar to the one assured to the Rumanians in the wartime treaty of August 17, 1916. Though the Western Powers had reached this decision as early as February 21, 1919, it was not until several weeks later, on March 20, 1919, that it was presented to Hungary in the form of an ultimatum by the French Lieutenant Colonel Vyx, Chief of the Allied Military Mission in Hungary.

On March 19, Colonel Vyx asked the Chiefs of the three other Allied Missions to meet him at his headquarters at nine o'clock the following morning, prior to making a collective demarche with the Hungarian government. Captain Nicholas Roosevelt, the ranking member of the Budapest branch of the American Mission, arrived fifteen minutes early in order to explain

---

11 Magyar was 80 percent and Slovak was only 11 percent. See U. S., National Archives, Inquiry, No. 108.

12 Ibid. It may be interesting to note in this connection that at the Paris Peace Conference the American Peace Delegation advocated an ethnic boundary for Czechoslovakia until April 4, 1919, when, during a period of the President's illness, Colonel House gave in to the French demand for the retention of the historical boundary of Bohemia and Moravia. See Charles Seymour, ed., The Intimate Papers of Colonel House (4 vols.; Boston: Houghton Mifflin, 1926—1928), III, 152.

to Vyx that he was not empowered to take any action of a diplomatic or military nature. Vyx pointed out that the note about to be presented by the mission chiefs to Hungary incorporated a decision taken by the Allied Powers at the Paris Peace Conference, with which Roosevelt was connected. Having failed to reach Archibald C. Coolidge, his chief at Paris, by phone for instruction, and at the urging of the British and Italian representatives, Roosevelt decided to go along.(13)

The four Allied representatives arrived at Károlyi's office sometime between 10:00 and 11:00 A.M. Vyx handed the note to Károlyi. In handing over the ultimatum to Károlyi, Vyx remarked that the new line of demarcation, which once again took purely Magyar districts from Hungary, would be the provisional political frontier. He warned that the rejection of the Allied demand would be followed by the withdrawal of the Allied missions from Budapest, which was generally interpreted as a threat to renew the state of war with the Hungarian republic.(14) This ultimatum destroyed the Democratic Hungarian Republic within the next few hours.

Károlyi did not have to read through the entire document to realize its full import. Károlyi pointed out to Vyx that the note was against the Belgrade agreement and to accept it could lead to anarchy and Bolshevism. He urged him to make a last attempt in Paris to postpone the matter. Vyx merely shrugged his shoulders and declared that it did not matter to him how the Károlyi government would respond. Károlyi continued to stress that the note was a matter of the greatest internal political importance; and that neither his own government nor any other government would last a day if it signed such a humiliating agreement. Vyx promptly replied in German: "Das ist mir ganz egal" ("I couldn't care less") either about the growth of Bolshevism, the consequences of resignation, or the composition

---

13 U. S., For. Rel. Peace Conference, XII, 413—14.
14 Böhm, Im Kreuzfeuer, pp. 268—69.

of a new government. In conclusion, should Károlyi fail to accept the ultimatum by 6:00 P.M. on March 21, the Entente Missions would immediately leave the country.(15)

Károlyi met with his cabinet during the afternoon of March 20; he confessed that the Allied note, as interpreted by Vyx, vividly demonstrated the failure of his Western orientation which had been based on Wilson's policy. In his answer to Colonel Vyx on March 21, Count Károlyi emphasized that the Hungarian government, "finds itself unable to accept this decision of the Peace Conference and unwilling to safeguard its execution." He charged that it ran counter to the armistice provisions of November 13.(16)

Count Károlyi resigned assuming that a purely socialist cabinet would be formed which would refuse to accept the new ar-

---

15 For full details see "Presentation to President Károlyi of Peace Conference Decision Regarding Evacution of Transylvania," March 20, 1919, in U. S., For. Rel. Peace Conference, 1919, XII, 413—14.

Vyx, like Franchet D'Esperey, offended the Hungarians unnecessarily by the form in which he issued his orders. The Hungarian opinion is expressed in Cecile Tormay's words: "Taking advantage of his position, Colonel Vyx has trodden on our self-respect. He has treated the Eastern bulwark of Europe as the French officers treat the savages in their own colonies." An Outlaw's Diary (New York: Berko, 1924), p. 39.

Peter Pastor is of the opinion in a recently published study that Vyx and some other French generals can be considered as pro-Hungarian. According to Pastor, the strongly anti-Hungarian French government and the Supreme Council — and not the French military — were responsible for the rise of a communist regime in Hungary. See "The Vyx Mission in Hungary, 1918—1919: a Re-examination," Slavic Review, XXIX, No. 3 (September, 1970), 481—98.

16 See Károlyi, "Die Geschichte meiner Abdankung," Arbeiter-Zeitung (Vienna daily), July 25, 1919.

Also a document is quoted by Francis Deak: "The Hungarian government, not being in a position to bear the responsibility for the execution of this decision, as it was not invited to the Peace Conference and could not participate in taking this decision, found itself today obliged to hand in its demission." Hungary and the Paris Peace Conference (New York: Columbia University Press, 1942), p. 409.

mistice line and would possibly threaten to fight a patriotic war. He now believed that the Social Democratic Party was the only political force capable of controlling the army and of ordering it to the front as well as the only party capable of gaining new friends for Hungary in East and Central Europe. Count Károlyi had reached the bitter conclusion that Hungary had little to expect from the victorious Western democracies.

The socialist ministers, however, without Károlyi's knowledge, had entered into an agreement with Béla Kun, the imprisoned Bolshevik leader, for a union betveen the Social Democratic Party and the Communist Party. In consequence of this fact Béla Kun moved directly from the prison into public office as head of the new government and commissar for foreign affairs. The new course was based upon the expectation that "we ought to get from the East what the West denied us."(17)

The Hungarian Communist Party had been founded on November 24, 1918. Béla Kun, who before the war had been an insignificant provincial journalist and had lost his job in a workmen's insurance office because of embezzlement, had arrived in Budapest from Moscow on November 17, 1918.(18) He and other war prisoners returning from Russia constituted the Bolshevik nucleus. In Russia, these Hungarians had become faithful converts to Leninist principles and tactics. Immediately after the foundation of the Hungarian Communist Party, they began publication of a communist organ, **Vörös Ujság** (Red News). Béla

17 **Pester Lloyd**, March 22, 1919. (This publication was a well-known Budapest Liberal daily written in the German language.)

18 About Béla Kun, see: Géza Herceg, **Béla Kun: Eine historische Grimasse** (Berlin: Verlag für Kulturpolitik, 1928); or Árpád Szelpál, **Les 133 jours de Béla Kun** (Paris: Fayard, 1959); or Albert Kaas and Fedor Lazarovics, **Bolshevism in Hungary: The Béla Kun Period** (London: Grant Richards, 1931). The communist opinion is expressed in the following works: Béla Kun, **La République hongroise des conseils** (Budapest: Editions Corvine, 1962); or The Hungarian Communist Party, ed., **Kun's Speeches, Articles and Official Statements, 1918—19** (Budapest: State Publishing, 1958).

Kun began his propaganda work through this newspaper and in speeches among the demobilized soldiers and officers, the unemployed, and the poor farm laborers.(19)

The communists held the Károlyi cabinet accountable for the plight of the poor, for the neglect of their grievances, and for blocking the road to Socialist paradise. Mainly because of this propaganda, violence and terrorism occurred widely throughout Hungary in early 1919. On February 20, a mass of unemployed workers congregated at Budapest in the center of the city. Béla Kun called on the workers to procure arms for themselves and summoned them to a mass meeting in front of Parliament for the following afternoon to protest against the existing social and economic order.(20) There was a heavy exchange of fire, with the security forces using machine guns. Who fired the first shot remains a mystery. At any rate, when the shooting was over, there were seven dead policemen and eighty wounded. The number of the injured workers is unknown. Béla Kun and the leaders of the Communist Party--a total of sixty-nine activists-- were thrown into jail. (21)

Now Károlyi's cabinet was afflicted by yet another problem. Lenin expressed his displeasure over events in Hungary by arrest- ing three members — all Social Democrats — of the Hungarian mission, which happened to be in Moscow to negotiate the re-

19 According to Von Fürstenberg, the chief German envoy in Budapest, in March, 1919, the Bolshevik Party had 10,000 members in Budapest and 25,000 in the provinces, and had spent about 1.5 million crowns of Soviet Russian origin over the last three months. German Foreign Ministry (Microfilm of records) 92/I/27/9294.

According to other records, on March 19, 1919, Colonel Vyx told the members of the American Mission in Budapest that there were "about 1,000 Russians, more c ess, in Hungary." U. S. Department of State 184.01102/254.

20 See Kun's speech as reported in Népszava (People's Voice; Budapest daily), February 21, 1919.

21 Wilhelm Böhm, Defense Minister of the Károlyi government, wrote later on that the government received an urgent message from the Allied Missions to jail all Bolshevik agitators. Im Kreuzfeuer, p. 198.

patriation of some 100,000 prisioners of war. Lenin notified the Hungarian government that these men would be put to death if anything happened to the communists in Budapest. This external pressure brought about the release of twenty-nine of the sixty-nine prisoners, while Béla Kun and those who remained in jail with him were classified as political prisoners and treated as gentlemen.

On March 21, 1919, as stated above, Béla Kun moved directly from prison into public office as head of the new government and commissar for foreign affairs. Kun promised a new course for foreign policy. Territorial integrity and defense would be achieved not through bidding for American help, but rather through an alliance with the revolutionary proletariat of Russia. In any event, to save Hungary, the Hungarian proletariat would fight a revolutionary war with Russia against predatory neighbors.

The proletarian revolution in Hungary had its own peculiar characteristics. It was, as the Vienna Social-Democratic daily, the **Arbeiter-Zeitung**, quickly pointed out, not so much a revolution against her own bourgeoisie as one against the Entente bourgeoisie.(22) **Izvestiia's** explanation of the political turnorver in Hungary, as serving the purposes of national defense, followed virtually the same lines.(23)

The prevailing view among the communists and noncommunists, both in Hungary and abroad, was that the Entente was largely responsible for the radical turn of events in Hungary. In addition, it was felt that the communist seizure had come as a direct consequence of the allied ultimatum — not as the result of victory in the internal class struggle.(24) The **Pester Lloyd** flatly

22 "Ungarn und wir," **Arbeiter-Zeitung**, March 23, 1919.

23 **Izvestiia**, March 25, 1919; similarly **Pravda**, of the same day .

24 Although the Social-Democrat Wilhelm Böhm held that the fall of the Károlyi government had been due largely to internal causes, he wrote later: "The responsibiáty for having brougt about the downfall of government must mainly be attributed to the behavior of the Entente and its representative Vyx. Hungary and the Hungarian Social Democratic Party had been pushed onto this new road by the Entente Imperialism." **Im Kreuzfeuer**, p. 181.

declared that the creation of the Soviet Republic was the reply of the Hungarian proletariat to the reckless, booty-seeking imperialism of the Entente and her satellites. This paper attributed the economic crisis to the loss of the wealthiest provinces and charged that the proposed Rumanian line of demarcation crudely violated Wilson's principles: "The answer to the peace of violence which the Conference of Paris seeks to dictate is the Red flood which, starting from Russia, now will spread from Hungary toward the West."(25) In Világ (The Globe) Louis Biró insisted that Hungary would have "signed her own death warrant by accepting the ultimatum which clearly proved the bankruptcy of bourgeois policy to everyone." In this same inflamed nationalist spirit, Thomas Kóbor, the editorialist of the conservative Az Ujság (The News) claimed that Hungarians have set their own house on fire in order to set fire to the whole world. The bourgeois Az Est (The Evening) seemed proud that Budapest "was shaking up the world," notably Paris, and that together with the Russian giant, "the courageous and vigorous Hungarian proletariat was at the forefront of progress." All these papers and editorials refrained from commenting on internal developments, preferring to justify the revolution in purely nationalist terms.

Not only in Hungary, but also in Western Europe, everyone traced the Hungarian explosion back to the Peace Conference. While the main line of criticism was directed at the error of the Conference in imposing such harsh policies on the Hungarian nation as to drive her into the arms of Bolshevism, the French press blamed Wilson's idealism. The Temps was shaken because Wilson was on the point of yielding to the enemy.(26) Figaro took the view that the Hungarian revolution was sheer blackmail, the Red spectre being the chosen weapon and Germany being the thinly disguised mastermind.(27) The Echo de Paris stated that with the

---

25 This Hungarian paper and those following are cited in Bulletin Périodique de la presse hongroise (Paris), No. 31, pp. 2—3.
26 Le Temps, March 24, 1919.
27 Le Figaro, March 23, 1919.

Hungarian revolution the "door to the heart of Europe was wide open to Bolshevism" and that instead of Wilsonian leniency towards the enemy the Conference should face up to the danger.(28)

Except for the charge of German complicity, the British press stressed the same themes as the French press. **The Times** (London) stated that Hungary lay well on the western side of the sanitary cordon against Bolshevism, and by the terms of the Armistice she indubitably submitted to the authority of Paris. The paper called the attention of the President to the fact that "between the Red League of Lenin and the ideals of the League of Nations there was a chasm which no compromise could bridge."(29) The **Daily Mail** vented its rage on Wilson whom the paper held "directly responsible for the nervous inertia of the Conference."(30) The **Morning Post** wanted to give Clemenceau the supreme direction of allied diplomacy in order to counter the Hungarian "try on" and, further, to wrest security and reparations from the enemy at once.(31)

The communist seizure of power in Hungary made the Hungarian question the first item on the agenda of the Paris Conference. The first impact of the news that a Soviet republic had been established in Budapest was disturbing. Furthermore, there were authentic reports of an imminent collapse in Vienna; a Soviet-type republic was proclaimed in Bavaria; strikes broke out in the Ruhr, in Hamburg, and in Saxony; the sailors of the French squadron at Odessa mutinied, thus hastening the evacuation of this strategic Black Sea port; and the Russian Red Army stayed Kolchak's advance and continued to push ahead in the Ukraine. To make matters worse, there was labor unrest in Britain, France, and Italy.

---

28 **Echo de Paris,** March 25, 1919.

29 **The Times** (London), March 25, 1919.

30 **Daily Mail** (Paris edition), March 23, 1919.

31 "The Need for a Generalissimo," editorial in the **Morning Post,** March 25, 1919.

President Wilson was alarmed. Lansing plied him with telegrams about Hungary from Vienna and also provided the President with analyses of Hungarian events.(32) General Tasker H. Bliss, the President's military adviser, directly accused the French military of having planned and anticipated the Hungarian reaction to the Vyx ultimatum, thus being responsible for Bolshevik radicalism. He even went so far as to claim that every evidence in the secret documents clearly proved that the French military and diplomatic authorities not only welcomed but stimulated the Soviet revolution in Hungary with the idea of forcing military action and military settlements. General Bliss held it probable that these militarist intrigues took place behind Clemenceau's back and by elements hostile to him. He charged that the Bolshevik seizure of power in Hungary was the direct result of action by the Supreme Council on February 26, 1919, an action politically unwise and one that could not be morally justified to the poeople of the United States. He also urged that the United States not only refuse participation in any armed intervention for the purpose of enforcing the decision of the Supreme Council of February 26, but also that it insist on reversal of this decision.(33)

Marcel Cachin, member of the American Peace Delegation, reinforced General Bliss. According to Cachin, Károlyi's fall was precipitated by the affronting and narrow-minded actions of local French generals who claimed to act for the Peace Conference. In Cachin's opinion the only sure way to arrest Bolshevism was to stick to the Wilsonian principles and not allow them to be compromised by French militarism.(34) William C. Bullitt, another member of the American Delegation, immediately after his return from Moscow on April 6, 1919, told the President in a letter that now that the Hungarians had followed the Russian example he was face to face with a European Revolution:

---

32 U. S., For. Rel., Peace Conference, 1919, XII, 416—19, 424.

33 U. S., For. Rel., Paris Peace Conference, VI, 281—89.

34 U. S. Commissioners to Wilson, March 28, 1919, **Woodrow Wilson Papers** (in the Library of Congress).

For the past year the people of Europe have been seeking a better way to live for the common good of all. They have found no guidance in Paris. Now, they are turning towards Moscow; but the impulses are remote from theoretic communism. . . Six months ago all the peoples of Europe expected you to fulfill their hopes. They believe now that you cannot. They turn, therefore, to Lenin.(35)

Professor Philip Marshall Brown, the second-ranking member of the Coolidge Mission, who stayed at his Hungarian post throughout the reign of Béla Kun, also characterized the Hungarian Communism as a national protest. He wired to Paris that since the mass of the people were not even remotely Socialist and since Soviet Russia was too far off to assist local radicals, by prudent action the Allies could still prevent Hungary from becoming completely Bolshevik. Personally he preferred a conciliatory course spearheaded by an assurance that the Peace Conference "had no intention of mutilating Hungary or of breaking her up without due regard for the wishes of the people."(36)

President Wilson himself was firmly convinced that certain French circles were responsible for the communist seizure of power in Hungary. Ray Stannard Baker, Press secretary of the President, informed him that he was blamed on all sides for the events in Central Europe. Baker suggested that the President would have to show what the real causes of the chaos were. "If I were to do that," the President replied, "it would immediately break up the Peace Conferencee — and we cannot risk it yet. . . I should have to tell the truth and place the blame exactly where it belongs — upon the French."(37)

---

35 William C. Bullitt Papers, April 6, 1919 (in the Sterling Memorial Library of Yale University: Edward M. House Collection).

36 U. S., National Archives, Document 184.01102/286.

37 Ray Stannard Baker, Woodrow Wilson and World Settlement (Garden City, N. Y.: Doubleday, 1923), XXII, 135—36.

Among the members of the American Peace Delegation Professor Robert J. Kerner, one of the junior experts on Eastern Europe, had the distinction of being the only one to attribute more importance to the internal causes of the Hungarian turmoil. In his view the occupation of additional Hungarian territory was only the ostensible cause. The real cause was the fear of the Social Democrats, especially the radicals among them, that they would fail to get an absolute majority in the coming elections. Among contributing internal causes he also cited peasant unrest over land reform as well as Károlyi's undue mildness toward "Bolshevik agitators, editors, press agents and politicians."(38)

Kerner's observations, however, were not unfounded. While the Entente's responsibility for Hungarian communism could not be denied, the entire Hungarian people, all Hungarian political parties, and especially Károlyi himself, must share the blame for a singularly unjustified optimism they held in regard to the country's boundaries and peace terms. Károlyi, furthermore, realizing the failure of his Wilsonian orientation and the misjudgment of his political advisers, in all probability believed that Bolshevism could conquer all over Europe. Mainly because of this belief, he handed over power to the Communist-dominated Hungarian Socialist Party and legitimized the peaceful transformation of Hungary's "People's Republic" into Europe's second Dictatorship of the Proletariat. Doing so, he became a "traitor" to Hungarians, who never forgave him. As one of the most scholarly Hungarian historical books puts it:

Michael Károlyi, the Hungarian Kerenszki, stole away from Hungarian history on March 21, 1919. Ruins marked his coming, and ruins remained after him. His sin is, that in the most critical period of his nation's history, he claimed the leadership for himself, to which he had no qualification. He

---

38 Robert J. Kerner, "The Question in Hungary," in **Edward M. House Papers**, March 24, 1919 (in the Sterling Memorial Library of Yale University).

forced this leadership for himself by such illusions, which were unfounded. The judgment of history given against him never will be softened.(39)

On the other hand, some historians recognize Károlyi's good will. His naivete, however, is beyond question. Károlyi did not realize that no one of the victorious nations in Europe took Wilson's ideas seriously. Hungary's neighbors, for example, organized their new national armies with great haste, while Károlyi abolished the Hungarian army under such slogans as: "We do not want to see soldiers anymore! We are pacifists! Wilson makes order! We want Wilsonian peace!" and so on.

It is also true, and be it said in Károlyi's defense, that the whole Hungarian nation was very much influenced by Wilson. Count Julius Andrássy, the last Minister of Foreign Affairs of the Austro-Hungarian Monarchy, wrote later:

> We were particularly hard hit by Wilson's action. Demagogues and some naive souls asked whether it was not revolting treachery to continue the war if Wilson declared, in the name of the great American Republic, that the war is not conducted against nations, but against the autocratic system which caused the war and which the people did not wish to tolerate any longer anyhow . . . Anyone who did not believe the promises of the American President was mercilessly stamped as an agitator for war. Wilson, "the enemy", was more popular than the very statesmen of the people.(40)

On March 21, 1919, Budapest, in the heart of Europe, became the second capital of Bolshevism. The Council of People's Commissars, in which Béla Kun was the real power, declared martial law, appealed for law and order, and called for maximum economic effort. At the same time, the Council decreed a

---

39 Miklós Asztalos és Sándor Pethö, **A Magyar Nemzet Története** (The History of the Hungarian Nation) (Budapest: Lantos, 1933), p. 532.

40 Count Julius Andrássy, **Diplomacy and the War** (London: Grant Richards, 1921), p. 243.

number of revolutionary measures: the abolition of titles and privileges; the separation of church and state; the preparation of elections of Workers', Soldiers', and Peasants' Councils; the establishment of a revolutionary tribunal; and the socialization of factories, apartment houses, and latifundia. The Council also announced that it would make an allience with Soviet Russia; that it placed Hungary under the protection of the Red Army; and that it was resolved to defend the Soviet regime to the last drop of blood.(41)

In foreign policy, the new course, as we have seen, was based upon the expectation that "we ought to get from the East what the West denied us." In a radio dispatch to Soviet Russia, the new rulers dutifully reported to Lenin that a proletarian dictatorship had been established in Hungary and simultaneously saluted him as the leader of the International proletariat, thus clearly subordinating themselves to Moscow's authority. The Hungarians then asked for a treaty of alliance with Russia and requested pertinent instructions. Lenin, in turn, told the Hungarian comrades of the huge enthusiasm which their revolution had aroused in Russia.(42)

---

41 Népszava (Budapest daily), March 23, 1919.

42 At 5:00 P. M. on March 22, 1919, Radio Budapest called Lenin. Twenty minutes later, in the Moscow station, he said, "Lenin at the microphone. I want to speak to Comrade Béla Kun." Budapest replied that Kun was at a meeting. Ernest Por, Kun's substitute, declared:

"The Hungarian Soviet Republic offers the Russian Soviet government an armed alliance against all the enemies of proletariat. Please inform us immediately about the military situation."

Lenin understood that Hungary needed military assistance to survive. But he wanted assurance before he acted. Lenin, therefore, sent a radio dispatch to Béla Kun on the next day:

"Please state concrete guarantees you have that the new Hungarian government is actually communist and not merely socialist, that is, social-traitors. Do the communists have a majority in the government? When will the Congress of Soviets meet?... I should like to know what, in your opinion, are the real guarantees."

From its inception, Hungarian communism not only looked eastward but also turned to her immediate neighbors, to Germany, and to all the workers of the world. In an appeal "TO ALL," the Hungarian Socialist Party (as the party called itself after the fusion of Social Democrats and Communists) extended its greetings to the working classes of Great Britain, France, Italy, and America and called on them not to tolerate the infamous campaign of their regimes against the Soviet Hungarian government. It also appealed to the workers and peasants of the adjoining victorious countries: Bohemia, Rumania, and Serbia, encouraging them to form an armed alliance against the Boyars (estate-owners) and dynasties. Finally, it called upon the workers of the vanquished states, Germany and German-Austria, to follow the example of the Hungarian proletariat, to make a final break with Paris and to link up with Moscow. The Soviet Hungarian regime appealed to the European proletariat not only to prevent an attack of their bourgeoisies upon Soviet Hungary, but also extend the base of social revolution throughout Europe. Kun and the Hungarian Soviet government stressed that Soviet Hungary could be secured and saved through international proletarian solidarity.(43)

Béla Kun knew that propaganda was a very important weapon in saving communism in Hungary. He also saw with equal clarity the importance of military strength. The absence of a reliable army was one of his major problems. The organization of a Red Army, both patriotic and loyal to socialist ideas, was a

---

Collected Works of V. I. Lenin, ed. by N. I. Bukharin, V. M. Molotov, and M. A Savelev (Moscow-Leningrad: State Publishing, 1929), XXIV, 768. The German original, in Lenin's handwriting, is printed in ibid., opposite p. 180. Lenin's doubts were due to the participation of several Social Democrats in the Béla Kun cabinet.

43 Népszava (Budapest daily), March 27, 1919.

necessity. Due to very skillful propaganda, patriots and thousands of Trade Unionists volunteered for military service. Hungarians were summoned to fight against both imperialism and robber neighbors, and in May the Hungarian troops had been increased to 200,000.

The proclamation of the dictatorship of the proletariat in Hungary was quickly followed by the withdrawal from Budapest of all Entente missions. Official diplomatic relations between Soviet Hungary and the Entente were thus virtually nonexistent. A few remaining contacts were provided by the presence of various individual Allied officials, although these were not authorized to act as Allied spokesmen or to make any binding agreements. Among the most prominent agents of Western powers in Hungary were Lieutenant-Colonel Romanelli, previously member of the Italian Military Mission in Hungary, and Philip Marshall Brown, previously member of the American Military Mission in Hungary, who stayed in Budapest at his own request. The British Sir Thomas Cuningham and Professor Coolidge used neighboring Vienna as a base for their operations, visiting Budapest rather frequently. These men served as eyes and ears for the Allied Powers, and their reports to Paris were given close and careful attention.

On his arrival in Paris on March 26, 1919, Captain Nicholas Roosevelt reported to the American Peace Delegation on the Hungarian revolution. He told the Delegation that the revolution was precipitated by the presentation of the Vyx note; that it was accomplished with comparative quiet; and that there were unconfirmed rumors of German as well as Italian complicity. In his judgment the revolution was essentially nationalistic, making use of Bolshevism for national goals. Hungary was openly defying a decision of the Peace Conference by holding the club of Bolshevism over the Allies and asking: "What are you going to do about it?" According to Roosevelt there were three alternatives: the Czechs and Rumanians could advance and occupy Hungary, but this would be bloody and, besides, they might not be up to the job. Secondly, the Allies could undertake this task themselves. Lastly, the Allies could rely on a rigorous blockade. (44)

Clemenceau wanted an immedite Allied intervention. President Wilson was firmly against it. An intervention, according to the President, raised the question of whether the Western Powers possessed the necessary troops and sufficient material means for military action, and whether public sentiment supported such a policy. The use of American troops was imposible, according to the President, and public opinion in America would definitely be opposed to any aggressive Allied move. There was doubt in the President's mind whether the revolutionary movements could be arrested with the help of the army. Wilson concluded that nobody knew fully what actually caused this movement. He felt that one of the causes was no doubt the misery of the people and their insecurity in regard to their frontiers and their government; the only means to kill Bolshevism was to fix the frontiers and open all avenues of commerce. Lloyd George strongly supported the position of President Wilson.

On March 26, 1919, Philip Marshall Brown sent two dispatches from Budapest to Paris. He reported that the new regime was styled on the Soviet Russian model. The communist faction of the government, which was in constant communication with Moscow, was pressing for extreme measures. In Brown's view "this was not an amateur, but a professional revolution." It all "looked like Red Terror." In Brown's judgment the mass of the people were "neither extreme nor even socialistic"; they were "intensely nationalistic"; and only the threat of dismemberment had brought about the "unnatural partnership of nationalism and communism." The mass of Hungarians would welcome "military intervention by British and American troops combined with conciliatory assurances, but not by others." Brown estimated that not more than 30,000 troops would be required for this intervention. (45)

---

44 U. S., National Archives, Document 184.01102/254.
45 U. S., National Archives, Documents 184.01102/266, 276, 282, and 286.

On the next day, however, the Council of Four clearly rejected intervention against Soviet Hungary either by their own forces or those of Hungary's neighbors. This Allied decision was the result of numerous factors and considerations. Demobilization was already proceeding at too fast a pace and public opinion was adverse to intervention.

The situation became more confused when, on March 29, 1919, Kun's first message reached Paris. This first communication of the new Hungarian Government to the Great Powers was significant and revealing both in its assertions and in its denials.

The new Government of Hungary, the Council of Commissioners of the People, recognize the validity of the Treaty of Armistice signed by the former government in Belgrade and do not think that the non-acceptance of the note presented by Colonel Vyx has infringed it. When the new Hungarian government had asked Russia to enter into an alliance with the Soviet Hungarian republic, it had not thought that this might be interpreted as an expression of its desire to break all diplomatic intercourse with the Powers of the Entente. The alliance with Russia is not a formal diplomatic alliance. It is a natural friendship justified by the identical construction of their respective constitutions, and has in no way any aggressive purpose. The new Hungarian Republic, on the contrary, has a firm desire to live in peace with all the other nations and to devote its activities to the peaceful social reorganization of its country. The Hungarian government wishes to negotiate specifically on the basis of self-determination, a principle as important to President Wilson as to Lenin. The Hungarian government would gladly welcome a civil and diplomatic mission of the Entente in Budapest and would guarantee to it the right of extra-territoriality and provide for its absolute safety.(46)

---

46 U. S., For. Rel., Paris Peace Conference, V, 18.

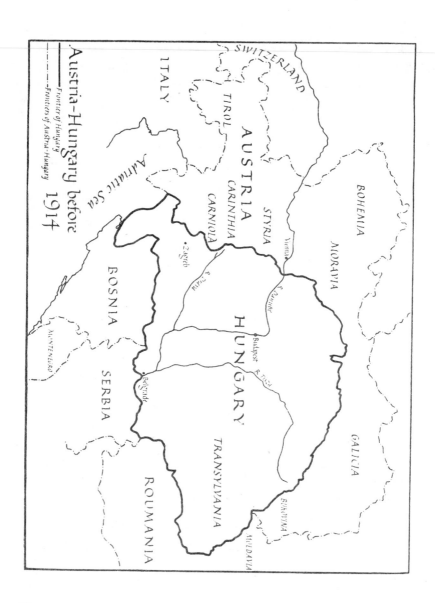

Austria–Hungary before 1914

——— Frontier of Hungary
------- Frontier of Austria-Hungary

SWITZERLAND

ITALY

TIROL

AUSTRIA

CARINTHIA

CARNIOLA

STYRIA

Adriatic Sea

Zagreb

BOSNIA

MONTENEGRO

SERBIA

Belgrade

Vienna

R. Drave

R. Danube

Budapest

HUNGARY

R. Tisza

BOHEMIA

MORAVIA

GALICIA

TRANSYLVANIA

BUKOVINA

MOLDAVIA

ROUMANIA

The major purpose of this message transmitted by Budapest was to persuade the Allies regarding the moderate character of Hungarian Bolshevism in external and internal affairs. The communiqué found the Allies in a receptive mood and contributed to their early restraint in their dealings with Soviet Hungary. If Hungarian Bolshevism was reasonable and moderate, Allied policy had to be similarly marked by reasonableness and moderation.

After the reception of Kun's note, the Allies sent a delegation headed by Field Marshal Jan Christian Smuts to Budapest. This mission, without recognizing the new Hungarian government on behalf of the Allies, was to enter into discussions with it about matters of Allied concern. However, by sending Smuts to Budapest and having him talk with Béla Kun and his government, the Allies had risked lending prestige to the new regime. Béla Kun, nevertheless, made the most of General Smuts' visit to Budapest. The Hungarian press maintained that Smuts dealt with Kun not in his capacity as soldier, but as diplomat. Népszava observed that until recently the Entente had refused to engage in any negotiations and had merely sent ultimatums; now, however, "the same Entente which had not deigned to have any dealings with the half-bourgeois Government of the People's Republic except through the medium of ultimatums," had entered into negotiations with the Hungarian Soviet Republic.

No doubt a Hungary governed by a bourgeois administration would have pleased the bourgeois Entente better than a Soviet government. But Imperialism had no use for sentiment in politics . . . Bourgeois Hungary had been feeble; therefore, she had to feel the whip. Because the Soviet Republic was powerful, negotiations were in order.(47)

General Smuts and his party arrived in Budapest in the morning of April 4, 1919. On the same day Smuts reported to Paris in

47 Népszava, Budapest, April 5, 1919.

a telegram about his first meeting with Béla Kun and two important members of the government, President Alexander Garbai and Sigismund Kunfi, Commissar for Education. In a second telegram to Paris, on April 6, Smuts referred to a plan of the Hungarian government relating to a conference of states bordering on Hungary. According to this telegram, while the Hungarian government recognized the principles of nationality laid down by President Wilson, it made clear that the definite settlement of the boundary questions ought not to be reached by the Great Powers at the Paris Peace Conference. Rather it should be agreed upon at meetings between representatives of the Hungarian, Austrian, Bohemian, Serbian, and Rumanian governments. Here the Entente Powers were not represented. Béla Kun suggested, furthermore that Smuts himself might preside at these meetings and Vienna or Prague would be the meeting place for this conference. In return for acceptance of the decision of the Peace Conference, Smuth held out a promise of territorial negotations; and he implied a degree of recognition and economic concessions. (48)

The two parties could not agree. The conversation broke off between Smuts and the Hungarians on the same day, and Smuts left Budapest for Paris. In conclusion, Smuts expressed his conviction that the Hungarian Soviets were weak and were rent by internal divisions likely to lead to their fall at an early date. The Hungarian cabinet held that many of the concessions made by Smuts represented merely personal promises and would not be binding on the Paris Peace Conference. Furthermore, the acceptance would provoke a nationalist reaction which might well lead to a counter-revolutionary coup. At the same time it would call for a break with Soviet Russia and thereby endanger the revolution.

In May, 1919, the Hungarian Soviet Republic was politically isolated. Russia's Red Army was far from the Hungarian borders;

---

48 U. S., For. Rel., Paris Peace Conference, V, 62.

the Austrian government survived only as a satellite of the Entente; and three hostile neighbors were eager to occupy further Hungarian territories. A counter-offensive against the Czechs promised a small chance of a link-up with Russia's Red Army across the Carpathian Mountains in the northern direction. The war against the Czechs proved successful beyond all expectations. By early June, more than one third of Slovakia had been lost to the Hungarian troops; and the Czechs were still retreating along the entire front. However, it became clear that Soviet Russia was in no position to extend military assistance to the Soviet sister republic. On June 18, 1919, Lenin sent a code message to Béla Kun, advising him to negotiate an armistice with the Entente.(49)

Meanwhile, the Paris Peace Conference terminated its work relating to Hungary's frontiers. In response to Eduard Benes' three desperate appeals for help, Clemenceau sent two sharply worded ultimatums to Béla Kun. In his second note on June 13, he informed the Soviet Hungarian government of the new Hungarian frontiers and demanded, under threat of penalties, the immediate withdrawal of the Red Army from Czechoslovakian territories. Clemenceau promised in exchange for evacuation of Slovakia that the Rumanians would withdraw from Hungarian territories. But, while the Hungarians left Slovakia, the Rumanians made no move to withdraw from Hungary; and the Peace Conference made no effort to compel them to carry out its orders. What was more, the Allies demanded a reduction of the Red Army to six divisions as a precondition for Rumania's withdrawal. Considering this fact, Béla Kun claimed now to fear a Rumanian

---

49 "It is necessary to make the maximum use of every opportunity to obtain a temporary armistice or peace, in order to give the people a breathing space. But do not trust the Entente powers for a moment. They are deceiving you, and are only attemping to gain time in order to be able to crush you and us." Béla Kun, La République hongroise, p. 216.

offensive, whose troops were at the Tisza River about eighty miles from Budapest. He took into consideration a preventive blow before the Rumanians could be ready for an offensive and started an attack against Rumania on July 21, 1919. The breakdown of Soviet Hungary on August 1, 1919, came in consequence of the failure of this offensive against Rumania.(50)

---

50 Béla Kun, La République hongroise, p. 214. On August 1, 1919, Béla Kun left Hungary and went to Austria. After remaining there about a year, he was smuggled out of the country. Austria put him into a transport with prisoners-of-war returning to Russia, and dispatched him through Bohemia and Germany toward Russia. In Moscow he was received with honor. The Soviet party leaders, the Trade Unions, and the Red Army met him at the railway station in Moscow with words of welcome. He was sent on an important mission to the Southern Russian Army of which he was appointed Political Commissar. He went on important missions during the following years. Finally, during the great purge of Stalin in 1937, his life ended before a firing squad in Moscow.

CHAPTER III

STRUGGLE FOR SURVIVAL:
THE RUMANIAN OCCUPATION

On July 21, 1919, Béla Kun sent a radio message to the Supreme Council announcing that his forces were crossing the Tisza River "to try to make the will of the Entente respected by the Rumanians."(1) The Rumanians, however, not only won the battle but crossed the Tisza and their advance towards Budapest was quick. On August 4 they marched into the Hungarian capital without opposition under the anti-Bolshevik banner.

The next months saw a period of great confusion. The Hungarian government had previously been taken over by a self-appointed Socialist government. On August 6, however, some fifty royalist gendarmes took advantage of the apathy of the Rumanians and staged a **coup d'état** in favor of the Habsburg Archduke, Joseph. Archduke Joseph became the "Head of State": the Socialist government was thus replaced by a nationalist one under Prime Minister Stephen Friedrich, who had originally been a democratic Republican and an ardent personal follower of Michael Károlyi. During the Bolshevik terror he had changed his opinions completely to become one of the most active pro-Habsburgs. The Supreme Council found itself face to face with the return of a Habsburg which was contrary to Allied policy. The Supreme Council also received reports about the Rumanian terrorism, loot-

---

1 U. S., For. Rel., Paris Peace Conference, VII, 236.

ing, and destruction, which exceeded even their worst fears and predictions.(2)

Two issues now faced the Supreme Council: how to prevent a "White terror" in Hungary and how to restrain the Rumanians. In accordance with a decision of the Supreme Council, an Inter-Allied Military Mission arrived in Budapest on August 7, 1919, to save Hungary from herself and from the Rumanians. It had been decided that this mission should be composed of generals rather than diplomats. Of the latter there had already been too many. Four generals representing the four chief Allies were appointed to head this Military Mission to Hungary: General Harry Hill Bandholtz of the United States Army, General Reginald Gorton of the British Army, General G. Graziani of the French Army, and General Ernesto Mombelli of the Italian Army.(3)

The Inter-Allied Military Mission received the following commission from the Supreme Council: keep the Rumanians under control and force them to leave Hungary as soon as possible; prevent atrocities and build up a police force in Hungary; help Hungary to establish a responsible government which could be acceptable to the Supreme Council; and force Hungary to accept the new boundaries fixed by the Peace Treaties and to sign the Peace Treaty.(4)

The problems of the Inter-Allied Mission were manifold. First of all, the Mission appeared to be a house divided. Although the American and British members followed strictly the instructions of the Supreme Council, and usually agreed in every case, the two Latin members were under the influence of the politics of their own governments. Furthermore, in the principal Allied countries and in the United States, public opinion was divided concerning the situation in Hungary. Liberal public opinion in England and in the United States was strongly opposed to Rumania's in-

2 **Ibid.**, pp. 604—5.
3 **Ibid.**, p. 529.
4 **Ibid.**, pp. 530—33.

vasion of Hungary, but in the French and Italian press there was a pre-disposition to justify Rumania's action.(5)

The differences of the Mission were evident from the very beginning. The French representative had come with the full intention of presiding over and dominating the Mission. Upon arriving in Budapest, he prepared a message requesting that each of the other Inter-Allied Generals report to him. Going to the regular meeting room, Graziani introduced himself and explained that seniority should govern in the question of chairmanship, adding that his government had undoubtedly expected him to be the presiding officer. This was not accepted by Bandholtz, who pointed out that accidential individual seniority should not outweight the qestion of national equality in representation. To secure national equality it would be better to organize the Inter-Allied Military Mission on the basis of daily rotation of chairmanship. The French general reluctantly agreed to the proposition, stating, however, that he must inform his government that he was not to be the permanent presiding officer.(6)

The Mission's second problem was Rumania, who stated that her little private war with Hungary was separate and distinct from the big war. She considered her victory over Hungary to be highly significant, completely ignoring the fact that she could never have touched Hungary had not the Allies first crushed both Germany and Austro-Hungary. The Rumanians considered themselves as crusaders against Hungarian Bolshevism and, therefore, felt entitled to do as they wanted. Furthermore, they

5 See "War of the Nations," New International Year Book for 1919 (New York: 1920), p. 748.

6 Harry Hill Bandholtz, An Undiplomatic Diary, ed. by Fritz Konrad Kruger (New York: Columbia University Press, 1933), p. 6. According to his diary, Bandholtz was of the opinion that the French attitude of favoring Rumania and being anti-Hungarian was on account of a desire to oppose England and make it difficult for the latter to gain headway in East-Central Europe. Italy, on the other hand, was trying to accomplish some kind of union between Romania-Hungary-Austria and Italy, with a view to isolating the Yugoslavs. See pp. 45, 331.

questioned why they should obey the Supreme Council when Italy refused to do so, and even such a prostrated nation as Turkey refused obedience.

On August 12, Constantine Diamandi, the Rumanian High Commissioner to the Peace Conference, accompanied by General Mardarescu, Commander-in-Chief of the Rumanian Army, and General Holban, Rumanian Commander in Budapest, appeared before the Mission. In view of the fact that it was decided to rotate the chairmanship in alphabetical sequence, Bandholtz, the American representative, presided at this meeting. Diamandi listened to the instructions which the Supreme Council had given the Military Mission. When asked if Rumania recognized them as valid and was prepared to follow them, Diamandi became enraged, jumped from his chair, and started to leave the room. Finding that his progress was not impeded by Bandholtz, he calmed down and returned to his chair. He finally agreed that the Rumanian government was prepared to accept the instructions as valid. Bandholtz handed over to the Rumanians the telegram of the Supreme Council ordering them to: 1) Immediately cease requisitioning; 2) Return all confiscated private property at once to the owners; 3) Return to the Hungarian Government the railroad, postal, and telegraph systems; 4) Evacuate as rapidly as possible all schools and colleges; 5) Cancel promptly all shipments of rolling stock or Hungarian property of any kind whatsoever to or towards Rumania, and return to Budapest any rolling stock or property already en route or held at outside stations; 6) Limit supervision over public or private affairs in the city.(7)

Bandholtz wired the American Mission in Paris that in his opinion the Rumanians were doing their utmost to delay matters in order to complete the looting of Hungary, and that as far as he could see, their progress to date in complying with the Supreme Council's desires was negative rather than positive.(8)

---

7 Ibid., p. 10.
8 Ibid., p. 11.

During the next months the Supreme Council sent several ultimatums to the Rumanians. Rumania always promised to fill them, but she never did. Eventually, the ultimatums became habitual. On August 26 Bandholtz sent a telegram to the Supreme Council in the name of the Mission, stating that:

In our opinion the Rumanians are looting Hungary as rapidly as possible, and at the same time, they are disarming everybody and refusing to organize the police. In general, intentionally or unintentionally, every move they make is in the direction of turning Hungary over to Bolshevism and chaos.(9)

The next day, Bandholtz sent the following coded message to Frank Lyon Polk, Assistant Secretary of State and leader of the American Peace Commision in Paris:

The Rumanians certainly could not continue their arrogant and haughty attitude unless backed by someone. I believe it is the French and Italians who are trying to accomplish some kind of political or other union among Rumania, Hungary, Austria, and Italy with a view of isolating entirely the Yugoslavs.(10)

A month later on October 1, 1919, Polk reported to Bandholtz:

It is now known that either Clemenceau himself or the French officials had always notified the Rumanians immediately after the dispatch of an ultimatum that such ultimatums could be ignored and that the Supreme Council really did not mean it.(11)

Rumania, occupying Hungary, had a far reaching political plan backed by France and Italy. In August, 1919, the whole Rumanian royal family moved to Budapest. On August 21, the Crown Prince of Rumania, as "future King of Hungary", received a num-

---

9 U. S., For. Rel., Paris Peace Conference, VII, 836.
10 Bandholtz, Diary, p. 45.
11 Ibid., p. 125.

ber of Hungarian aristocrats. Rumania wanted to force Hungary to make with her a separate peace which practically amounted to annexation. On August 11, Archduke Joseph, as temporary head of Hungary, received from the Rumanian government an ultimatum to the effect that Hungary must yield to all Rumanian demands, give up all war material and supplies of whatever nature, agree to back Rumania in taking the Banat county from the Yugoslavs, and, finally, consent to political union with Rumania, with the Rumanian King as ruler, along the same lines as the former Austro-Hungarian monarchy. The Archduke sent a negative response to these demands. On August 29 Rumania sent a second ultimatum, similar to the first, and including demands for immediate peace between Hungary and Rumania, the occupation of Hungary by Rumania for one year, and, finally, the annexation of Hungary to Rumania. The Archduke handed it over to Bandholtz. It was coded and ciphered and sent to the American Commission in Paris with a request that a copy be sent to the British Commission. Then Bandholtz turned to the Archduke and told him briefly: "Tell the sender to go plumb to Hell."(12)

A third problem was the reorganization of the Hungarian police and the establishment of a government acceptable to the Supreme Council. On September 5 the Inter-Allied Military Mission put the task of the reorganization of the Hungarian police into the hands of Colonel Halsey E. Yates of the United States Army. The Rumanians, however, tried to prevent such a reorganization. In spite of the fact, Yates organized a police force of six thousand men in Budapest and obliged the Rumanians to give them arms. Upon completion of his work six weeks later, Yates was officially congratulated by the Supreme Council.(13)

The first problem in organizing a government was to decide who would be head of state. Among the three Habsburg pre-

---

12 See the full text of the Rumanian ultimatums, U. S., For. Rel., Paris Peace Conference, VII, 567—68.

13 Bandholtz, Diary, p. 234.

tenders, the former King Charles had never resigned as sovereign of Hungary, and so long as he lived the people would have no other king, since he had been crowned. Furthermore, in case of return, he would take Croatia with him because this country was fanatically loyal. The second Habsburg who could be invested with the royal authority was Charles' popular relative, Archduke Joseph, temporary head of state. Archduke Albrecht, the third Habsbrug, had large holdings in the North and could promise to return Slovakia if he were elected, since he was in favor with the Slovaks. But it was clear that the Allies would not have permitted Charles or any other Habsburg to be King of Hungary; they did not even accept Archduke Joseph as temporary head of the country. On August 23 Clemenceau sent a telegram to the Military Mission at Budapest insisting that as long as Hungary had at her head a member of the House of Habsburg, no peace was likely to be lasting, nor could the Allied governments give her the economic support which Hungary so sorely needed. (14) The Archduke resigned on the same day, and Hungary was without a head for several months.

The Peace Conference wanted a permanent popular government established in Hungary. But it was impossible to hold elections in Hungary because of the Rumanian occupation. Although the Entente sent three ultimatums to Rumania to leave, she did not budge.(15) Yet Hungary had to organize some cabinet that would be recognized by the Entente, which would not accept or acknowledge the de facto Hungarian government as sufficiently permanent to guarantee a treaty of peace. When Archduke Joseph resigned, the entire cabinet did the same, stating that everything was now in the hands of the Inter-Allied Military Mission. In fact, there was now no government, and no one had the power to appoint a new one. To avoid this situation the Mis-

---

14 See the debats of the Supreme Council, U. S., For. Rel., Paris Peace Conference, VII, 679—81, 694—98, 707—8, 709—10, 775—76, 791—92, 803—4.
15 U. S., For. Rel., Paris Peace Conference, VIII, 110.

sion informed the Prime Minister that it did not want to mix in the internal affairs of Hungary, except to such an extent as it might be definitely instructed by the Supreme Council, and added that it was the duty of the present cabinet to continue temporarily in office until a new government could be organized within a few days. Bandholtz reported to Paris on August 22 that the Hungarian political situation was believed to be critical, but not beyond remedy, provided the Rumanians withdrew behind their own recognized boundaries.(16) But Rumania did not withdraw and Hungary was without an "acceptable" government during the next months. In the confusion, of course, many politicians tried to organize a cabinet of their own and obtain acceptance by the Entente. Bandholtz wrote in his diary on August 31: "Business is decidedly poor in Hungary, if we do not have from three to five cabinets per week." The Hungarian cause was hopeless; the country, prostrate; the Rumanians, pillaging; the Entente, doing absolutely nothing. On September 20 the Mission sent the following telegram to Paris:

At the present rate of progress, the Rumanians will continue indefinitely with their occupation and attendant looting in which they are daily becoming more expert. The Hungarians, on the other hand, are becoming more and more discouraged; famine, suffering, and disorder are approaching. It is recommended that either the Friedrich cabinet be recognized or that explicit instructions be given as to what will be recognized.(17)

The reply of the Supreme Council stated that it was not thought the Friedrich government was a real representation of all Hungarian parties; he should in his cabinet have a member from each party. In case Friedrich could not do so, the Entente could not recognize his cabinet nor make a treaty of peace with it. In view of the fact that there were eighteen different political par-

---

16 Bandholtz, Diary, p. 26.
17 U. S., For. Rel., Paris Peace Conference, VII, 777.

ties in Hungary from Socialists and Radicals to Royalists, it was apparent that such an order could not be carried out. The Hungarian Government responded to the order of the Supreme Council by a message sent to the Inter-Allied Military Mission on September 23 stating that there was nothing else left for Hungary but to come to terms with Rumania because otherwise she would be absolutely ruined. The Entente either could not or would not help her.(18) This is exactly what the French and the Italians wanted. Bandholtz called the Hungarian Minister of Foreign Affairs and told him that he was very foolish for two reasons: the first being that the Rumanians would demand so much that it would ruin Hungary in perpetuity; and secondly, that the Rumanians, for their part, would not carry out any contract which they made. Then he inquired if the Minister of Foreign Affairs had been approached at all by the French. He said no, but that the Hungarians knew that the French were winking at the Rumanians in all they had been doing. Then Bandholtz asked him if he had had any transactions with the Italians. Yes, the Minister answered, General Mombelli himself had suggested that the Hungarians come to terms with the Rumanians.(19) But the subsequent negotiations reached no agreement and the Rumanians responded with terror. They arrested some of the Hungarian officials, and the Crown Prince of Rumania himself, as the "future King of Hungary," had ordered the arrest of Prime Minister Friedrich. Such an action, of course, could not be tolerated by the Supreme Council, and the Military Mission sent a memorandum to the Rumanians calling their attention to the fact that the Mission considered it indispensable that the conduct of affairs by the Hungarian cabinet be not interrupted for a single moment. Therefore, in the name of the Supreme Council the Mission demanded that the Rumanian authorities leave the members of the Hungarian government entirely alone.(20) In any event, the attempt to

---

18 Bandholtz, Diary, p. 108.
19 Ibid., p. 109.
20 Ibid., p. 155.

arrest the Primer Minister failed, but relations between Rumania and the Mission became so unfriendly that Mardarescu, taking the memorandum from the Mission, declared to the Allied Generals: "Gentlemen, you have four telephons but I have 80,000 bayonets."(21)

Meantime something changed in the relations between France and Italy. On November 7, Polk sent a code telegram from Paris to Bandholtz, which indicated that the French were up to something and for some reason the French and the Italians were not working together. "It will now be up to us to see just exactly what the cause of the separation is."(22) It was, of course, the Fiume question. Gabriele d'Annunzio seized Fiume on September 13, 1919, and Zara on November 4, in defiance of the decision of the Allies. French and Italian soldiers were hostile toward each other, almost to the point of war.

As previously noted, the Entente did not recognize the Hungarian Government of which Friedrich, as representative of the Habsburg dynasty, was the head. So long as Friedrich was Prime Minister, even though an election was held and resulted triumphantly for him, nothing would convince the Entente to recognize the Hungarian Government. Therefore Bandholtz advised Friedrich to resign. But Friedrich was unwilling to do so and stated he thought it was the policy of the Supreme Council to allow the Hungarian people to do what they wanted and that they should have their own way. Bandholtz told him that the Hungarian people knew or should know that America had nothing whatever to gain there in the way of indemnity or territorial acquisitions, but that it was interested in a square deal for everybody, in having peace ratified between Hungary and the United States, and in having a well-organized government in control of the destinies of the country. Bandholtz proposed to speak to Friedrich frankly and in the manner of one gentleman to

21 Ibid., p. 249.
22 Ibid., p. 210

another. Bandholtz stated that he did not want to defend the Supreme Council or any allied countries. He would grant Friedrich that they were all wrong. If given sufficient time, a year or two, Friedrich could by propaganda and by demonstration of his own worth convince the American and British people that he was right, but in the meantime where in hell would Hungary go? It was up to the Hungarians to organize as quickly as possible a government that would be acceptable to the Entente, so that Hungary could be recognized.(23) Two weeks later Friedrich resigned and a coalition government was formed under Charles Huszár, a Christian Democrat, as Prime Minister. The function of this government was to act until the people had been consulted through the medium of general elections by secret vote. This temporary government was recognized by the Supreme Council and, finally, Hungary had some kind of government!

In the meantime the Rumanians continued to loot Hungary removing all automobiles, locomotives, cars, and other rolling stock. They took possession of, and shipped to Rumania, all the arms, munitions, and war material they could find, as well as private automobiles, farm implements, cattle, horses, clothing, sugar, coal, salt, and everything of value. Even after they were notified by the Supreme Council to cease such requisitioning, they continued their depredations. They had taken possession of all branches of the government, all railroad, telegraph, telephone, and postal systems. They stole everything movable: plates, pictures, carpets, linen, furniture, even the cloth from billiard tables. They took twelve hundred locomotives, leaving the Hungarians only four hundred. In the Ritz Hotel, headquarters of the English member of the Molotary Mission, Béla Kun had done five million crowns' worth of damage; the Rumanians did seven millions' worth. They took literally everything! A member of the English Mission, sent into the East of Hungary to investigate the facts, said that the Rumanians had not even left the nails in the boards.

23 Ibid., p. 211

In September, with 6,000 kilometers of railroads, Hungary had only 4,500 cars available. Budapest, which contained one-fifth of the population, required 4,000 a day to feed its people. It was not difficult to imagine the result when winter set in! The rolling stock had been so thoroughly cleaned out that transportation was insufficient for local food and fuel requirements. In October the Rumanian administration had reduced the food reserve to one-third of what it was in September. On October 10, two thousand laborers were put out of work when the machinery from the firm of Schmitt and Társai was seized and removed. In Budapest they looted the Weiss factories to the value of eight million dollars. They desired to loot the National Museum; that they did not was due to the fact that the doors were sealed and signed by Bandholtz. In all towns occupied by Rumanians the Mission found an oppression so great as to make life unbearable. Murder was common; youths and women were flogged and imprisoned without trial, or arrested without reason; theft of personal property went under the name of requisition. Bandholtz reported to Paris on Ocotber 13: "Conditions prevail which are difficult for Western Europeans to realize, if they had not seen and heard the evidence." Experienced Hungarian Directors of Hospitals had been replaced by inexperienced Rumanian doctors. Petitions had to be written in the Rumanian language; one had to employ Rumanian lawyers, who charged enormous fees. At Boros-Sebes, two hundred fifty Hungarian soldiers were taken prisoner and killed in the most barbarous manner: stripped naked and stabbed with bayonets — a lingering death.(24)

The Armistice of August 2 between Rumanian and Hungarian forces provided that after the Hungarian officers should supervise the disarming of their own troops, the officers would then be given freedom with retention of arms, but such was not the

---

24 Further details on the looting of Hungary by the Rumanians can be found in U. S., For. Rel., Paris Peace Conference, VII, 774—75, 836—39, et passim. Also see Bandholtz, Diary, pp. 151—55 (on requisition), pp. 187—89 (on Rumanian brutalities), et passim.

case. After the Hungarian troops were disarmed, officers were required to report daily and in the first week of August, many officers were arrested and sent to Arad. Nearly all so-called prisoners-of-war were arrested and disarmed! During the transfer from the place of arrest to prisons both officers and men were beaten, maltreated, and robbed by Rumanian officers and soldiers; moreover, prisoners' female relatives were insulted when visiting prisoners. The Mission's Committee sent to investigate prisoner-of-war camps consisted of Colonel Raymond Sheldon of the American Army, Doctor Hector Munro of the Internatinal Hospital Relief Association, Captain Georges Brunier of the Swiss Army and delegate of the International Red Cross, and First Lieutenant Francesco Braccio of the Italian Medical Corps. The report of the Committee accused the Rumanian soldiers, and in some instances officers, of stealing the clothes, boots, and private property of the prisoners. They found 121 civilian prisoners among the war prisoners. Among the civilians were six women, one evidently an educated woman who had written poetry; four boys, two were thirteen and two were fourteen years of age; and one old man of seventy-six. Many were suffering from serious disease. They reported that at present the Rumanian-Hungarian situation was the most serious in Europe. Bandholtz noted in his diary: "It is not possible to describe conditions in a city or country occupied by an enemy, but judging from conditions in Budapest and Hungary, while occupied by the Rumanians, we Americans should promptly take every measure possible to avoid any such catastrophe."(25)

Conditions were going from bad to worse each day. Bandholtz decided to go to Rumania to meet the Rumanian King on behalf of the Hungarians. The meeting took place in Sinaia in September, 1919. The King went into detail regarding the Rumanian grievances, protesting especially the fact that the Rumanians were considered robbers because they were looting Hungary, whereas the Serbs had looted and had never been called to account.

25 Bandholtz, Diary, p. 18.

He also complained that the Serbs had received some of the Danube monitors, whereas Rumania had received nothing. But his main grievance seemed to be due to the "Minorities Clause" in the Treaty of Peace which Rumania was called upon to sign. He explained that some fifty years ago, as a result of the pogroms in Russia, a great Jewish migration to Rumania had taken place. These immigrants belonged entirely to the commercial class and came into a country where commerce had hitherto been almost nonexistent. In the Treaty of Berlin of 1878 the Powers had imposed upon Rumania certain conditions in regard to the Jews, but when Rumania bought the railroads which had been built by German capital, these restrictions were removed, and Rumania was left as independent as any other nation. Now she wished to maintain her independence. He added that the Jewish question was not the only one touched by the Minorities Clause. Rumania had acquired about one million Hungarians as well as many Bulgarians and Slavs, by their recent acquisition of territory. He felt it was administratively wrong to have these minorities come into a government when they felt no obligation on their part to assimilate themselves to the new nation but rather felt themselves protected by the strong powers in any opposition they might make. He considered that no independent and sovereign state could accept the conditions which were being imposed on Rumania. The King stated, furthermore, that he was pleased to have an opportunity to meet an American who would probably have influence with the American government and deplored the fact that the United States was so far away as to be in relative ignorance of Rumania and things Rumanian. He added that Bratianu, the Rumanian Prime Minister, was treated badly by the Americans in Paris and particularly so by Wilson. He added also that it was unfortunate that the American officers sent after the war had been selected from those who had not liked his country.

Bandholtz explained to His Majesty that, of course, the Inter-Allied Military Mission had nothing whatever to do with any such matters He assured the King that Americans had no ill feeling toward Rumania and that they had nothing to gain financially or otherwise in treating her badly.

At breakfast Bandholtz met Her Majesty, the Queen. She turned to him and said: "I didn't know whether I wanted to meet you at all. I have heard many things about you." Bandholtz replied: "Your Majesty, I am not half so bad as I might look, nor one quarter so bad as you seem to think I am." The Queen smiled and said that the King had told her that the American General wasn't exactly a heathen. During the conversation the Queen said that she felt keenly the fact that Rumania had fought as an ally and was now being treated as an enemy. "I feel that we are perfectly entitled to do what we want to. You may call it stealing if you like, or any other name." The King intruded upon the conversation by saying that at any rate the Rumanians had taken no food stuffs. Bandholtz wrote in his diary: "As it is bad form to call a King a liar, I simply informed His Majesty that he was badly mistaken, and that I could give him exact facts in regard to thousands of carloads of food stuffs that had been taken out of Budapest alone."

After breakfast the Queen said that Bandholtz was a very pleasant gentleman and she desired to give him one of her photographs, so that whenever he felt hard towards the Rumanians, he could look at it and, she hoped, it would make him feel more kindly. Bandholtz remarked in his diary: "Her Mjesty certainly seems to think that she can control any man whom she meets and it must be admitted that she has considerable foundation for that opinion. I am inclined to think, however, that she realized that it took more than a signed photograph to cause me to wander from the straight and narrow path of military duty."(26) After the departure of Bandholtz, the Queen explained her true feelings. She told Colonel Poillon that Bandholtz was a Jew, his aides were all Jews, and that everybody in his office was a Jew.(27)

26 **Ibid.**, pp. 65ff.
27 **Ibid.**, p. 320.

Arriving at Budapest Bandholtz found a telegram from Clemenceau suggesting that the members of the Mission engage in no diplomatic discussions. Apparently the French felt that Rumania came within their sphere of influence and, in anticipation of possible rivals, had done everything possible to make the Rumanians dislike the Americans.(28)

The Rumanian reports to Paris were entirely different from those of the Military Mission. They denied all stories of outrages and looting saying that their victorious march upon an enemy's capital had caused no more casualties than customary in time of war. They stated that all Hungary was clamoring for them, and that 150,000 workers gathered at Budapest to express their thanks to the Rumanian Army for feeding their children and for giving them political liberty. The Supreme Council directed Sir George Clark, the Director of the Oriental Department of the English Foreign Office, to go to Budapest and interview the Mission to determine whether Rumania or the four Allied Generals were lying. Clark was sent to Budapest on October 23, 1919, as a special diplomatic representative of the Supreme Council to deliver the ultimatum to the Rumanians and to bring about the formation of a coalition cabinet in which all the responsible parties of Hungary would be represented. From General Bandholtz' account, it would appear that Clark was at first decidedly prejudiced against the Hungarians and inclined to favor the Rumanians. The latter gave him a tremendous dinner at the Hotel Hungaria, during which there was much playing of "God Save the King" and much talking about Great Britain as the greatest power on earth, and much champagne flowed. Gradually, however, Clark modified his viewpont, strongly influenced, no doubt, by the statements of General Bandholtz and Gorton.(29)

The situation in Hungary required immediate decisions by the Supreme Council in order to re-establish the normal condi-

28 U. S., For. Rel., Paris Peace Conference, VIII, 135.
29 Ibid., p. 147.

tions necessary for the security of central Europe. Clark came to Budapest with a proposition of the Supreme Council to send into Hungary two divisions as an army of occupation under Inter-Allied officers—one division of Czechoslovaks and one division of Yugoslavs to replace the Rumanians. Against this proposition the Inter-Allied Military Mission unanimously protested that such procedure would stir Hungary into revolution and would destroy all prospects for an early solution of the Hungarian question. It was furthermore urged that the Rumanians, the Yugoslavs, and the Czechoslovaks all be required to retire at once behind their respective lines of demarcation.(30) Bandholtz, too, sent a personal message to Polk by Captain Richardson, one of his subordinates, who was in charge of the American Organization for feeding chidren in Hungary. The effect of these messages was that the Supreme Council gave up its original plan and sent its final ultimatum to Rumania of November 7, giving her eight days for reply. In general Rumania was invited to obey without discussion, reservation, or conditions, the following resolutions:

First:
> To entirely evacuate Hungarian territory as defined by the Conference.

Second:
> To cease her requisitions and restore all goods taken in the requisitions made in Hungary since the beginning of the Rumanian occupation.

Third:
> To sign the Austrian Treaty and the Minorities Treaty under the conditions indicated by the note of the Supreme Council of October 12, 1919.(31)

In conclusion, the ultimatum of the Supreme Council stated as follows:

---

30 Bandholtz, Diary, p. 204.
31 U. S., For. Rel., Paris Peace Conference, VIII, 269.

Should the reply not be satisfactory to the Supreme Council of the Allies, the latter has decided to notify Rumania that she has separated herself from them. They shall invite her to recall immediately her delegates to the Peace Conference, and they will also withdraw their diplomatic missions at Bucharest. As the questions concerning the settlement of boundaries are still to be made, Rumania will thus by her own action deprive herself of all title to the support of the Powers as well as to the recognition of her rights by the Conference. It would be with the profoundest regret that the Supreme Council of the Allies should see itself forced to sever relations with Rumania, but it is confident that it has been patient to the very last degree.

The ultimatum of the Supreme Council also noted that:

The Rumanian Government has continued for the last three and one half months to negotiate with the Conference from Power to Power, taking into consideration no other rights or interests than her own and refusing to accept the charges of solidarity although she wishes to enjoy the benefits of them. The Conference wishes to make a last appeal to the wisdom of the Rumanian Government and of the Rumanian people before taking the grave resolution of severing all relations with Rumania. Their right to dictate rests essentially on the fact that Rumania owed the priceless service of having reconstituted her national unity in doubling her territory and population to the victory of the Allies. Without the enormous sacrifices consented to by them, at the present time Rumania would be ruined and in bondage without any possible hope. Rumania entered the struggle at the end of the second year of the war, making her own conditions. It is true she made great sacrifices and suffered heavy losses, but she finally consented to treat separately with the enemy and to submit to his law. She owes her liberty and her victory, as well as her future, to the Allies. How can such a situation be lost sight of and so soon forgotten by the Rumanian statesmen.(32)

Rumania understood that it was bad policy for her to force the Supreme Council into this position. She accepted this last ultimatum. She signed the treaties with Austria and Bulgaria on December 10, 1919, containing the obnoxious Minority Clauses. She evacuated Hungary, first west from the Tisza River, and later the eastern part of the country. For the requisitions and fcᵢ other calamities in Hungary she accused her own Generals General Mardarescu, Commander-in-Chief of the Rumanian Army, and General Holban, in Budapest. The Rumanian Government resigned. Mardarescu did the same. General Holban committed suicide on the eve of the investigation ordered by the new government after Sir George Clark had come to look into the situation.

Admiral Horthy's Nationalist army entered Budapest on November 16, 1919. The bells began to ring in the early morning to indicate the arrival of the troops.(33) There was a big public Mass in front of the Parliament Building and a huge celebration at the Opera house. But the work of the Inter-Allied Military Mission was not yet over. It had to prevent the atrocities which could arise from the new situation. Bandholtz as early as October 29 explained to Horthy that Hungary was about to appear

32 Ibid., pp. 270—71.

33 A good biography of Admiral Horthy is in English: O. Rutter, Regent of Hungary (London: Rich and Cowan, 1939). Also there is a good detail about Horthy and the whole Hungarian political situation in John F. Montgomery, Hungary: The Unwilling Satellite (New York: Devin-Adair Co., 1947). As a scholarly work see C. A. Macartney, October Fifteenth: A History of Modern Hungary, 1929—1945 (2 vols.; Edinburgh: Edinburgh University Press, 1961).

before a jury of all the nations; she was to a certain extent discredited on account of having allowed Bolshevism to exist within her borders for over three months. Should any disorders result after the Rumanian evacuation, her standing with the Allied Powers would be practically nil. On the other hand, if she conducted herself with the dignity of a civilized nation and permitted no serious disorders to ensue, she would raise herself highly in the estimation of the Entente. Bandholtz explained to Horthy that there would undoubtedly be some young hot-heads in the Hungarian Army who would be anxious to shoot a Rumanian or hang a Jew, and that one or two such incidents could bring discredit upon the whole country. He further explained that the workmen of Budapest feared the so-called "White Army" and that Horthy therefore should show that his army was not made up of a gang of "White Terrorists" but was a well-disciplined and organized National Hungarian Army. The Admiral said that he had his forces absolutely in hand and would guarantee no disturbances. The Admiral promised Bandholtz that it would be his constant and earnest endeavor to prevent any and all excesses on the part of his countrymen that would affect the situation.

In the meantime almost the whole country was clamoring against the Jews, who were being beaten and maltreated in Budapest while some were killed in the countryside. Report from western Hungary indicated all sorts of atrocities on the part of the Hungarians who were torturing the Jews. Colonel Nathan Horowitz, a Jewish member of the American Military Mission in Budapest, was sent by the Inter-Allied Military Mission to visit western Hungary, and, in his report concerning the general conditions there, he stated that in his opinion, Admiral Horthy's army had done everything within reason to prevent any such persecutions. He added that no more atrocities had been committed than would ordinarily happen under the stress of such circumstances.

He stated that a great many "rascally" Jews under the cloak of religion had committed crimes, that there really was a great deal of anti-Semitic feeling on account of so many Jews having been Bolshevists, but as to there being a real White Terror, there was nothing of the kind—this danger was a figment of the imagination of politicians. He affirmed that Jews and Gentiles alike united in maintaining order and was absolutely sure there was no danger from the Hungarian National Army.(34)

Before World War I there existed no anti-Semitic movement in Hungary. The large percentage of Jews felt as strongly Hungarians as the German Jews felt German. In contrast to their racial brothers in Rumania and Russia, Hungarian Jews did not suffer from persecution or exceptional legal treatment.(35) But a disproportionate number of Jews helped to establish Bolshevism in Hungary and were its most cruel exponents. Ninety-five percent of the Communist leaders were Jewish; and, of the twenty-six Commissars, eighteen were Jews, though there were only one and a half million Jews among the twenty-one million inhabitants in Hungary. Furthermore, all the leaders of the Red Terror Corps were Jews, among them Tibor Szamuely, Cserney, and Korvin. A very large number of Jewish Bolshevik leaders had only recently emigrated into Hungary and could not be called Hungarians in any sense. The conservative and national Jewish-Hungarian element despised these foreigners as did their Christian compatriots. It is deplorable but quite natural that the reaction against the Red Terror was accompanied by excesses and persecution of the Jews, though the account of it is generally greatly exaggerated.(36)

Perhaps there were fanatics who committed atrocities. According to Bandholtz, a Catholic priest at a public meeting on November 30 in Budapest said:

---

34 Bandholtz, Diary, p. 120.
35 For further details see Macartney, October Fifteenth: A History of Modern Hungary, 1929—1945.
36 Ibid., I, 29.

The Bible tells us we must forgive our enemies. I say we can personally forgive our enemies as Christians, but not as Hungarians. The Hungarian people must never forget and the Jews must be punished. They say it is shameful to have pogroms, but we say it is just as shameful to have communism in the twentieth century, and we had it!(37)

The second speaker was a professor by the name of Zarkany, who, after giving some left-handed compliments to the Entente, stated: "The Jewish question is a natural one for the Hungarian people to settle, and we will settle it."(38)

Editorials in Budapest papers strongly advocated progroms and persecution of the Jews.(39) On December 10 a Jewish printing office was wrecked by a mob. Four days earlier a couple of young Jewish boys, who had been beaten by Hungarian soldiers, were brought to Bandholtz' office at the Railroad station. Bandholtz sent for General Soos, Hungarian Chief of Staff, and told him that he was "damned sick" of such conduct. Although he could understand that Hungarians naturally felt resentful because of the fact that most of the Bolshevist leaders had been Jews, nevertheless, neither America nor England could tolerate such barbaric conduct. One of England's greatest Prime Ministers, Benjamin Disraeli, he continued, had been a Jew, and the present Chairman of the Military Committee in the American House of Representatives, Julius Kahn of California, was a Jew. If reports got out that Hungarians were lapsing into the same form of barbarism as the Russians, it would seriously affect their whole future. Bandholtz wanted the Hungarian captain punished. He also informed the General that other reports had come to him from outlying districts where pogroms were openly advocated. General Soos promised that he would take immediate and drastic action to cut short this growing evil.

---

37 Bandholtz, **Diary,** p. 257.
38 **Ibid.,** p. 256.
39 **Ibid.,** p. 274.

There was an alleged attempted Bolshevik uprising in January, 1920, in the Ganz-Danubia Works at Budapest in the suppression of which twenty Bolsheviks were supposedly killed. Rumor has it that Bolshevism had reigned for a few hours in Szolnok on the Tisza River about forty miles east of Budapest, but that it was vigorously and thoroughly suppressed by Horthy's troops, who killed several hundred Bolsheviks while only four of his officers were killed. Some days later these reports proved to be untrue. The persistent rumors of Bolshevik uprisings and killings in Hungary were due to unfriendly propaganda, but it was difficult to find out who spread them.

The Communists had a well-organized organization in Vienna which had become the center of their activities for East-Central Europe. Four Communists, who had infiltrated Hungary from Austria, endeavored to blow up the Gellert Hotel in Budapest where Admiral Horthy had his headquarters, the Royal Palace occupied by General Gorton and General Bandholtz, the Prime Minister's residence, and other Government buildings, the Coronation Cathedral, and the Opera House. Fortunately they were discovered before they did any damage, and one of them was captured. Moreover, they confessed Moscow's plan to have general uprisings on Thursday, January 22, 1920, in Hungary, Czechoslovakia, Austria, and Italy, and gave evidence showing Vienna to be the center of Communist operations in Europe.(40)

As a result of this confession, fourteen Bolsheviks were hanged in Budapest. The government itself had in December authorized the internment of any person who, even if not guilty of an indictable offense, might present a danger to the public order. Under this ordinance many thousands had been interned, including nearly all the more prominent Social Democrats who had not escaped abroad. This action presaged the "White Terror" to come. Outside Hungary, many people thought this area of the Inter-Allied Military Mission's work was a failure, a question we will discuss later.

40 Ibid., p. 284.

On November 19, 1919, the United States Senate definitely rejected the Treaty of Versailles, and the American Commission left Paris. Bandholtz remained in Budapest as the United States representative in Hungary until the arrival of Ulysses Grant Smith, whom the Department of State sent to replace him. Grant Smith arrived on January 22, 1920. He had worked in Vienna in the diplomatic service for a number of years, and Hungary warmly welcomed him.

The Inter-Allied Mission held its last meeting on January 21, 1920. The Chairman that day was General Reginald St. George Gorton, Head of the English Military Mission. The members had decided to send a telegram to the Supreme Council informing that honorable body that it was their opinion that the Mission had been treated with superciliousness and contempt from the beginning and proceeded to give concrete cases in which telegram after telegram containing inquires and requests for decisions addressed to the Council had never been even acknowledged. The Mission considered that its duty was to dissolve. Major General Harry Hill Bandholtz left Hungary with the Hungarian Peace Delegation on February 10, 1920, for Paris.(41)

41 **Ibid.**, p. 341.

CHAPTER IV

FIGHTING FOR JUSTICE:
THE TRIANON PEACE TREATY

None of the Paris Peace Treaties was more drastic in its terms than the Treaty of Trianon. By it Hungary was not so much mutilated as dismembered. Even if we exclude Croatia, which had stood only in a federal relationship to the other lands of the Holy Crown of St. Stephen—although one of eight hundred years' standing—Hungary proper was reduced to less than one-third of her pre-war area, and a little over two-fifths of her population. Territories and peoples formerly Hungarian were distributed among no less than seven states. Rumania alone secured, at Hungary's expense, an area larger than that left to Hungary herself.(1) These losses were proportionately far greater than those inflicted on Germany or Bulgaria. The Austria of 1920 was, indeed, an even smaller fraction of the State which had borne

---

1 Of the 325,411 sq. km. which had composed the area of the Lands of the Holy Crown, Hungary was left with only 92,963. Romania alone had received 103,093; Czechoslovakia 61,633; Yugoslavia the 42,541 sq. km. of Croatia-Slovenia and 20,551 of Inner Hungary; Austria 4,020; Italy 8 sq. km. (the area of the city of Fiume); and even Poland small fragments. Of the population of 20,886.487 (1910 cenzus), Hungary was left with 7,615,117. Rumania received 5,257,467, Czechoslovakia 3,517,568, Yugoslavia 4,131,249 (2,621,954 + 1,509,295), and Austria 291,618. In addition, the Treaty required Hungary to pay in reparations an unspecified sum and limited her armed forces to a long-service force of 35,000 (officers and men), to be used exlusively on the maintenance of internal order and on frontier defense.

that name in 1918, but the old Austria had not been a unitary state, but only a federation of kingdoms, duchies, and provinces, the hereditary estates of a super-national dynasty. The Treaty of St. Germain simply divided this federation into its constituent elements. Turkey retained almost intact the Turkish core of her Empire, losing only outlying portions.

The Hungarian State, on the other hand, had existed for a thousand years within frontiers which had shown a very remarkable degree of stability. The political state enclosed within those boundaries had been unitary long before most of the states of today. Moreover, its geographical structure had imposed upon it also a very close economic coherence, obviously beneficial to almost all its inhabitants. The unity of Hungary was thus something of an entirely different order from that of the Austrian or the Ottoman Empire. It was even far more firmly established than that of Germany.

These issues were never seriously denied. But the real reason for the partition of Hungary was, of course, that the racial diversity of its population was at least as undeniable as its historic or geographical unity. The majority of the population of the periphery was German in the west, Slovak in the north, Ruthene in the northeast, and Rumanian in the east, while in the south there was a large contingent of Serbs, mingled with the Magyars and with German and other colonists. It was, broadly speaking, the principle of self-determination which was invoked in 1919 to bring about the dismemberment of Hungary. The German area in the west was assigned to Austria; the north, both Slovak and Ruthene, to Czechoslovakia; the east to Rumania, and the south to Yugoslavia, with Italy taking the Port of Fiume; Poland got some in the far north, while the center remained with Hungary.

The ethnographic boundaries were not, however, followed exactly. The successor states and their advocates took their stand on the simple right of self-determination of peoples, which, according to them, automatically justified the non-Magyars in leaving Hungary to form their own national states. This right seemed so obvious that it was hardly argued at Trianon. The doctrine of self-determination was used to detach not only the Rumanians and Serbs from Hungary, but also the Slovaks. The Ruthenes were assigned to Czechoslovakia as a more natural home for them than Hungary. But the assumption was carried even further. It was supposed that the neutral or third-party minorities, such as the Germans in Northern, Eastern, and Southern Hungary, ought also to be reckoned in the non-Magyar camp. Thus in Southern Hungary, for example, the Germans were added to the Serbs; whereas, if the Germans had been added to the Magyars, it would have been the Serbs whose claim might have appeared thin. Moreover, evidence was presented to show that Magyar rule in Hungary had been unjust, oppressive, and tyrannical. Because of this oppressive Magyar rule, it was argued that the new national states were automatically justified, and that even where it was necessary to assign minorities to them, this did little harm, because they were more democratic and socially more advanced than Hungary. Furthermore, because of economic and strategic considerations, three and a half-million Hungarians, one-third of the Hungarian speaking people, were transferred to the successor states, and many of these were living in compact blocs contiguous to the new frontiers.(2)

Hungary did not altogether deny the right of national self-determination, but she protested strongly against the conclusions drawn from it. She admitted as valid only the decision taken by the Diet of Croatia. For the rest, she questioned the representative character of the local popular meetings, and maintained stoutly that the nationalities never really wished to separate from her at all. If the point was uncertain, it could be settled by plebiscites, which she requested, but in vain. Hungary was confident that their result would be favorable to her for she contended that the nationalities had no reason to desire a change, as was proved

2 Of the 10,050,575 persons of Magyar mother-tongue, according to the 1910 census, no less than 3,219,579 were allotted to the Successor States: 1,704,851 of them to Rumania; 1,063,020 to Czechoslovakia; 547,735 to Yugoslavia and 26,182 to Austria.

by the remarkable cohesion shown by the Hungarian state throughout history. And although the Magyar nation had predominated in Hungary, it had never in any way oppressed the non-Magyars. The Magyars' only postulate had been the political unity of the state. A non-Magyar had been left entirely free to enjoy his own national culture in private and local affairs. Therefore to speak of oppression was absurd, and to parcel up the old historical and economic unit of Hungary was to inflict not merely injustice but also disaster upon the peoples concerned.(3)

It must be emphasized that the Treaty was not negotiated but dictated. Hungary was not even invited to Trianon until the Allies had agreed among themselves, and the mass of maps, historical essays, and statistics which her delegates brought with them represented, from the point of view of the Conference, so much wasted labor.

Although in most respects there was little difference between Trianon and the other Peace Treaties, there was at least one pe-

---

3 Pre-World War I Hungary is accused by many non-Hungarian historians, especially by Hugh Seaton-Watson, of having oppressed the non-Magyar minorities. Others, like Carlile Aylmer Macartney, have a different point of view. Also there is a very interesting report on the situation of the minorities in post-World War I Yugoslavia sent by John Dyneley Prince, Minister of the United States to Yugoslavia, to the State Department on June 15, 1933, which admits that pre-war Hungary did not oppress the minorities. It says:
"I can state of my own experience that although the Croatians, stimulated by Pan-Slav agitators under the influence of old Russia, chose to regard the very light Hungarian rule in Croatia as a 'tyranny,' one finds many persons in Yugoslavia today who look back upon their former status as having been much better than the iron hand of Belgrade which is clutching the whole of Yugoslavia by a well organized and successful system of repression. I cannot find, for example, that the former Austro-Hungarian Government compelled the study of the Magyar language in Croatia except in the case of persons in government service, who were relatively few in number. After all there was little tyranny in insisting that railway and customhouse officials should be able to speak some Hungarian — and that is really all that was requested."
U. S., For. Rel., Department of State, FP 864.00/786.

culiarity. The Treaty could not be presented in Hungary until 1920. At that time many who participated in the work of the Peace Conference admitted without reservation the errors committed by the conference and the defects of its conclusions. One had only to refer to the Senate of the United States, whose attitude toward the treaties is well known. On November 19, 1919, the Senate, after months of debate, rejected the Treaty of Versailles. As a consequence of this, when William C. Bullitt, geographic and economic expert of the American delegation at Paris, saw the first drafts of the peace treaty with Hungary, he left the conference in order to voice in the United States his opposition to what was happening in Paris.(4) In England several members both of the House of Lords and of the House of Commons spoke openly for revision of the Trianon Treaty.(5) In 1919, John M. Keynes published a book in London entitled **The Economic Consequences of the Peace.** Although he dealt with the German treaty, he concluded that the treaties must be revised.(6) The movement for revision reached a more significant stage when Signor Nitti, former Premier of Italy, appeared on the scene. When Nitti resigned the premiership, he, having regained his freedom, pointed out frankly that the Allies would have been horrified if anyone else had used the tone which they had adopted toward the defeated nations. The article in which these views were set forth was originally intended for publication in the United States but was ultimately printed in Italian newspapers.

Soon after, Nitti raised his voice in a meeting of the Union of Democratic Control in London, urging the revision of the Versailles Treaty.(7) Lord Newton stated in the House of Lords that

---

4 **Papers and Documents Realting to the Foreign Relations of Hungary, 1919—1920** (Budapest: Hungarian Ministry for Foreign Affairs, 1939), p. 954.

5 For full details see **The Hungarian Question in the British Parliament, Speeches, Questions, and Answers in the House of Lords and in the House of Commons** (London, Grant Richards Publ., 1933).

6 (London: Harcourt and Brace, 1919). See Introduction.

7 **Papers and Documents,** p. 1002.

the Trianon Treaty was the scandal of civilization. Senator de Monzie, member of the French Senate, came to the conclusion that Central Europe had been balkanized by the Trianon Treaty, that this created a new danger zone for Europe, and that revision of this treaty was imperative in France's own interest. M. Danielou stated in the French Chamber of Deputies that the French were extremely uninformed about the situation in the Danubian states, that the French Parliament should not approve this stringent Treaty and that a way ought to be found to remedy its injustice.(8)

In 1920 many articles were published in the French, British, and Italian newspapers which advocated treaty revision in the general interest of mankind. On the first of May, 1920, the New York Herald stated that Europe was rapidly approaching ultimate destruction because of the Peace Treaties.(9) It appeared from the article that although peace was presumably re-established in the world, nine countries were still engaged in war, armed forces still occupied nineteen fronts, four states were threatened with imminent danger of hostilities, and in seven countries there was active or imminent civil war. Furthermore, Turkey was fighting with all her strength against the treaty. The New York Herald quoted Pioncare, who, in an article published in the Revue des deux Mondes, characterized the Turkish peace treaty as "broken Sevres china."(10)

There was much talk of revision, but the treaty remained the same. Millerand, the new French Premier, declared that the Trianon Treaty could only be accepted or rejected because all the peace treaties constituted a single organic structure which would be impaired by any change.(11)

The Hungarian Peace Delegation, headed by Hungary's "Grand Old Man," Count Albert Apponyi, arrived at Paris on January 5, 1920. It was lodged in the Hotel Chateau de Madrid,

---

8 **Ibid.**, p. 1002.
9 Column A, p. 3.
10 **Ibid.**
11 **Papers and Documents**, p. 1003.

in Neuilly, one of the suburbs of Paris, perfectly isolated. The members of the mission were not permitted to communicate with any foreign diplomat or embassy in Paris. Apponyi informed the Hungarian government in his first telegram to Budapest of the fact that the Hungarian Delegation was indeed interned. This isolation was so near total that when the Japanese ambassador in Paris expressed the wish that the Hungarian Delegation should seek contact with him, it was all but impossible. Colonel Paul Henry, the representative of the French Government, declared that personal contact with Allied diplomats was impossible until after the signing of the peace treaty.(12)

Although Hungary had no allies in 1920, she still had some personal friends. Among them were some influential members of the British Parliament. Before the peace delegation left for Paris, Lord Bryce advised the Hungarian Government that it would be most important to establish contact with the United States Government.(13) The United States was not bound by Rumanian's secret war-time treaty; therefore, she could take a position against the annexation of Transylvania by the Rumanians and could demand that final decision in this matter be conditioned upon the findings of a commission appointed to deal with this problem. Such a demand on the part of the United States would be supported by numerous members of the British Parliament.

The Hungarian Minister for Foreign Affairs raised this question with the representative of the United States in Budapest. The Foreign Minister emphasized to Grant-Smith that the United States' ambasador in Paris was not participating in the preliminary negotiations concerning the peace treaty with Hungary and that, consequently, the conditions of peace were being determined without the knowledge and approval of the United States. The Foreign Minister stated:

---

12 **Ibid.,** p. 854.
13 **Ibid.,** p. 859.

We do not know whether, under these circumstances, the United States will feel bound by that treaty. It would be most important to have the American ambassador in Paris participate in discussions of the peace conditions and to have his support on behalf of our justifiable demand for a plebiscite based on the idea of self-determination.(14)

In a reply to this request, Grant-Smith suggested that the Hungarian Government endeavor to induce the Department of State in Washington to participate in the discussion of the Hungarian peace conditions. He suggested this because it was apparent that if he (Grant-Smith) himself undertook official steps to that end, it would at once arouse the Yugoslavs and the Czechs who would doubtless effectively counteract his move. On the basis of this suggestion, the Minister of Foreign Affairs instructed the Hungarian Legation at the Hague to initiate such action at once through Consul János Perényi. Also a special note was sent to the Supreme Council pointing out that owing to the fact that the United States was no longer represented in the Supreme Council, Hungary's position was different from that of the powers with whom peace had heretofore been concluded. Hungary could not leave her position toward the United States unsettled, especially as there were many thousands of Hungarians in the United States whose interests must be protected.(15)

Clemenceau's answer to the letter of the Hungarian Delegation was written in a very abrupt tone. It concluded that if the Hungarian Delegation desired to cause delay by some pretext, there was no necessity for it to remain in Paris.(16)

The first meeting of the Hungarian Delegation with the delegates of the Supreme Council took place in the office of Colonel Henry at the Chateau de Madrid on January 14, 1920. M. Jules Cambon presented the credentials of the Allied plenipoten-

---

14 **Ibid.**, p. 893.
15 **Ibid.**, p. 859.
16 **Ibid.**

tiaries. When he read the list of names, no representative of the United States was among them. Count Apponyi asked Cambon whether the United States was represented, and Cambon replied that they were not. The whole ceremony was rather frigid. Cambon introduced himself as well as the Allied representatives, whereupon Count Apponyi introduced himself and the other Hungarian delegates. Apart from that related above, no conversation took place. Count Apponyi accepted the credentials and that ended the ceremony. There was no hand-shaking. Thereafter Count Apponyi wrote a letter to Clemenceau. He stated in this letter:

Having taken note, through the comminications made by M. Jules Cambon, of the novel fact that the United States of America are not represented at the Conference to which we were sent by our Government, entrusted with the mission of preparing peace with all the belligerents, we beg you, Mr. President, to open the way for us to enter into direct relation with the Government at Washington and its representative accredited in Paris. The Allies can in no way resent our desire to conclude peace with the United States.(17)

The letter stated furthermore that the members of the Hungarian delegation were not treated as diplomats because they could not communicate with the other diplomats in Paris. Therefore, the members could not negotiate as was usual between diplomats. In such circumstances the Hungarian Delegation could not remain in Paris, although its desire was to negotiate with the Allied Powers. Next day, perhaps because of other political reasons, the French Government relented. The new French Government permitted free communication to the Hungarian Delegation and Clemenceau himself promised to mediate between the Peace Delegation and the United States.

On January 15, 1920, the Allies handed their peace conditions to Count Albert Apponyi, the President of the Hungarian Delegation. Next day, in the name of the people of Hungary,

17 Ibid., p. 857.

Apponyi addressed an appeal to the Supreme Council. He referred to the great principle so happily phrased by President Wilson. namely, that no group of people, no population, may be transferred from one state to another without being first consulted. In the name of this great principle, he said: ". . . We demand a plebiscite in those parts of Hungary that are now on the point of being severed from us; I declare we are willing to bow to the decision of a plebiscite whatever it should be."(18) Alexandre Millerand, the President of the Supreme Council, argued that having acquired the certitude that a consultation of the people would not offer a result different sensibly from those which the Allies arrived at, plebiscites were considered unnecessary.(19)

The peace treaty was signed between Hungary and the Entente Powers on July 4, 1920. Signed at Versailles in the Trianon Palace, it is known as the Treaty of Trianon. It was ratified by the Hungarian Parliament on November 15, 1920, but no Hungarian could accept it as valid and Hungarian official and unofficial politics were determined by the fight against Trianon during the inter-war period of Hungary. During these years it was the aspiration of nearly every Magyar to end the sad state of affairs imposed upon them by the peace settlement. It is no wonder then that revisionism, as the movement for the alteration of the terms of the Treaty of Trianon was called, became a very important factor in Hungarian politics. It also became a declaration of faith, a measuring rod for every Magyar's patriotism and loyalty.

To serve as an instrument of this cause, the "Hungarian League for Revision" was organized. The League collaborated with the influential British politician and newspaper magnate, Lord Rothermere, and with other influential persons, who conducted a personal campaign for the peaceful revision of the Treaty of Trianon. The campaign, however, led to little, if any, visible success.

18 U. S., For. Rel., Paris Peace Conference, IX, 872—884.
19 Ibid.

The international reputation of Hungary and her regime could improve only very slowly and, as a result, revision had very small prospect. But the overwhelming majority of Hungarians could never acquiesce in the Judgment of Trianon. Time and time again their spokesmen argued against the injustices of the Treaty. They pointed out that since its provisions were arrived at without Hungary having been consulted, it could hardly be called a treaty, but only a "ukase". They argued that the principle of self-determination of nations was not adhered to, principally because the people involved in the transfers of territory had never been consulted. The fact that the governments of the Czechs, Rumanians, and Serbs rejected the idea of plebiscites for the disputed areas for many Hungarians constituted the best proof that these regions did not desire to separate from Hungary at all. It was argued furthermore that the Treaty left nearly one out of every three Magyars outside the country, and that the boundaries of the new Hungarian state were illogical, both from the geographical and the ethnographical standpoint. They pleaded that there was neither historical nor economic justification for dissolving Hungary, which had existed for the past thousand years and which had a high degree of geographic unity because of its location within the Carpathian Basin. Hungarian historians have always been quick to point out that, in contradiction to the principle of national self-determination, the successor states were multinational entities. They point out that peoples were put into one state (for instance, in the cases of Czechoslovakia and Yugoslavia) on the basis of linguistic relations, without any political, economical or cultural foundation for the action.(20) Furthermore, the Hungarians argued, nationalism is not the only form of self-determination. It can be political, economic, and religious self-determination, and so on. In the late eighteenth century the United States itself had an economic basis of self-determination and not a national

20 For a good, scholarly written work on the minority question in Eastern Europe, see C. A. Macartney, National State and National Minorities (New York: Russel & Russel Publ., 1934).

one. So the Wilsonian ideas of self-determination, carried out as nationalism, were far from the American political ideas.(21)

Why Hungary accepted the peace treaty is an open question. Many historians argue that, in June of 1920, Hungary had no choice but to accept the peace treaty. They argue that the more powerful Germany, as well as the other states, accepted the peace treaties for the same reason. This argument is not accepted by others, who point out that the Hungarian treaty was signed a year later than the other treaties and at a time when the United States had, as we have seen, already rejected the peace treaties. Japan, Argentina, and some other Latin American states did the same. Moreover, Poland refused her signature on the Treaty of Trianon arguing that she had not been at war with Hungary. It is also a fact that after Italy, the Soviets were the next power to identify themselves openly with the Hungarian demand for revision of the unjust Trianon Treaty in the 1920's. The fact has almost passed into oblivion that the Fifth Party Congress, held in the Soviet Union in 1924, included in its program the approval of the demand "that the Hungarian-populated Czechoslovak, Rumanian, and Yugoslav territories be reannexed to Hungary.(22) In England, too, there was a loud debate about the Treaty of Trianon, both in the House of Lords and in the House of Commons. MP Adam Herber, supported by others, declared in the House of Commons, "The Treaty of Trianon is a vindictive one and it holds the seeds of future wars."(23)

In connection with the ratification of the Trianon Treaty, Hungarian Communist historians have produced a most unusual version of the famous "stab-in-the-back" theory. They claim that the "reactionary regime" of 1920 accepted the Treaty of Trianon

21 For fuller details on this question, see Baron Julius Wlassics, "The Right of Self-Determination," The Hungarian Nation, I, No. 4, 65 (Budapest: Quarterly, Pub. in English, 1920).

22 Tibor Eckhardt, Regicide at Marseille (New York: American Hungarian Historical Society, 1964), p. 145.

23 The Hungarian Question, p. 145.

in return for imperialist support against socialist revolution in the country. In doing this, the Communists argue, the rulers of Hungary betrayed their people, "stabbed them in the back." Stating this, they argue that the Entente was looking for a Hungarian government which from the very begining could accept the peace treaty.(24)

As a matter of fact, Hungary accepted the peace treaty with reference to Millerand's Covering Letter and to Article XIX of the League of Nations, which promised the possibility of peaceful revision when injustice was done.(25) The government declared:

---

24 For fuller details, see Gyula Juhász, **Magyarország Külpolitikája,** 1919—1945 (Hungary's Foreign Policy, 1919—1945) (Budapest: Kossuth Könyvkiadó, 1960); or J. Adám, Gy. Juhász, and L. Kerekes, eds., **Magyarország és a Második Világháború, Titkos Diplomáciai Okmányok a Háború Elözményeihez és Történetéhez** (Hungary and the Second World War, Secret Diplomatic Documents on the Origin and History of the War) (3d ed.; Budapest: Kossuth, 1966).

25 In early 1920, negotiations took place between France and Hungary. In connection with these negotations, on April 15, 1920, France addressed a note to the Hungarian Government. The French High Commissioner in Budapest, Maurice Fouchet, declared that France was determined to support Hungarian claims aimed at correcting some of the territorial provisions of the Treaty of Trianon. In return Hungary was expected to give important concessions to France. These included leasing the Hungarian State Railways and Railway Locomotive Works, the exploitation of navigation on the Danube by a French concern, the building of a Danube port in Budapest by Schneider-Creusot, and the transfer of control over the Hungarian Credit Bank to a French financial syndicate. This bank owned a considerable part of Hungarian industry. The French-Hungarian negotiations provoked Italian and British protests, and Hungary's neighbors were greatly alarmed. Lloyd George declared in the House of Lords that the Hungarian peace treaty was rather a formality and he was convinced that a revision of it would take place within a year.

M. Millerand, Prime Minister of France, delivered the peace terms to the Hungarians on May 6, 1920, with the letter mentioned above. It is quoted in Montgomery, **Hungary, The Uuwilling Satellite,** pp. 50—51.

For further details of the acceptance of the Trianon Treaty, see also "The Peace Debate in the Hungarian National Assembly," **The Hungarian Nation,** I, No. 4 (1920), 1ff.

"The Hungarian Government does not consider itself able to refuse signing the Treaty of Peace." As we have seen, this act was accomplished on June 4, 1920, in the Grand Trianon palace, located in the park of Versailles.

In fact, the Treaty of Trianon was "cruel and unjust," to use the words of Jászi.(26) Its princnples were mistakes of the historians and philosophers of those nations whose politicians committed the error. Hungary realized this, and she tried to remove this error from the very beginning. The first question was, how could it happen that Hungary, which was the symbol of liberty some decades earlier, was now war-guilty before the jury of the nations? President Wilson assessed Hungary's position in the Austro-Hungarian Monarchy in the following words:

> Dominant in a larger country than Bohemia, perhaps politically more capable than any Slavonic people, the Magyars, though crushed by superior force on the field of battle, have been able to win a specially recognized and highly favored place in the dual monarchy. Although for a long time a land in which the noble was the only citizen, Hungary has been a land of political liberties almost as long as England herself has been.(27)

Theodore Roosevelt, on his visit to Hungary in 1910, found this country the most progressive and, in her dynamism, the most closely resembling the United States in all of Europe. President Roosevelt praised the Hungarians for their role in Europe's history in a speech delivered in the Hungarian Parliament. The **Catholic Hungarian's Sunday**, vol. 81, no. 28, printed the following excerpt of that speech:

> I feel it my duty to say thanks to the Hungarian Nation for protecting Europe against the barbarous invasions of the East. In point of fact, Hungary protected not only Europe, but the

---

26 Oscar Jászi, "Neglected Aspect of the Danubian Drama," **Slavic Review**, XIV (July, 1934), 65ff.

27 Woodrow Wilson, **The State** (Boston: Hearth and Co., 1898), p. 336.

whole New World, as well as the United States of America, which, at that time, was in Europe's womb. Had I not known this, I would not consider myself to be an educated man. But, I know it and I say thanks to the Hungarians for protecting my nation although it was not yet born.

Arthur Griffith, the founder of the Sinn Fein, the organization which fought for the independence of Ireland, wrote a series of articles on the "Resurrection of Hungary", which originally appeared in **The United Irishman**, a Dublin newspaper. They were published in a book in 1902 entitled **The Resurrection of Hungary: A Parallel for Ireland.** A second edition was published in the same year, and a third edition appeared in 1918. Hungary's position was given to the political program of the Sinn Fein as an example. Griffith wrote in the preface to the first edition: "The despised, oppressed, and forgotten province of Austria is today the free, prosperous and renowned Kingdom of Hungary."(28)

Perhaps, after World War I, Hungary had maneuvered herself into a most unfavorable situation. Károlyi's efforts to reverse the position in October, 1918, were incredibly naive. President Wilson preached the necessity of democracy, but when Károlyi tried to follow his advice he was insulted for his pains by the French general in command in Belgrade. The Liberal-Socialist experiments in disbanding the old army and organizing a new force on democratic lines only led to chaos and weakness, and allowed Hungary's neighbors to press forward into her territory. While she never could have organized a successful resistance to the whole treaty, as Turkey did, yet it is quite possible that, had she a determined military force at the end of 1918, she might have made considerably better terms for herself. When at last she did undertake a more active resistance, it was highly unfortunate for her that this should have been done in the name of the Third International. The help which Moscow had promised never came,

---

28 Arthur Griffith, **The Resurrection of Hungary** (Melbourne: Cassel and Co., 1904), Preface.

and the Western Powers were only frightened by the spectre of Bolshevism and strengthened in their resolve to exorcise it. Finally, when the reaction came, it came again in such form as to give an easy handle to Hungary's enemies. Hungary realized this situation. She saw war-time propaganda, especially Czechoslovak propaganda, as the chief cause of the harsh peace treaty. (29) Hungary, between the world wars, fought with all her might against this propaganda with a counter-propaganda, under the slogan: "Justice for Hungary".

Yet this idea, "Justice for Hungary" originated with an American journalist. On April 7, 1920, an unknown American journalist went for information to the Hungarian Peace Delegation in Neuilly, France. The Delegation proceeded to give him statistics, maps, and other data. Instead of taking them, the journalist stated frankly that it would be too much to assume that the Americans would be willing to devote days and hours to the study of statistical data, maps, and arguments concerning a matter so remote as Hungary's case. He suggested that the American public could never be interested in these details. One or two catchwords, like "Justice for Hungary", would be much more effective than a whole volume of notes and information.(30)

The most prominent advocate of the movement for revision of the Trianon Treaty was also a non-Hungarian. In fact, it was an Englishman, Lord Rothermere, the newspaper magnate, who became interested in the consequences of the mistaken Paris Peace Treaties. He went incognito to Hungary with an expert staff to inspect the new frontiers. Finding them more foolish than he had expected, he published on Easter Sunday, 1927, an article about them in his paper, the **London Daily Mail,** under the headline: "Hungary's Place Under the Sun". From then on, the

---

29 On the war-time Czechoslovak propaganda in the United States, see Victor S. Mamatey, **The United States and East Central Europe 1914—1918. A Study in Wilsonian Diplomacy and Propaganda** (Princeton: Princeton University Press, 1957).

30 **Papers and Documents,** p. 221 (name is not given).

London Daily Mail published a series of articles about the injustices of Trianon. Hungarian public opinion replied to the campaign with enthusiasm. Lord Rothermere suddenly became "the Saviour of Hungary". The English Government was somewhat vexed by the campaign. The **London Daily Mail** stated on August 20, 1938, that it had received a request from the Foreign Relations Committee of the United States for copies of Lord Rothermere's articles, as well as the **Daily Mail** editorials dealing with Hungary, for further study.(31) As a result of this campaign, a group of about two hundred forty members of the House of Commons in England, composed of men from each of the three parties, to the annoyance of the Foreign Office came out for a revision of the Trianon Treaty. France declared "any step toward revision of the Peace Treaties is courting war". Thomas Masaryk, President of Czechoslovakia, called Lord Rothermere a dilettante in Central European politics. But, in the Parliament at Prague, he stated his feelings in a softer view:

> I myself admit without hesitation that the peace treaties are in need of some explanation. This, however, must be done in a loyal, open and honest way. Agitation which has a hostile tendency, which arrays an army of untruths and even lies, will not achieve the desired correction.(32)

The shrillest voice, however, came from Austria and Germany. On July 27, 1928, the Vienna Daily, the **Neue Freie Presse,** wrote in an article:

> Not only six million Austrians, but also 70 million Germans are the pledge that the plans of Lord Rothermere shall never come true. We say this not in the name of the German Government, but most certainly in that of the German people.(33)

A month later the **Kölnische Zeitung** in Cologne, Germany, wrote in reply to the Austrian paper:

31 U. S., **Nat. Arch.,** Micr. No. 708, RO11 No. 10—0207.
32 U. S., **Nat. Arch.,** Micr. No. 708, RO11 No. 10.
33 **Ibid.**

The Germans of Western Hungary, and wherever they may be, are supported by 70 million Germans. Germany, however, fully sympathizes with Lord Rothermere's campaign for the restitution of purely Hungarian territory on the basis of self-determination of the peoples.(34)

Historians usually refer only to the territorial and material losses of Hungary at Trianon, but they do not make mention of the cultural loss, which was great. The Hungarian Protestant churches suffered the greatest losses. For instance, the Hungarian Lutheran Church had lost all of her three colleges.(35) Since there was little hope of regaining these colleges, it was to be feared that the Lutheran Church would remain without any school for the training of their clergy. This fact gave another interesting aspect to Hungarian Revisionism. The Hungarian Protestant Churches and the whole nation discovered the fact that the United States was in the main a Protestant country. Hungarians deduced that the Treaty of Trianon was an offense against religious toleration and against Protestantism, placing so many Protestants under the Orthodox yoke of Rumania. They stated that Transylvania was the most important outpost and fortress of European Protestantism. It was in Transylvania that, for the first time in the history of continental Europe, a law was enacted which secured liberty of conscience and freedom of religion for every man, woman, and child living in Transylvania.(36) Furthermore, it was Transylvania, alone in the entire history of Protestantism, which had a Unitarian ruler, an enlightened one, Gabriel Bethlen, who made Transylvania the country of religious toleration in seventeenth century Europe. Now it was natural that the Hungarian Protestant churches cried for help to their American brothers. American Protestantism responded seriously. In February, 1920, the

---

34 **Ibid.**

35 The Colleges at Poszony and Eperjes were given to Czechoslovakia, the College at Sopron to Austria. This latter city returned to Hungary by plebiscite in 1921.

36 The Diet of Torda enacted this law in 1571.

Evangelic Church of the United States sent a Committee to Hungary, under Professor John A. Morehead, to study the situation of the Evangelic Church there. Returning to the United States, Professor Morehead delivered many speeches about the sad situation of the Hungarian Lutheran Church. He collected 800,000 dollars for the relief of the Hungarian Lutheran Church and made a foundation for the maintenance of a Lutheran College to be established at Budapest.

In the same month, a group of the Bishops of the Methodist Church arrived at Budapest. Dr. John L. Nueton, the head of that committee, declared at a reception given by the Hungarian Prime Minister to the Committee: "The American heart has always beat for those fighting for truth. I, for my part, have always been friendly-inclined to Hungary, one of the pioneers in the struggle for religious liberty".(37)

The American Christian Church also formed a committee for the protection of religious minorities in Transylvania. Dr. Brown, the Chairman of that Committee, gave an account of his investigation in Transylvania on July 24, 1920, in the big hall of the Protestant Church at the Deák tér of Budapest. Dr. Brown stated on that occasion that he would carefully study the Foreign Ministers' communications relating to the status of religious minorities in Transylvania, and that the Hungarians might be assured of the Western Protestant nations' sympathies as to this question. He had become convinced that Hungarian Protestantism possessed strength. He pointed out that the information he had sent to different Protestant churches about their Hungarian brethren had in great measure already influenced public opinion in the Western Protestant states. "I have personally convinced myself", he said, "that Rumania is East and Transylvania is West".(38) One of the members of the mission, Joel H. Metcalf, went to London to give an account of his Transylvanian experiences. Another,

---

37 **The Hungarian Nation,** I, No. 8, 76.
38 **Ibid.,** p. 177.

Rev. Sydney B. Snow, said that with profound regret he would remember the terrible suffering the Transylvanian Hungarians had to endure at the hands of occupying Rumanians.

Indeed, the American Protestant Churches worked well on Hungary's behalf. The members of the United States Senate and the House of Representatives heard from their own prominent church leaders that something unjust was going on in Central Europe because of the Versailles Treaties. Hearings began as early as 1921 in the different committees and subcommittees of the Senate and House of Representatives about the facts caused by the Treaty of Trianon. Among others, Professor Eugene Pivany, Chairman of the American-Hungarian League for Hungary's Territorial Integrity, had the honor of appearing before the Senate's Committee of Foreign Relations on September 25, 1919, through the intervention of Senator Harding, later President of the United States. It is remarkable that no other conquered nation, neither the Germans, the Austrians, nor the Bulgars or Turks, had the honor to appear before the Senate of the United States. As is well known, on November 19, 1919, the United States Senate rejected the Treaty of Versailles, and it was probably due to these hearings that the United States did not make any reference to the territorial changes of Hungary in her separate peace with Hungary in 1921. (39)

The most prominent critic of the Treaty of Versailles was William E. Borah, the Senator from Idaho, chairman of the Senate Committee on Foreign Relations. Again and again, Borah emphasized that there could be no hope of improvement until the European states altered their evil policies. The most serious defect was their faith in the Treaty of Versailles, which Borah asserted was based upon militarism, secrecy, injustice, and imperialism. Under the terms of the treaty an impractical division of the territories of European nations had been fostered. "What Europe

39 For the Senate hearings, see **Inquire 1919** (Washington: Government Publishing, 1920). For the text of the treaty of peace between Hungary and the United States, see Appendix III.

needed after the war was unity. And what it got was dismemberment."(40) The League of Nations was not curing these ills, but perpetuating them by maintaining the status quo. It seemed to Borah that the Treaty of Versailles and its static territorial adjustments were the best way to start a new war. He was convinced that, in reality, permanent peace would not be possible until the way was cleared by a revision of the Treaty of Versailles. Borah charged that M. Clemenceau was the man responsible for the misery of Europe because he stood in the way of the American attempt to modify the peace treaty. His animosity for France was most strikingly shown when Clemenceau visited the United States in November, 1922. Borah refused to serve on the committee to greet him and arraigned French policy in the Senate, charging militarism at home and imperialism abroad.

Senator Borah not only expressed his feelings toward the Paris peace treaties on the whole, but at times he entered into details on the Trianon Treaty. On November 6, 1927, he gave an interview to Hungarian journalists touring the United States and stated among other things that he was pleased that the United States did not ratify the Trianon Treaty because of the stipulations contained herein. He stated furthermore that he was in possession of a great many facts, figures, and other data concerning the treaty and that he continued his interest in Hungary and her problems, particularly that of the Trianon Treaty.(41)

Exactly a year later, on November 6, 1928, the Budapest paper, Az Est (The Evening), published a cable from its American correspondent as follows:

Senator Borah, who is spoken of as a possible Foreign Secretary in the event of Hoover's victory, received me in Baltimore and made the following statement:

40 Fort Wayne News, March, 1922. Quoted in John Charles Vinson, William E. Borah and the Outlawry of War (Atlanta: Foote & Davies, 1957), p. 50.

41 U. S., For. Rel. 864.00 P.R./13.

"For a long time I have been thinking of the Hungarian problem. I may state that America sympathizes with Hungary's endeavor to regain her rights. I firmly believe that the Trianon Treaty cannot remain in its present form. I consider the action of the Hungarians, in which the whole nation joins like one soul, to be a very fine thing".(42)

Two years later, on June 14, 1930, the **Budapesti Hirlap** (The Budapest Newspaper) published another interview granted by Senator Borah to its special correspondent, George Ottlik. It should be stated in this connection that Ottlik, who was well-known in the United States, came for a tour of the United States as a member of a group of European press correspondents, under the auspices of the Carnegie Endowment for International Peace. Ottlik's interview with the Senator was of great significance in the journalistic world in Hungary, since he enjoyed the complete confidence of the Hungarian Foreign Office. He had frequently accompanied important official Hungarian delegations to Geneva, and his opinion carried considerable weight. He was also the Hungarian correspondent for the **London Times.**

According to Ottlik, it was Senator Borah who asked the first question as to whether the diplomatic situation in Hungary had improved, and whether better prospects existed in connection with its claims for revision. To this Ottlik replied that as far as he was able to judge, nothing had changed on the diplomatic front in Europe with the exception perhaps of the conclusion of the Hague and Paris agreements. He believed that the resulting liberation from reparation charges might be considered as a change in the mentality of the Allies. If this were really so, it might also mean that the Allies recognized that it was unjust to demand reparations from a country which had lost two-thirds of its territory and two-thirds of its population. Ottlik availed himself of the opportunity to ask Senator Borah whether he did not believe that America, even though insisting upon standing aloof from European complications,

---

42 **Ibid.**

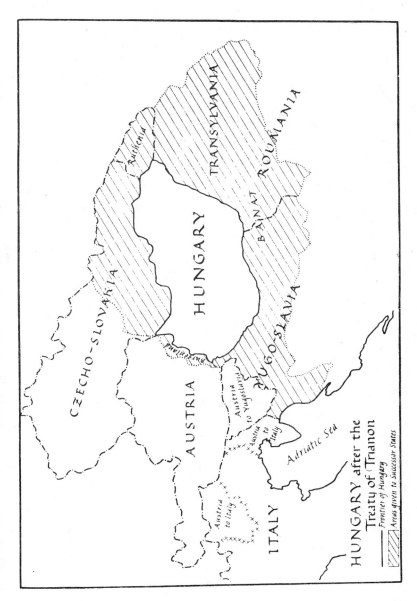

HUNGARY after the
Treaty of Trianon

───── Frontier of Hungary

////// Areas given to Successor States

CZECHO-SLOVAKIA

Ruthenia

TRANSYLVANIA

BANAT

ROUMANIA

HUNGARY

AUSTRIA

Burgenland

Austria to Yugoslavia

Austria to Italy

YUGOSLAVIA

Adriatic Sea

Austria to Italy

ITALY

could assist Europe in bringing about changes which were absolutely necessary. The Senator answered this question as follows:

America had a share in the drafting of the peace treaties; on account of this I deem America to be morally responsible for their development and consequences. I am convinced that, in spite of her insistence upon a policy of standing aloof from all further complications, she may well use her moral weight in telling Europe what she thinks of these questions and what American public opinion would consider a just settlement of the problems which created new danger zones in Europe. I am confident that such an American policy would not be without effect upon European public opinion, all the more because the United States of Europe cannot be established before the aforementioned changes take place. I have always had the impression that Briand, with his plan to found the United States of Europe, does not follow today any other aim than to provide new securities and guarantees for the actual conditions of power and political situation and the actual European frontiers. I do not think, however, that this is possible. I have always considered the Treaty of Versailles and its kindred treaties to be dangerous to the peace of Europe; I believe that their revision would put your continental peace upon a considerably safer basis.(43)

In reply to a question from the Hungarian correspondent as to whether Senator Borah intended visiting Europe in the near future, the latter replied that he would like to do so and hoped that in the spring of 1931, after the short session of Congress, he might go to Europe, in which case he would certainly visit Hungary.

The Hungarian press had not been silent in its reaction to the statement of Senator Borah, and articles had appeared in the more prominent newspapers attempting to analyze its probable effects. Gustav Gratz, Former Minister of Foreign Affairs, remarked in an article on Europe and the United States in the **Budapesti**

---

43 U. S., For. Rel., 711.6412/27.

Hirlap: "America is today the banker of the world as Britain was before the war. It would be hard if France and the Little Entente do not take American opinions into consideration".(44) The writer believed, furthermore, that American public opinion could be allied with that of Hungary in an endeavor to modify the Covenant of the League of Nations and in creating a new spirit which would eliminate the one-sided privileges of victorious states.

Senator Borah determined his policy toward Hungary in October, 1931, when Pierre Laval, the premier of France, visited President Hoover in Washington to discuss economic problems and French security. It was not to the White House nor the State Department, but to the Idaho senator's office that the thirty French journalists accompanying Laval flocked for an interview. Borah put his foot down against any French security pact, rumored as the real purpose of Laval's visit. France would have to determine for herself whether she was in danger of attack; Borah would not quarrel with her judgment. Europe would have to consent to a peaceful revision of the peace treaties with Germany, Austria, and Hungary or there would be another war. Questioned more closely on this, he admitted he wanted the arrangements relating to the Polish Corridor, Danzig, and Upper Silesia changed "by arbitration": he also wanted the restoration of Hungary's boundaries as they were before the Trianon Treaty, making possible Hungarian economic integration. He reiterated his hostility to any plan for collective security because it meant "making eternal the status quo."(45)

Borah's remarks created a sensation. When they were recounted to Laval, he replied acidly: "I have not come to engage in polemics with Senator Borah and to discuss the revision of the Versailles Treaty."(46)

---

44 U. S., For. Rel., **Department of State**, 864.00 P.R./36.

45 **Chicago World Examiner,** October 24, 1931, quoted in Marian C. McKenna, **Borah** ((Ann Arbor: University of Michigan Press, 1961), p. 275

46 **Ibid.**

Senator Borah undoubtedly was right when he stated that in the case of revision the whole Hungarian nation was joined like one soul. Between the world wars, every Magyar had inherited the subconscious conviction that the Carpathian Mountains were the God-given wall against the East, against barbarism, against Asia, Europe's eternal menace. No one could be in Hungary very long without knowing that **"nem, nem, soha"** meant "no, no, never", and that it referred to the boundaries fixed by the Treaty of Trianon. Hungary considered her revisionism as a fight for justice and never forgot the fact that when the United States concluded peace on August 29, 1921, all mention of the new frontiers was omitted.

CHAPTER V

EMIGRATION AS A FOE:
THE POLITICAL REFUGEES

Hungary was prey to innumerable problems in 1920, some of which derived from the immediate past, others created, or at least greatly aggravated, by the present. Four years of exhausting war in which the nation had suffered very heavy casualties, two revolutions, and a predatory foreign occupation would have been enough to repair within intact frontiers; but on top of all this had come the dismemberment of the country. As a consequence of these events, industrial unemployment was high; capital fled from the country; the currency was inflated. The revolutions had greatly embittered the land-owning classes (including all of the peasants), who ascribed to them the blame for all Hungary's misfortunes. Feeling ran particularly high against the Jews, who had played a disproportionely large part in both revolutions, especially Kun's.(1) The Social Democrats had also compromised themselves by their alliance with Communism, and even Liberal democracy was tainted by its share in Károlyi's regime.

The inflation threw a large part of the fixed income middle classes into great poverty. Worse situated still were the families

---

1 Although Jews numbered 909,500 or roughly 5 percent of the total population, Jewish radicals had formed almost the whole of Karolyi's intellectual General Staff. Nearly 95 percent of the active leaders of the Communist revolution under Kun were Jews. U. S., **National Archives**, Mic. copy no. 708, Roll 3, Doc. 0498.

who had fled or had been expelled from the Successor States, leaving all behind them. By the end of 1920 about 700,000 of these unfortunates, nearly all from middle-class families, had found refuge in dismembered Hungary, where many of them were existing under lamentable conditions, camped in old railway carriages and supported by American relief. That was all that the government could provide for them. These men were even more embittered than the land-owning classes against the revolutions and their authors, whom they regarded as responsible for their misfortunes.(2)

In any case, the violent days of the Communist rule and its aftermath left bitter hatreds behind. As noted in a preceding chapter, there were atrocities during the months following the collapse of Hungarian Bolshevism. While the Allies were still negotiating the formation of a government to allow representation to the Liberal elements, the mob lynched more than one local dictator who had not been fortunate enough to escape in time. With so much confusion the government was too weak to control the situation. The real strongholds were the patriotic associations, secret or otherwise, which were a power in the land in the early 1920's. These groups were the self-appointed avengers of the nation's sufferings. First among them was the **Awakening Hungarians**. They appointed themselves chief executors of the White Terror, although other bodies shared the work with them. The **Ragged Guard**, after beginning as an internal counter-revolutionary movement, was a guerilla group organized to prevent the Austrians from taking possesion of West Hungary (Burgenland) in 1921. The MOVE (Magyar Országos Véderő Egyesület—Hungarian Association of National Defense) was called into being by a group of military officers. It was an anti-Habsburg but also strongly counter-revolutionist and anti-Semitic movement. Later on it developed into a second-line defense force which controlled sports organizations. There were many other organizations which spread over the whole

---

2 C. A. Macartney, **Hungary** (Chicago: Aldine Publishing Company, 1962), p. 212.

country and which catered to every sort of interest. The official statistics show twenty-two patriotic associations as having been founded after World War I. Furthermore, it must be noted, that the government itself turned sharply against the Social Democrats and Trade Unions and imprisoned hundreds of alleged revolutionaries. All these events were carefully watched by the political refugees who left Hungary after the collapse of the Communist regime. Among those who did not or could not return to "White Hungary" were some prominent people; the chief figure among these was Károlyi's right-hand man, Dr. Oscar Jászi. Others were adventurers, politicians, and journalists.

The refugees were not unanimous in their political opinions. First of all, there were the followers of Károlyi who called themselves "Octobrists" and declared themselves bourgeois liberals. The second group was the left wing of the Social Democrat Party, cooperating openly with Béla Kun during the Bolshevik regime. Finally, there were the Communists who, despite Moscow's orders, did not go to Russia. Although neither the Octobrists nor the Social Democrats desired another Dictatorship of the Proletariat in Hungary, all of the different groups agreed that the home government which had raised a barrier against their return must be blackened. During the fall of 1919, a merciless press campaign against "White Hungary" was begun in Vienna where the refugees had their headquarters. A small Hungarian weekly paper in Vienna, Az Ember (The Man), edited by Francis Göndör, an adventurer journalist and once Béla Kun's commissar, was the center of this campaign. Fearful tales were printed daily-over-colored reports full of disgusting and revolting details. Although it happened, now and again, that the supposedly butchered Bolshevik appeared later in good health, these lapses did not disturb Göndör. Truth was not what he was after. The awakening of antipathy against Hungary was his aim.

Written in Hungarian, the sensational stories would not reach the ears of Europe, nor influence the opinion of the cultural world. Therefore, Göndör established a powerful organization to spread them in other tongues. In his confessions in 1922, he described his activities as follows:

> I translated the news from **Az Ember** and with the help of press agencies I placed it in the German papers in Vienna and in the foreign press. In a comparatively short time the whole world was full of the particulars which I had published in **Az Ember**. German, French, English and even American papers cited the disclosures of **Az Ember** and in a few months' time the whole world, shuddering, was convinced that black-mailers, robbers, and murderers were ruling in Hungary.(3)

As a result of this press campaign, a whole literature arose in Europe which those with normal sensibilities could not have read without horror. Details were given of a very regular, persistent persecution of the workers; any-one suspected of holding Democratic views was placed under arrest in "White Hungary". The European press no longer remembered any Hungarian Red Terror and it did not write of Communist terror in Russia; but it made noise about Hungarian "White Terror". After several years had passed, Sigsmund Kunfi, once minister of Károlyi's cabinet, stated with satisfaction that although Finnish White Terror had been more bloody, more unmerciful, and more dreadful than the Hungarian White Terror, yet, thanks to the propaganda of the refugees, the world had heard incomparably more of the latter.(4)

Indeed, the propaganda of the refugees succeeded beyond expectation. Hungary was defamed by this methodical, well-organized, and calumnious press campaign. A large section of European workers and statesmen adopted a point of view which not only offended the Hungarian nation but endangered its very existence. The Labor Party members of the European Parliaments, under the influence of reports and personal appeals, put questions to their governments. Did the governments know about the state of affairs

---

3 Francis Göndör, **Confessions** (Vienna: Arbeiter, 1922) p. 24.
4 Sigismund Kunfi, "Our Campaign," **Az Ember** (Vienna daily in Hungarian), November 18, 1923.

in Hungary and were they prepared to intervene? Those questions were asked in the Hague, in the Ital'an Camara, in the Swedish Parliament, and in the House of Commons and House of Lords. What was worse, Trade Unionists all over the world, and particularly the marine-transport laborers, boycotted Hungary. Furthermore, the **Rote Fhane**, a Vienna Communist paper, stated that the boycott was only the first step against "White Hungary": a "Workers Army" was already assembling in Austria and an invasion of Hungary was under way.(5) It seemed that the case of the refugees could triumph over White Hungary by the favor of western democracies.

Meanwhile, however, the social and political reconstruction of Hungary proceeded. As early as December, 1921, the government had concluded a formal treaty with the Social Democrat leaders under which they had been granted an amnesty, the cessation of persecution, and the same right of association as was enjoyed by other parties. The Trade Unions had had their confiscated funds restored to them with recognition of their right to pursue their legal activities. The workers' spokesmen were able to send representatives to Parliament. The White Terror was liquidated quietly, but effectively, and it became not much easier to preach active anti-Semitism than Marxian revolution. Mainly because of these facts, a large part of the European press, especially in England, Sweden, Switzerland, and Bavaria, became pro-Hungarian. The refugees had to realize that the fate of Hungary no longer depended on their politics but had developed into a problem of European interest for all the Great Powers: namely, to maintain order and peace on the European Continent after so many troublesome years. It also meant that, after so many successes, the refugees lost their case in Europe.

After their fiasco in Europe, the refugees turned to the United States. They judged that the majority of the population was ignorant of the political circumstances of Central Europe; conse-

---

5 "Workers' Solidarity," **Rote Fhane** (Vienna daily), May 20, 1920.

quently, they, the "champions of Freedom and Democracy", hoped with well-chosen catchwords to make a great impression on the Americans. Dr. Oscar Jászi, the most prominent leader of the refugees, devoted all the energies at his disposal to affect American public opinion. He himself undertook to direct the work in America. He even decided to send the greatest name among the refugees, Count Michael Károlyi, to America. According to Jászi's calculation, Károlyi's name would serve to mislead the unsuspecting population of America.(6)

Jászi was attracted by two other things; one was the hope of winning over to their cause several hundred thousand Hungarian emigrants who, although naturalized Americans, still spoke their mother-tongue; the other was the chance to prevent America from subscribing to the loan applied for from the League of Nations, a loan necessary to the economic reconstruction of Hungary.

Economic reconstruction of Hungary was possible only by means of a foreign loan and, because of the unsettled question of reparation, the agreement of the League of Nations was necessary to obtain it. The League of Nations, however, though it could vote for a loan, had no money. Only the United States could give money for the Hungarian cause, through the channels of the League. The refugees hoped to provide against that eventuality by influencing public opinion in America against Hungary.

Perhaps the first question was how could the refugees, many of them Progressive Radicals or even Communist, reach the United States at all. It was no easy task for a Hungarian to reach America in the early 1920's. Strictly enforced emigration laws and the coldly reserved behavior of the American authorities towards revolutionary agitators presented insurmountable obstacles. In fact, the State Department refused to grant immigration licenses to several leaders of the refugees. Many of them, however, evaded the emigration law and the vigilance of the authorities. Most of these

---

6 For details see Elemér Mályus, **The Fugitive Bolsheviks** (London: Grant Richards, 1931), pp. 183—204.

had come over first to South America with Austrian passports and South American visas, and had gradually crept up from South America to the United States. They never openly called themselves Communists or even Radicals. They formed organizations in New York, St. Louis, Chicago, and other cities, organizations such as "The Hungarian Engineers' Social Organization" and the "Octobrist Republicans' Circle". Others reached the United States with Czechoslovak, Rumanian, and Yugoslav passports.

The first among the political refugees who appeared in America was a man of no real political standing. His name was Dr. John Török, who in 1921 represented himself as a Roman Catholic priest. According to some reports, he managed, upon landing, to evade in some mysterious manner the vigilance of the American authorities. According to others, a Yugoslavian passport had secured him a free entrance.(7) However that may have been, his past life was evidence that the emigrants had done well in choosing him as the most suitable pioneer of their cause. His father, John Toch, had been a traveling merchant. He himself was twenty years of age when, in 1910, he was baptized and chose a Hungarian name. He became Roman Catholic and even took Orders, but in a short time became a convert to the Greek Catholic religion because he thought that it would be easier to carve a career in the hierarchy of that church. In 1917 he turned Roman Catholic again and became chaplain in the Army. He was arrested for embezzlement after he had been for some time under suspicion of spying for the enemy. Revolution threw open the doors of his prison. Subsequent to the downfall of the Soviets, he made his living in Vienna by trading and smuggling. After such a chequered past it would have been a surprising thing had he not managed to enter America.

On January 7, 1921, the Radical Hungarian New York paper, the Elöre (Forward) published a long article on the results of his endeavors. According to the paper the workmen of New York at

---

7 **Ibid.**, p. 195.

the meeting where Dr. John Török, Roman Catholic Priest, was the speaker, had made a demonstration against White Terror in Hungary. Dr. Török was able to mislead people with impunity. His ecclesiastical vestments surrounded him with a halo in their eyes. They could not know that in 1921, the Holy See in Rome had ordered all American bishops to forbid his wearing a soutane. This did not disconcert him. He continued professing to be a bishop, sometimes a Protestant bishop, sometimes a Greek Catholic one. It would seem the latter Church appealed to him as being particularly suited to his impostures. Once a Ruthenian bishop, once a Greek bishop, in 1925 he had the audacity to return to Europe with the intention of procuring a real bishopric for himself in Czechoslovakia. On March 17, 1925, the **New Yorski Dennik**, a Slovak Journal in New York, strongly protested against that attempt and stated that Török was a Jew and had belonged to various other denominations as well. In spite of these disclosures the refugees did not break with him. On the contrary, he was provided with money by the Czechoslovak Government and sent back to Cleveland in 1926 with a Czechoslovak passport.(8)

The pioneer work of the emigration was done by this man whose life was but sketchily described in the few foregoing sentences. His work was well done, too. He knew how to organize demonstrations against the White Terror as well as how to get anti-Hungarian articles into various newspapers and journals. Moreover, amidst his other activities, he was a real estate agent in Pittsburgh.

This adventurer, who stuck at nothing, was followed by another man in clerical garb. Although the name of the second was well known at home and by the Hungarians of America, he was not the most conspicuous of the emigrant politicians. John Hock had really been an ordained Roman Catholic priest in Budapest. He was a famous orator and had been a Member of the Hungarian Parliament before the War. As a bosom friend of Károlyi's and Jászi's he had become one of the leaders of the revolution in 1918

---

8 **U. S., Nat. Arch.**, Micr. No. 708, Roll No. 10.

and out of respect for his vestments was elected chairman of the Revolutionary National Council. During the first few years of exile he had lived more or less in retirement. He wished to come to the United States in 1921, but the State Department had refused to grant him an emigration license. It was only in the following year that he managed to reach the United States with a Czechoslovak passport. Arriving there, he was joined by John Török who accompanied him on his journeys in the role of secretary and helped him to arrange public meetings. John Hock spoke only at secular meetings, for the American Catholic clergy had unanimously protested against his using the pulpits of the churches as a medium for his agitation. The churches were therefore closed to him. His tour did not result in the success he hoped for either from a financial or from a political point of view. The Hungarian settlements showed but little sympathy for Hock's speeches. At a meeting in Chicago, on January 21, 1923, only about 250 to 300 people turned up, and the results in the Eastern States, Los Angeles, and San Francisco were still poorer. Cleveland, for instance, convinced that his visit would be a failure, did not even invite him. Because of this lack of sympathy, Hock could not realize the fantastic plan of the refugees, which was to organize an elite group of miners and workers of Hungarian origin in the United States and afterwards induce the American Hungarians to proclaim a Hungarian Republic in the hope of creating an upheaval at home and in Hungary.

That scheme was not successful, however, partly because the laboring classes belonging to Social Democratic and to Communist organizations did not consider the plan radical enough, and partly because the other factions turned their backs on such a fantastic plan. Even the small number of men who participated in the public meetings were not willing to make financial sacrifices for such an unreasonable plan. The results of extempory collections taken at banquets were, at the most, sufficient only to defray current expenses. In New York, for example, the takings were less than the expenses. The Hungarians of America had learned a lesson from the events at home and refused pecuniary assistance to those revolutionists who had proved unworthy of their confidence. The State Department, too, carefully watched Hock's every step. Such agitation could not be permitted in the United States where, at that time, bombs were mailed by leftist radicals to prominent American persons.(9) John Hock was forced to leave the United States, returning to Europe in June, 1923, with no financial or political success at all.

Jászi and the leading staff of the Emigration believed that Hock's failure was not the final defeat. He was ordered to turn his attention more to the workers--to establish better cooperation with them. In the autumn of that year, 1923, Hock returned to New York with these instructions, using a Czechoslovak visitor's passprot went to New York also, and the fact that he possessed a Rumanian diplomatic passport and a letter of introduction from Thomas Masaryk, President of the Czechoslovak Republic, shows in whose interest he undertook the journey acros the ocean.

Before starting, Jászi gave Count Károlyi all the instructions necessary for him to go to England, take advantage of any social connections he had there, and busy himself with the affairs of the Emigration until the time should come for him to come to America also. In June, 1923, Krolyi left for London from the port of Gravos on a cargo-boat. On presenting his Czechoslovak passport, he received permission to land in England and was issued a license to remain there for two weeks on condition that he leave for Canada at the expiration of that time. He was lodged in London by a Czechoslovak banker named Panast and, through the intervention of Eduard Benes, at that time Minister of Foreign Affairs in Czechoslovakia, his permission to stay in London was extended to the end of the year. Károlyi was anxious to prove himself worthy of Czechoslovak support. He kept up contacts with Czechs, with Seton-Watson, and with publicists known to be closely connected with the Little Entente. While Károlyi was in England, a Labor

---

9 The "Red Scare" radical movement after World War I.

Party Government came into power. This government would insist on a change in the existing Conservative Hungarian regime as a condition for granting the Hungarian loan.

Meanwhile Hock and Jászi were busy working in the United States. Jászi delivered about fifty speeches to English-speaking people while Hock addressed the Hungarian masses. Jászi "exposed" the terrible sufferings of Hungary and the great menace to the peace and culture of Central Europe lurking in the present rule of terror".(10) Besides this he openly admitted that he was a herald of the Danube Confederation, proposed at that time mainly by Czechoslovak politicians. Success did not attend his footsteps, for he was a poor orator. His scientific, abstract lectures were listened to, but not understood by the students of universities in St. Louis and in Chicago. Jászi was not able to reach an agreement with other factions of the emigration; for, while he was easily able to reach a complete agreement with the Socialists in New York, the Communist faction hesitated. They, strictly true to their principles of class-conflict and a dictatorship of the proletariat, refused to entertain the idea of a formal alliance, insisting that it was all the same to them whether Horthy or Károlyi ruled. They stated themselves willing, howeves, to render financial aid to the movement of the emigrants. These leftist radicals of the Hungarian emigrants hoped that with the help of the so-called Burgher (bourgeois socialist) emigrants it would be easier to send their agents to Hungary with American passports.

The hesitation of the Communists confined itself to principles rather than to deeds. In practice they worked shoulder to shoulder with the Emigres. This was quite evident when non-Communist and Cómmunist emigrants appeared on the platforms of public meetings. At such a meeting in Chicago on January 27, 1924, Hock was able to announce publicly their agreement and cooperation. In his speech he announced that the Socialists were ready to support the movement to the best of their ability and concluded that

10 **Az Ember** (Vienna Hungarian daily), June 29, 1924.

the Democratic, Progressive Radical, Socialist, and Communist shades of color blended in a harmonious whole. For his part he was not prepared to go the length of the Communists, but the latter would be sure to continue the work begun by Károlyi's party popularly known as the Octobrists. With the following parable he showed how important it was for the Communists to assist the bourgeois emigrants also:

> If a man wishes to scale a ladder he must do so step by step. It is impossible to reach the top at one step. We must unite forces in order to overthrow the Hungarian government, and, setting our feet on this lower rung, climb slowly.(11)

Armin Loevy, leader of the Communists, also spoke at that meeting and admitted that the Communists had shaken hands with Hock and his followers. He insisted, however, that they were not willing to cry a halt there, but intended to go further. This co-operation of the Emigration with the Communists was further evidenced at the public meeting held in St. Louis. In an article on February 8, 1924, in the **Saint Louis és Vidéke** (Saint Louis and District), a Hungarian newspaper published there, appeared the following:

> It was an uplifting experience to see how the various shades of color, the Democrats, the Progressive Radicals, and the Communists, were blended together in one harmonious whole to the lasting glory of the Hungarians of Saint Louis.(12)

The article made special mention of that part of Hock's speech where he explained that every section could take part in the republican movement without having to give up its own special principles and proudly referred to Hock as "The Apostle of the October Movement."

The price paid for the alliance with the Communists, however, was a heavy one: the loss of the more moderate elements. Many of the Hungarian-Americans who had shown sympathy for the cause of the refugees in former times turned away from the move-

---

11 **Chicago Hungarian Tribune** (Hungarian daily), p. 1.
12 "The Triumph of the October Idea," p. 1.

ment. Hock's trip to Los Angeles ended in a fiasco, as did his visit to San Francisco, and when he went back to Chicago in the spring of 1924, the **Chicago Hungarian Tribune**, which had espoused his cause, took no more notice of him, and only a few men appeared at the banquets arranged for him.

The struggle to prevent the financial reorganization of Hungary proved abortive. It was a failure both in the United States and in Europe. On the New York stock exchange the shares of the Hungarian loan were over-subscribed in a few days' time. This fact definitely proved that an anti-Hungarian propaganda was powerless to mislead American public opinion. A faint hope remained that the refugees would still be able to win over some of the Hungarian-Americans: Károlyi's journey to the United States·

Before the war, when Károlyi was but the leader of a small political faction in the opposition, he had been taken on a tour of the United States to collect money for a campaign against the Conservative Hungarian Government of that time. A considerable sum was collected from the Hungarian-Americans for the purpose of covering electoral expenses. The greater part of that was still lying in an American bank under Károlyi's name. The chief reason for sending Károlyi to the United States was to make a new collection and at the same time to persuade the United States to remove the embargo from the sum already collected but sequestered since the War.

In fulfillment of Jászi's instructions, Madame Károlyi came over to the United States first to prepare the way for her husband. Jászi's supposition was that the wife of the President of the People's Republic, the democratic Countess, with her arresting personality, would easily be able to gain the sympathy of the American masses (famous for their worshipful attitude towards women) for the cause of the refugees. In this he was mistaken. H. L. Menken, president of the anti-Communist American Security League, demanded Madame Károlyi's deportation because of her connection with the Communists. This was a very bad letter of introduction for her. Madame Károlyi's entourage served only to strengthen Americans' suspicions against her. Besides Simon Szerényi, a representative of the emigrants' leftist journalists, her most zealous adherent among the pressmen was John Lékai-Leitner whose drama entitled "Man" had deified Béla Kun. At this time he was collaborator of the radical journal **New Forward**, and he wrote under the name of Lassen. Becoming advised of this, Mrs. Gerard, wife of the American Ambassador to Germany, cancelled her name on the list of the reception committee, and her example was followed by many others. The memory of her connection with Communism hampered Madame Károlyi all along her journey. For instance, at a public meeting in Chicago on November 29, 1924, only one hundred and fifty people were present.

If Madame Károlyi's journey had ended in failure, the one of Károlyi himself, following on it, seemed a lost cause. His permission to land in the United States was qualified by a condition restricting his freedom of speech, not on the grounds of his behavior in Hungary, but because of deeds perpetrated by him in other lands. Upon his arrival in the United States, the Hungarian Conservative newspaper, **Amerikai Magyar Népszava** (American-Hungarian Voice of the People), published in New York, put the following questions to him:

> Is Count Karolyi willing to take this opportunity of rendering an account through the medium of the press of the money collected for the purposes of the Independent Party in Hungary? Count Károlyi had $37,004 banked in his name. He extracted $20,694 before the war. What became of that sum? What induced Count Károlyi at the time when the money was collected to make over $5,000 of the sum subscribed to Sigsmund Kunfi, Radical Social Democrat? What induced him to grant $1,000 to the Előre, a Hungarian newspaper, published in New York, which even at that time was extreme? What is the Count's answer to the charge that he and the rest of the refugees are receiving pecuniary aid from the Czechoslovak Government.(13)

13 **Amerikai Magyar Népszava**, January 9, 1925.

To these questions Károlyoi refused to give any answer. His journey proved to be a failure. The pre-War money-making tour was not repeated. Károlyi returned to Europe and settled in Paris, being regarded as a traitor to his nation.(14) Dr. Oscar Jászi also realized the failure of the refugees' propaganda and, ceasing his extensive activities after so many failures, worked to retire quietly. In October, 1925, he became assistant professor of Sociology at Oberlin College in Ohio.

In spite of all of this, the work of the refugees was not altogether without results. As was noted before, the most prominent man among the refugees was Dr. Oscar Jászi. An effective publicist, he was able to inflict enormous damage on post-War Hungary's international reputation. Jászi's articles appeared in many periodicals, and his books, **Revolution and Counter-Revolution in Hungary** and, even more, **The Dissolution of the Habsburg Monarchy** went through several editions in different languages.

It might be asked why a man like Dr. Oscar Jászi insisted on castigating the government and political system of his country when, he hurt his political foes, he also did a great disservice to his nation as a whole. The fact was that Jászi, who possessed all the sensivity of a proud and high-strung intellectual, left Hungary as a greatly disillusioned and offended man. He could not forgive the "Whites" their treatment of the Jews; he could not forgive the aristocrats, who ruled the country, their stifling of progressive leftist political movements; and he could not forgive his compatriots their rejection of his dream of a federated Hungarian state. Thus for many years Jászi heaped invectives upon Hungary and her regime. In his anger he extolled the political systems of her enemies: Czechoslovakia, Yugoslavia, and Rumania. He contrasted the

---

14 Károlyi returned to Hungary after World War II where he served as a diplomat until 1949, when the increasingly totalitarian character of the Communist regime made him return once more into exile.

John Hock appealed for amnesty to the Hungarian Government in 1931. He died some years later as a broken man.

"liberalism" and "pacifism" of the governments of these states with the "militant nationalism" of that of his own country.

With the passage of time, however, Jászi's bitter resentments gradually dissipated. After a visit to his favorite successor states in 1935, he admitted that these were plagued with the same nationality problems as Austria-Hungary had been only two decades ago. What went on in Eastern Europe at the time, according to Jászi, was a "hidden bellum omnium contra omnes." By this time he saw that no one in Eastern Europe was immune from the bacilli of chauvinism. After 1945 Jászi went even further in admitting how unfair he had been to his country and countrymen during the early years of his exile. All this, however, could not undo the damage which he and his colleagues had inficted upon Hungary in the early 1920's.

Other political refugees of the 1920's, however, could not reconcile themselves to "white Hungary" at all. Some of them were still active when World War II came. They endeavored once more to rally western statesmen, and American-Hungarians too, for their political goals. New Left-wing Hungarian organizations appeared in the United States (and elsewhere too) such as the **Hungarian-American Council for Democracy** under the chairmanship of Béla Lugosi, the film actor, and **The New York Council of Hungarian-Americans for Victory** under the chairmanship of Professor Louis Toth, a recognized authority on accounting.

One of the more serious organizations was the **Movement for a New Democratic Hungary**, founded by Armin Rusztem Vánbéry, leader of the Left-radical group of the Hungarian political refugees at that time. This movement attempted to create an official representation for Hungary, a representation in exile. It failed to achieve that object, but it prepared memoranda for American government agencies and published an informative periodical **Harc** (Fight). Vánbéry also reached the ears of the Hungarians at home by the Voice of American broadcasting. This propaganda line of the Voice of America, however, was the most unfortunate possible for the cause of democracy in Hungary: it advised Hungary, probably through Eduard Benes' inspiration, that her road to democracy led through Prague and Moscow; thus it was only natural that the Hungarians went in fear of such a democracy. On the whole, their fear was not unfounded. After so many years fighting against "White Hungary", the "New Democratic Hungary" did not give a home to many of the political refugees of the 1920's, or, still worse, the refugees found it unsuitable for themselves. And, as a result of the new war, their one-time political foes were also forced to go into exile, with hundreds of thousands of their countrymen, in spite of the fact that these did not concern themselves with politics at all.

CHAPTER VI

EMIGRATION AS AN ALLY:
HUNGARIANS IN AMERICA

The United States emerged from World War I as potentially the strongest power on earth. Although the war created a new isolationism in the United States, it made clear for Europeans that no political affairs could be settled henceforth without the involvement of America. This fact created a new situation in Eastern European politics too. During the war and later, the Eastern European nations realized more and more the uniqueness of the United States. No nation in history ever had such a large number of people who were citizens by choice and not by birth. Furthermore, a considerable number of this large pre-war immigration came from Eastern Europe.

It is a fact that an emigrant, whatever the cause of his emigration, always preserves something from his past. Relations and sentiments toward the old country do not cease by the mere fact of emigration. The fact is that by emigration one can choose a new country as his home, but one cannot choose a new nationality. Eastern European politicians realized this fact as early as the war, and they began to look upon Americans of different nationality as their own national stock who had left their mother country for good or ill, but had in the meantime maintained their original nationality. For many Eastern European politicans, it seemed to be in the national interest to maintain the ties and friendship of the emigrants with their mother country. In America, propaganda was started on a large scale, and American citizens from different Eastern European stock, especially the Slavs, cried for justice for the oppressed peoples of their mother country.(1)

After World War I, it was quite natural that Hungary, too, should follow the same political tactics and try to make the Hungarian emigration an important part of her revisionist politics. Hungary realized immediately after the war that the United States was the only state--except the successor states--which had a large Hungarian population. This fact was quite significant, for, after Budapest, New York was the largest "Hungarian city", with a population of 115,098 Hungarians. Cleveland had 39,545; Chicago 30,420; Detroit 22,312; St. Louis 21,110; Philadelphia 14,321; and Milwaukee 6,848 Hungarian speaking inhabitants.(2) The fact was at hand for future politics. This large Hungarian emigrant population could and must be used in diplomacy concerning Hungary's case. Before discussing this question, let us examine the Hungarian immigrant in America.

Historical Survey of the Hungarian Immigration

The Hungarian emigration has a colorful past although it was small in number until the late nineteenth century.(3) The first recorded American Hungarian was Michael Kováts, Colonel Comman-

---

1 For full details of Slav propaganda in the United States during World War I, see Victor S. Mamatey, **The United States and East Central Europe 1914—1918** (Princenton, N. J.: Princenton University Press, 1957).

2 Dezső Halácsi, **A Világ Magyarságáért** (Budapest: Pub. by the author, 1944), p. 116.

3 For details on Hungarian emigration, see Emil Lengyel, **Americans from Hungary** (Philadelphia: J. B. Lippincott & Co., 1948); Géza Kende, **Magyarok Amerikában; Az Amerikai Magyarság Története** (Hungarians in America; a History of the American Hungarians) (Cleveland: Szabadság Pub., 1927); and Eugene Pivány, **Hungarian-American Historical Connections,** "A treatise read on the occasion of assuming his seat as a foreign member of the Hungarian Academy of Sciences by Eugene Pivány, Budapest, October 4, 1926" (Budapest: Published by the Hungarian Academy of Science, 1927).

dant of the Pulaski Legion during the War of Independence. Kováts was born at Karcag, Hungary, in 1724, and died in the battle of Charlestown on May 11, 1779. Dr. Joseph Johnson, Charlestown physician, recorded in his **Traditions and Reminiscences**: "The British buried him where he fell, on the west side of the road, in the land now owned and enclosed by John Margart, at the corner of Hugar Street. He was an officer of great merit, a Hungarian by birth".(4) His widow, unable to visit her husband's grave, erected a memorial chapel to his memory near the church of Szinne, Hungary. There it stands to this day, surrounded by old lime trees, recalling the memory of the Hungarian officer of hussars who died in action for the liberty of the United States of America.

The other Hungarian officers of the War of Independence were the Benyovsky brothers; Count Maurice Augustus Benyovsky and Count Ferenc Benyovsky. Count Maurice A. Benyovsky turned up at Philadelphia in 1872 with a letter of recommendation from Benjamin Franklin which he transmitted to General Washington, offering his blood, skill, and courage to America. The Count stated furthermore that he would raise an army of 3,483 men in Germany, clothe, arm, and transport it into the United States, all for the sum of 518,000 livres. America would agree to pay his men monthly stipends and provide them with grants of land.(5) Congress referred the plan to a committee headed by James Madison. It was rejected. His younger brother, Count Ferenc Benyovsky, was an officer in Lausun's Legion and died as a veteran in America in 1798.

News of American events penetrated Hungary more effectively during the first part of the nineteenth century through travelers and writers. One of the most successful among them was Sándor Bölöni Farkas. Bölöni Farkas came to America in 1831 as the secretary of Count Ferenc Béldy. He covered 2,450 miles in the United States and wrote an instructive book about his experiences,

---

4 Aladár Póka-Pivny, "A Hungarian under Washington," **The Hungarian Quarterly** (Budapest), No. 10 (March, 1939), pp. 90—105.

5 Lengyel, **Americans from Hungary**, p. 30.

Utazás Észak-Amerikában (Journey in North America) published in Koloszvár, Hungary, in 1835. The book was so popular that it reached two editions in a short time. Bölöni Farkas painted contrasting pictures of the American and Hungarian ways of life and revealed America's attractions for prospective immigrants. He found Philadelphia attractive and distinguished and observed incredulously that there was no police force in evidence at the Mint, confiding to the director that every single person in such a place in Europe would be watched by three other persons.

Visiting Washinton, he and his employer called at the White House as a matter of routine courtesy, and were surprised to be offered an audience with President Jackson, whom they found to be a gay and friendly elderly man, wearing only a black business suit with no badge of office.

In Boston, Bölöni Farkas remarked that his host's table was appointed with as much luxury as that of a European aristocrat. He marveled at how school-minded Americans were: while they did not like to pay taxes, they readily taxed themselves to support their schools. In every town, no matter how small, he found public libraries. Inquiring about wages, he was told that unskilled labor was paid as much as a dollar and sometimes two dollars a day; in comparison with Hungary, this was fabulous, indicating one of the main causes of the large immigration to come. The message Hungary received from his book was that "America is a happy land, America is progressive, America is young". As his 500-ton ship, **Albania**, set sail for Europe, he exclaimed: "Farewell, glorious country. Keep on being the eternal defender of man's rights. Keep on being the inspiration of the oppressed".(6)

Another Hungarian, not many years later, also found an America he had never expected to find. This man was Ágoston Mokcsay Haraszthy, author of the two-volume book **Utazás Észak-Amerikában** (Journey in North America) published by Gustav Heckenast in

---

6 Ibid., p. 33.

Pest, Hungary, in 1844. Haraszthy found that "nothing daunts the American and no impediments can halt him in carrying out his design. The boundless energy and self-assurance characterizing the American above all other nationals are truly breathtaking. He seems to live twice the span of others and to accomplish a hundred times more. He rises early and he begins his work without delay. He reads his paper while having his breakfast, so as to waste no time".(7)

Ágoston Mokcsai Haraszthy translated his admiration for America into deeds. He returned to Hungary and then came back to the United States with his family. Haraszthy chose to settle in a fertile region of Wisconsin and bought a tract of ten thousand acres from the government. There he established a village which was named for him--Haraszthy--it later became Westfield and is now called Sauk City, twenty miles from Madison.

Haraszthy was active in settling immigrants and left his mark in Sauk City before he departed in 1849.(8) He founded a Humanist society in 1845, an organization of free thinkers which spread throughout Wisconsin. The society, established for intellectual and cultural purposes, had such far reaching results that Sauk City became known widely in Europe as "Free Thinkers Heaven", The organization still exists there and a related group is active yet in Milwaukee.(9)

In 1849, Haraszthy ran into debt and was forced to sell his land in Sauk City. He went to California and was among the first to notice the great wine-growing potentialities of California. The eighteenth century Franciscans had already laid out vineyards and the missions had their wineries. Haraszthy decided to work on that foundation. He introduced cuttings of Muscat Alexandria grape and Zinfandel red wine grape. Later he imported two hundred

---

7 Ibid., p. 34.

8 "From Many Lands," The Milwaukee Journal (Daily), January 25, 1967, p. 4.

9 Ibid.

114

thousand vine cuttings, including the most important European varieties. Due largely to Haraszthy's initiative, California was to produce most of the nation's wine. Half a million California acres were to be turned over to viticulture, second only to orange growing in the State's agricultural economy.(10)

If American Hungarians ever had a hero it was Lajos Kossuth, the leader of the Hungarian war of independence in 1848. Americans sympathized with all the liberal revolutionary movements, but the Hungarian struggle particularly appealed to them. One reason may have been that the Hungarian republic was supposed to be modeled on the United States. Among the western powers, only the United States of America intended to recognize Kossuth's regime as a **defacto** government, but independent Hungary was destroyed before the American agent reached the country. The American government next turned its attention to Kossuth himself, who had escaped from Hungary into Turkey where he was held prisoner for two years. America helped secure his release and sent a naval vessel to bring him to the United States. Arriving in New York on December 5, 1851, he met with great popular enthusiasm and official honors. In Washington, Kossuth dined with President Fillmore and received a special banquet from Congress. There Daniel Webster, Secretary of State, said that Americans would rejoice in seeing a model of the United States on the lower Danube and that Hungary ought to be "independent of all foreign powers".(11)

Kossuth visited several cities and delivered over three hundred public addresses throughout the United States. America fell in love with him. Books were written about him; streets, cities, and counties were named after him. To this very day Iowa has a

---

10 **California: A Guide to the Golden State**, American Guide Series, Sponsored by Mabel R. Gillis, California State Librarian (New York: Hastings House, Inc., n. d.).

11 Alexander De Conde, **A History of American Foreign Policy** (New York: Charles Scribner's Sons, 1963), p. 218.

Kossuth County, and there is a Kossuth in Pennsylvania, in Ohio, and in Mississippi. Children were named after him. There was a gentleman in Cleveland whose name was E. K. Willcox — Éljen (Long Live) Kossuth Willcox. (12)

Some of the Kossuth soldiers also came to America. Among them the most interesting figure was László Ujházy, former Lord Lieutenant of County Sáros, and ex-government commissioner of the Danubian fortress, Komárom. Ujházy conceived a political idea which, at that time, was unique. He wanted to build up a large Hungarian community, a New Hungary, in the United States which, by its votes, would exert a pressure on Washington to back the Kossuth solution of the Hungarian problem. Ujházy wanted all of the Hungarian refugees to come over to America. To encourage Hungarian immigration to the United States, an American Society was founded in London. However the plan did not appeal to Kossuth. Nevertheless, a Hungarian settlement was founded some 110 miles from the Missouri in Iowa. Ujházy himself bought twelve sections of the land, and a small Hungarian colony of five families started there in 1850. They called their new home New Buda, in remembrance of their old country. New Buda carried on fifty years. But a great statesman or strong general was not necessarily a good frontiersman, and "New Hungary" failed.(13)

By the time of the Civil War there were approximately four thousand Americans of Hungarian descent in the United States. Their number was not large, but the ratio of those who volunteered

---

12 There is a considerable literature devoted to Kossuth's stay and activities in the United States. For example, **Report of the Special Commitee of the City of New York for the Reception of Governor Louis Kossuth** (New York, 1852); Ph. Skinner, **The Welcome of Kossuth** (Philadelphia, 1852); **Kossuth in New England** (Boston, 1852); F. M. Newman, **Selected Speeches of Kossuth** (New York, 1854); Denis Jánossy, "Kossuth and the Presidential Election, 1852," **Hungarian Quarterly**, VII (1941), 105-11; and Stephen Gál, "Kossuth, America and the Danubian Confederation," **Hungarian Quarterly**, VI (1940), 417—33.

13 Lengyel, **Americans from Hungary**, pp. 50—51.

March 15, 1939

My dear Mr. Vasvary:

I am glad to learn that The Hungarian Reformed Federation of America is planning to hold commemorative services on June fourth next in connection
with the seventy-fifth anniversary of the battle of
Piedmont, Virginia where Major General Julius H. Stahel
exemplified such bravery that he later received the
Congressional Medal of Honor. Men of Hungarian blood
-- many of them exiles from their fatherland -- rendered
valiant service to the cause of the Union. Their deeds
of self-sacrifice and bravery deserve to be held in
everlasting remembrance.

Very sincerely yours,

Franklin D Roosevelt

Reverend Edmund Vasvary,
The Hungarian Reformed Federation of America,
1726 Pennsylvania Avenue, N. W.,
Washington, D. C.

117

for war service was considerable. Eight hundred Hungarians served in Lincoln's army and about a hundred of them were officers. Such a high ratio of soldiers to the total number was not reached by any other nationality in the United States.

Two of the Hungarians became major generals and five reached the rank of brigadier general. The Hungarian-born immigrants furnished the Union armies with fifteen colonels, two lieutenant colonels, fourteen majors, fifteen captains, and a number of subaltern officers and several surgeons. (14)

The Hungarian-born soldiers played an important part in the Western Department, comprising Missouri, Kansas, Illinois, and Kentucky, under the command of General John C. Fremont. His chief-of-staff was a Hungarian, Brigadier General Alexander Asboth. Three of his aides were also Hungarians: the commander of Fremont's Body Guard, Major Charles Zágonyi, his chief topographical engineer and his chief of ordinance. (15)

The high tide of the Hungarian migration to America started with the "new immigration" at the turn of the century. The United States immigration statistics began with three lone Hungarian immigrants in 1871. Three years later the figure rose to 1,347. In 1880, with 4,363 immigrants, the rush began. In 1884, 14,797 emigrants left Hungary for the United States. From this time on, the number was between 10,000 and 37,000 a year until the last year of the nineteenth century. Then the figures began rising. In 1900, there was a migration of 54,767 people from Hungary to the United States. The peak was reached in 1907 with 193.460, about 1 percent of the total population of Hungary. The yearly number rose from 76,928 to 122,944 between 1908 and 1912. In 1913, just before World War I, 117,580 immigrants left Hungary. About 1,700,000 immigrants came to the United States from pre-war

14 Edmund Vasváry, **Lincoln's Hungarian Heroes** (Washington, D. C.: Published by the Hungarian Reformed Federation of America, 1939), p. 290.
   15 **Ibid.**

118

Hungary, including not only the Magyars but the national minorities.(16)

A comparison of immigration from Hungary with immigration from other countries is instructive. During the fifteen-year period beginning in 1895 the ratio of Hungarian immigration to the total increased from 5 to 16 percent. Another interesting figure is that 87 percent of the Hungarian immigrants were between fourteen and forty-four years of age.

The occupational statistics of the Hungarian immigrants, in the period preceding World War I, show that 67 percent of the total were farmers, 12.5 percent were unskilled workers of all kinds, 12.4 percent were miners and factory workers, 5.5 percent domestic servants, and the remainder belonged to "miscellaneous occupations". The size of the professional group was microscopic. It increased very slowly, amounting to one-half of 1 percent just before World War I. In spite of the fact, there are some remarkable names among them.

The name of Janos Xantus was becoming known in scientific circles just before the Civil War. He collected many specimens of California's fauna and flora and wrote a book on his explorations titled **Journey in the Southern Parts of California.**

Tivadar Puskás became one of the original collaborators of Edison, who praised him highly. Eventually, he became director of the Edison World Exhibition and general manager for Edison's business interests aboard.

Another Hungarian, Joseph Pulitzer, the newspaperman, is well known to every student of American history. In 1903 Pulitzer founded the School of Journalism at Columbia University, one of the most famous institutions of its kind, established the Pulitzer Prizes which are among the most coveted distinctions of writers and artists all over the United States.

---

16 These statistics and those following are based on Lengyel, **Americans from Hungary,** pp. 123ff.

Two further facts characterized the Hungarian immigration. First, it was largely a male immigration. In the years around the turn of the century more than 73 percent of all Hungarian immigrants were male. Secondly, once the Hungarian immigrant left home he underwent a remarkable change. At home he had been a peasant, but when he reached America he never thought of going to work on the farm. He turned his back on the soil and turned toward the mine and factory. He did this possibly because he considered himself a transient. He hoped to make money quickly in the mine and in the factory and to return home and buy a piece of land. The best proof of this is the size of the remittances to the Old Country. At the height of the immigration the immigrants sent home sometimes as much as one hundred to two hundred million crowns a year. The highest annual remittance was a quarter of a billion crowns — the equivalent of $50,000,000. An investigation in County Torontál, South Hungary, showed that until 1907 the immigrants had sent home eight and a half million crowns to this county alone. The proposed disposition of this sum was: two million to buy land, an equal amount for savings and kin, and the rest to pay off mortgages. All of this indicates that many of the immigrants planned to return to Hungary. (17)

In fact many of them did return. The figures show that one-fourth of the immigrants returned to Hungary in the fifteen years up to 1914. Most of these ex-Americans were racial Hungarians and not members of the minorities. Between 1908 and 1924 the number of Hungarian reemigrants from the United States to Hungary ranged between ten thousand and thirty tousand annually. The total of all returning Hungarians between 1908 and 1924 amounted to 149,906.(18)

Others never returned to their homeland. They settled in the neighborhood of mines and steel furnaces. Physically, they were

17 For full details, see Pál Farkas, Az Amerikai Kivándorlás (Budapest: Singer & Wolfner, 1907).

18 Lengyel, Americans from Hungary, p. 128.

in the United States but spiritually they were not. They were living in the Hungarian colony, in the ghetto. Here they understood each other's language and felt somewhat more secure.

The main cause of the Hungarian emigration was neither political persecution nor religious discrimination. These were unknown in pre-war Hungary. Most of the emigrants were Catholics, the dominant religion in Hungary. Others were Protestants; but Protestantism enjoyed perfect freedom in Hungary. Many great leaders of the nation belonged to that faith. Others were Jews. But neither were Jews persecuted in Hungary at that time; pre-war Hungary was considered by many as a paradise for the Jews in that part of the world. Pre-war Hungarian governments saw in the Jews useful allies for the future, both economically, and owing to the Jews' willingness to assimilate linguistically, in the national struggle. To these considerations of expediency were added entirely sincere ones of principle, for the Hungarian Liberals (not only the political party which bore the name but the whole generation) were convinced that it was morally wrong to draw a distinction between man and man on grounds of religion or etnic origin. All the Hungarian governments of that era were therefore at pains to admit the Jews to full civic and political equality and to give them their share of social reward.

The arrival of the Jews in Hungary, as in the United States, had been mainly a nineteenth-century phenomenon. In 1785, when they were first counted, they had numbered only 75,000. Immigration, chiefly from Galacia, had raised their figures to almost 1,000,000 before World War I. It would have been in the interest of the nation that this influx be stopped. Hungary was, however, altogether too liberal in this matter; the eastern gates of the country were left wide open and Hungary's economic prosperity attracted new masses of orthodox Jewry from its primitive surroundings beyond the Carpathians. Their first generation settled in the northeastern counties of Hungary; the second and third moved to the cities; the fourth generation in many cases migrated further west to other countries or overseas. About

110,000 Jews left Hungary between 1870 and 1890.(19) In this procedure, Hungary mostly lost the assimilated European-type educated Jewish element and received instead ever new waves from the east, raw and unassimilated as they were. This resulted around 1880 in a short-lived movement of anti-Semitism. The government, however, turned its batteries on the movement, and it soon disintegrated.

Mention must be also made of those who belonged to the ethnic minorities and left Hungary for America. They were numerous, but not one of them left Hungary because of political persecution or religious discrimination. Generally, pre-war Hungary is presented to the English reader as a feudal land dominated by rich and powerful Magyar landlords who oppressed both the peasants and the ethnic minorities. Many historians, English and French among them, have condemned pre-war Hungarian policies, accusing the Magyars of being "born oppressors", "the Prussians of the Danube", while the different nationalities of Hungary were innocent, gentle, and defenseless people.(20) In spite of this accusation (although some bombastic journalists and politi-

---

19 For full details see Aloys Kovács, **A zsidóság térfoglalása Magyarországon** (Expansion of the Jews in Hungary) (Budapest: no publisher, 1922).

20 For full details on this subject from a Hungarian point of view, see Dominic G. Kosáry, **A History of Hungary** (Cleveland—New York: Benjamin Franklin Bibliophile Society, 1941). Professor C. A. Macartney of Oxford is considered to be fundamental on this topic in English. Professor Macartney is one of the few who has made on-the-spot a thorough study of conditions among nationalities in Eastern Europe. See **The Habsburg Empire 1790—1918** (New York: Macmillan Company, 1969), pp. 687—740. Also see Professor Macartney's other works: **Hungary and Her Successors** (Oxford, 1937); **Problems of the Danube Basin** (Cambridge, 1942); **National State and National Minorities** (London, 1934). Professor Macartney does not shut his eyes to the faults of either party. On the other hand, Professor R. W. Seton-Watson's works are admirably written from the anti-Magyar angle. See **Racial Problems in Hungary** (London, 1908); **The Southern Slav Question in the Habsburg Monarchy** (London, 1911); **A History of Czechs and Slovaks** (Hamden, Conn., 1943); **A History of the Rumanians** (London, 1934).

cians who were for "magyarization" provided excellent material for anti-Magyar historians to denounce), the Hungarian generation of that age attempted to arrive at a settlement with the national minorities. This was the motive of Francis Deák and Joseph Eötvös, the two great Hungarian statesmen of the era, in creating the Bill of Nationalities of 1868. In this they attempted, in a true Liberal spirit, to balance the security of the state with the principle of free development for the nationalities. (21)

The Nationality Bill of 1868 stated that "all citizens of Hungary compose one nation, politically speaking an indivisible unified Hungarian nation, in which every one, no matter to what nationality he or she should belong, enjoys equal rights before the law".(22) Accordingly, the idea of the "political nation" did not recognize any difference or privileges based on the racial background of its citizens. The official legislative and parliamentary language was Magyar, yet in dealing with the lower spheres and offices of administration every one could use his mother tongue. The bill was explicit in stating that its aim was to serve every one's freedom and cultural advancement.

The social conditions of pre-war Hungary also were characterized by Conservative Liberalism, professing the principle that no development was to be interfered with beyond the granting of equality before the law. It refused to interfere even when this would have meant positive assistance and protection for the lower classes. It allowed free passage for the sudden growth of Capi-

---

21 The name of Francis Deák is well known to Eastern-European historians. Joseph Eötvös was one of the outstanding contemporary writers of political philosophy, having devoted several of his books to the question of the equal rights of nationalities. In his voluminous work, **The Reigning Ideas of the Nineteenth Century and their Influence on the State,** he revealed with shocking clarity where European developments would lead. He pointed out that the three leading ideas of the day, Liberty, Equality, and Nationalism, clashed with each other in the long run, and that without sufficient balance this would lead to disturbances, social revolutions, and war.

22 Kosáry, **Hungary,** p. 330.

talism, but for a long time it left agricultural and industrial laborers to their fate. About one-third of all arable land in 1890 was in the hands of owners holding above 1,000 yokes (1,422 acres). A few reform-spirited landowners made a study of the homestead system in America, launching a movement to prevent further disintegration of small farms, but the expropriation of landed properties was not suggested at that time, because the public was made to believe that all official intervention would be injurious.(23)

The poorer section of the peasantry, with little or no arable land, found employment until the end of the century in large scale government works projects, such as building railroads and canals. When, at the end of the century, these large public works were completed, marginal agricultural labor lost its outstanding source of income. Before World War I, Hungary was not a country of large industries, with the exception of some large flour mills and sugar factories (Budapest was the largest flour milling center in Europe and the second largest in the world, next to Minneapolis). But the country was rich in agrarian resources. It produced wheat of good quality. As to quantity, it closely followed the crops of the United States and Russia, with a yearly production average of nearly 200 million bushels. As long as world price of wheat was sufficiently high and American competition did not assume prohibitive proportions, Hungarian grain growers throve on this export. But when, around 1890, wheat-producing areas overseas grew enormously, and, besides the United States, Canada and Argentina entered world competition, a substantial slump of price resulted, seriously hampering Hungarian farming. Since more than half of Hungary's population earned its living by agriculture, the drop in the price of wheat in world markets was a serious blow to Hungary as a whole. Meanwhile the phenomenal growth of the American economy and the

23 For details see Michael Kerek, **A Magyar Földkérdés** (The Hungarian Land Problem) (Budapest, no publisher, 1939), pp. 64—65.

ascending prosperity of the United States prompted a flow of emigration from the eastern and southeastern parts of Europe to the New World. The Hungarian emigrant, being Magyar or belonging to the ethnic groups, left Hungary for no other reason than to acquire capital with which to purchase sufficient land to maintain a livelihood in the country of his origin. Migration was considered by many Hungarians as a temporary, money-making tour. A part of them, as was mentioned above, achieved this aim and returned.(24)

Hungarian authorities looked upon the emigration as a national sickness. In 1904, the Hungarian government signed an agreement with the Cunard Line to avoid illegal emigration. Indeed, anyone could leave the country, unless they were of military age (in which case they had to deposit a bond they forfeited if they failed to return home to perform their military service) or were subject to jail or fine. For the authorities. it was hard to understand why workers left the country in such great numbers, since living conditions seemed to be good. They stated perhaps the main cause of the emigration when they observed that "the measure of emigration does not depend on us, but on the power of attraction of American industry".(25)

Social and Cultural Structure of the Hungarian Immigrants

In the United States, the immigrants found themselves in a land where newspaper reading was a habit. It was natural that a Hungarian press was started in America. The immigrant, as was mentioned above, felt his home ties very strongly. National societies, the church, and the mother-tongue press kept him in touch with the political struggle at home and even gave him opportunities to take part in it. This applied also to the Hungarian-

---

24 This fact also proves that social conditions were not as bad, as some historians have described them. Had the social conditions been hopeless, emigrants would not have returned to that Hungary at all.

25 Lengyel, **Americans from Hungary**, p. 125.

language newspapers published in the United States; except for a small minority, they identified themselves with the home-land, representing it as the beloved fatherland.

As in so many other things, the name of Lajos Kossuth is associated with the beginnings of the Hungarian-language press in the United States. **The Hungarian Exiles' Journal** of the 1850's is the first Hungarian-language newspaper on record. It attempted to be the spokesman of Kossuth's followers, but there were never many of them, and this paper never had more than 118 subscribers.

The second Hungarian language newspaper was established in 1879. Its title was **Magyar Amerika** (Hungarian America) and the paper devoted itself to the cultural interests of Hungary and America. Its program reveals the contemporary mentality:

Magyar Amerika wants a mighty, thriving, happy Hungary. It wants universal well-being for all Hungarians wherever they may dwell. It wants to help raise Hungary's beautiful literature to the high place it deserves, wants to acquaint broad segments of American life with our fatherland, our national habits of thought, culture, spiritual and material resources, thus counter-acting the nefarious work of our malicious neighbors. We also want to depict our new country to our readers, providing them with a truthful picture.(26)

The paper went out of existence after a short period.

The first Hungarian-language newspaper with greater staying power was **Amerika Nemzetőr** (American National Guard), first published on February 1, 1884. It described itself as a "journal devoted to the cultural interests of Hungary and America". The following reasons were given by the editors for the existence of the paper:

------

26 **Ibid.**, p. 196. NB. After the Hungarian Revolution of 1848, a large anti-Hungarian propaganda campaign was carried on by Austria in order to counterbalance Kossuth's activities. The paper was probably referring to this in its mention of the "nefarious work of our malicious neigbors."

The Hungarians in the United States have no contact with one another. Our business and other interests have dispersed us all over the country. It is imperative that the Hungarians living in this country should have a newspaper to manifest their manly courage in defending the interests of their native country abroad. We may have lost our Hungarian citizenship, but no law can deprive us of our right to be devoted to our own fatherland. (27)

The editors of the paper had a thorough knowledge of the Hungarian immigrant mentality. The Fatherland must be defended against a real enemy and no more ideal foe could be found than Austria.

One of the most permanent Hungarian papers was the Szabadság (Liberty). It was founded in 1891 and celebrated the fiftieth anniversary of its foundation in 1941. The paper called itself liberal and took an effective stand for liberal democracy. It claimed to be the leader of the Hungarians in the United States and, in 1942, reported a circulation of 40,612. Ater that the paper sharply declined.

Another Hungarian-language daily, the **Amerikai Magyar Nép-szava** (American Hungarian People's Voice), was launched in 1899. The paper gave its readers what they wanted: news and patriotic stories from the old country.

The Left-wing press was represented by **Előre** (New Forward) which was transformed into **Uj előre** and, after a period of hibernation, emerged as **Magyar Jövő** (Hungarian Future) describing itself as a "Democratic, anti-Fascist daily" and claiming forty-five years of previous existence in 1946. Most of the time it was rather anticapital and sentimentally fond of the Soviet Union. It was one of the few Hungarian newspapers that did not attempt to pursue a nationalist Hungarian policy in the United States and never waged a war against the Trianon Treaty. **Előre**

---

27 **Ibid.**, p. 197.

was the publication of the American Hungarian Socialist Federation, which federation had many crypto-communist members.

Az Ember (The Man) had a unique history in Hungarian journalism. It was founded in Budapest before World War I, under the editorship of Ferenc Göndör. He supported the Hungarian Communist regime after World War I. From Budapest the paper was transferred to Vienna where it fought "White Hungary". Ferenc Göndör became one of the most hated men in Horthy's Hungary. While many of the former political exiles were gradually forgiven and some of them returned to their native country, Göndör moved his paper from Vienna to New York, where it was established in 1926. It became known as a fighter for liberal causes and a great admirer of the policy of President Franklin D. Roosevelt. The paper made many foes, and this was probably the reason that the main Hungarian centers usually voted for Republican candidates.

The principal Hungarian settlements were the main Hungarian-language newspaper publishing centers: New York, Cleveland, Detroit, Pittsburgh, Chicago, St. Louis, and Milwaukee. In 1884 the Hungarians in America had only one newspaper.(28) In 1898 the number rose to five. In 1913 the number increased to fifteen and it reached twenty-seven in 1918. Between the world wars, altogether about forty Hungarian-language newspapers were published in the United States. The Hungarian press grew because America was no longer a transit station. Three of these papers were dailies, most of the others were weeklies, and a few were fraternity publications. Most of them described themselves as "Independent" or "Non-party"; while a few called themselves "Democratic", "Catholic", or "Religious". There was a "Republican" paper and there was even a monarchist monthly publication, promoting the candidacy of Otto von Habsburg to the Hungarian

---

28 In that same year the number of German-language newspapers in the United States was 621.

throne. The combined circulation of the papers amounted to about a quarter of a million.(29)

All week long the new American worked in mine and mill, but Sunday was his day at home and at the church, where God understood his language, which men did not understand. He shepherded his children into the House of God where they heard the Hungarian tongue. The church was instrumental in keeping his children from becoming strangers in the parental house.

The Catholic Hungarians in the United States had their first church in Cleveland. It was built in 1895. Before World War I, Catholic churches were built in other Hungarian diaspora centers too, such as Bridgeport, Toledo, and South Bend.

The largest of the Protestant churches of Hungarian-born Americans after the war was the Reformed Church in the United States, consisting of the Eastern, Central, and Western districts. The American Hungarian Reformed Church comprised several parishes. The Episcopalian Church also had Hungarian-language parishes and so had the Southern Presbyterian Church. Small congregations were maintained by the Hungarian Baptists, Methodists, Seventh Day Adventists, and Unitarians.

As a national religious community the Jews of Hungary did not play an important part in the United States. Most Hungarian immigrants before World War I were non-Jews. If the Jewish immigrants joined any group, most likely it was a neighborhood synagogou without any special nationality affiliation.(30)

The immigrant came to the United States and was transplanted into an entirely different setting. America was a nation of "joiners". People were expected to join all kinds of organizations to meet like-minded people. It was natural that the American Hungarians, too, had their associations. In general, strong Hungarian national sentiment characterized the American Hungarian

---

29 N. W. Ayer & Sons, **Directory** (Philadelphia: N. W. Ayer and Sons, 1942).

30 For full details on the religious life of the Hungarian imigrant, see Géza Kende, **Hungarians in America** (Cleveland: Szabadság Publ., 1927).

organizations. Paradoxically, the nationalistic feeling increased, rather than declined, as a result of transplantation to the alien soil. Home became a much sweeter place when it was no longer theirs.

As the tidal wave of Hungarian immigration set in, the fraternal insurance companies came into existence. One of the first and most important of these was the **Verhovay Segély Egylet** (Verhovay Fraternal Insurance Association). It was founded in Cleveland on February 20, 1886. The Association was named after Gyula Verhovay, a member of the Hungarian parliament. The Association strated with a capital of $17,25, which thirteen ordinary miners collected themselves. Verhovay was chartered as a sick-benefit and burial association. A year after its foundation it had seventy-seven members and assets amounting to $126.83. The number of members increased as the number of Hungarians in America grew. The Verhovay Fraternal Insurance Association became the largest of all American-Hungarian fraternal orders. Its total membership in 1944 amounted to 52,292; it had total assets of $7,408,000 and 364 lodges.(31)

Another big Hungarian organization was the **Amerikai Magyar Református Egyesület** (Hungarian Reformed Federation of America). It started in 1896 at Pittsburgh with 320 members and a total of $272.15. The federation had such rapid growth that after World War I it established a Hungarian orphan asylum and a home for old people in Ligonier, Pensylvania. They called it **Bethlen Otthon** (Bethlen Home), after Gábor Bethlen, the great Protestant ruler of Transylvania in the sixteenth century. In the Golden Jubilee year of 1946 the membership of the Federation was more than 26,000 and its assets amounted to $2,652,357. The number of its lodges was 235, distributed throughout the main American-Hungarian settlements.(32)

---

31 **Journal of the Verhovay Aid Association,** February 21, 1946.

32 Alexander Kalassy, **The Hungarian Reform Federation of America,** in manuscript.

The third largest Hungarian fraternal organization, **The Rákóczi Segélyző Egyesület** (Rakoczi Aid Association of Bridgeport), started at Bridgeport in 1888 with an initial capital of $7.50. In 1946 the Association had 24,222 members in 144 lodges, and assets close to five million dollars.(33)

Besides these there were many small fraternal organizations all over the United States. The American Sick Benefit and Life Insurance Association was founded in 1892 in Bridgeport. In 1897 the Hungarian Catholics founded their association called "Virgin Mary, Patroness of Hungarians". Others were named for Hungary's historic figures, such as Louis Kossuth, Count Stephen Szechenyi (often called the greatest Hungarian), John Hunyadi and Nicolas Zrinyi (the two Turk-Beaters), then Francis Deák, whom his countrymen called the Fatherland's Sage. Many of the societies were named after saints revered in Hungary, such as St. Stephen, St. Emeric, and St. Elizabeth. Some of them were highly nostalgic, judging by their names, such as "First Hungarian Christian Sick Benefit Society Trusting in God" and "Akron God Bless the Hungarian Sick Benefit Society".

Some of those who came from Hungary joined American organizations. One of the largest was the I.W.O., International Workers' Order. Its Hungarian branch, **Testvériség** (Fraternity), claiming 2,790 members in 1945, was patronized by Left-wing followers.

American-Hungarians of the Jewish faith also founded many fraternal organizations. These organizations were usually given the names of historic Hungarian persons, such as Kossuth, or Joseph Kiss, a Hungarian poet of the Jewish faith, or Theodor Herzl, founder of modern Zionism.

The First Hungarian Literary Society was founded in New York before World War I. Similar societies were set up in Chicago, Cleveland, Bridgeport, Akron, Youngstown, Trenton, Passaic, and Perth Amboy. The object of the First Hungarian Literary So-

---

33 Laszló Lakatos, **Golden Jubilee Book** (Bridgeport: Ed. Rákóczi Aid Association, 1946).

ciety in New York was to arrange debates and lectures, to foster literature and social life among the members and to maintain a library. The Hungarian Cultural Association of Philadelphia set out to foster sympathy for Hungary, secure American interest for Hungary, foster the Hungarian language, and promote business contacts between the United States and Hungary. The Detroit **Magyar Klub** (Hungarian Club) entertained and was entertained by some of the most famous visiting Hungarian artists and welcomed some of the best-known Hungarian statesmen.

The end of the First World War saw the influx of a large number of college-bred Hungarians—physicians, scientists, and lawyers. Chicago Hungarians founded the **Egyetemi Kör** (University Association), for members with academic backgrounds, and they gave life to the **Amerikai Magyar Diák Egylet** (American Hungarian Student Association). In New York, the intellectuals got together in the early twenties and founded **Ady Endre Társaság** (Ady Endre Society), named after Hungary's greatest twentieth-century poet. The Ady Society served as a bridge between the Hungarian-born **inteligentzia** of New York and Budapest. It became a tradition for visiting Hungarian artists to appear on the platform of the Ady Society.(34)

The American-Hungarians and Hungary's Case for Justice

This was the past and structure of the Hungarian immigration which the home country wanted to use for the cause of the Revision of the Trianon Treaty. The organization of the American-Hungarians for the purpose of revisionism began immediately after the war. As noted earlier, the movement of the political refugees failed mainly because it was anti-nationalistic, accepting the support of the successor states, and because it did not emphasize the question of the revision of the treaty of Trianon. On the other hand, the nationalistic organizations had success among American-Hungarians for the simple reason that they seemed to be pro-

---

34 For details see Kende, **Hungarians in America**.

Hungarian. The social order of the mother country was a secondary issue for American-Hungarians when the real one arose: survival. Hungarians in America could belong to different religions and classes, could differ in world outlook, but there was one issue on which nearly all ex-Hungarians in the United States agreed after World War I: the question of Hungary's boundaries. Even the least nationalistic Hungarians agreed that the frontiers of Hungary were not just.

Hungarian **irredenta** swept all the American-Hungarian organizations. The activities of these organizations were manifold. They wrote letters to prominent Americans, including the members of the Senate and the President of the United States. On the occasion of President Harding's inauguration, the Hungarian Territorial Integrity League addressed a memorial to the chief of the United States of America, in which the League, on behalf of the mutilated Hungarian nation, referred to humanity and justice. The address stated that Hungary's enemies misrepresented her actions and history before the tribunal of the world. They charged Hungary with responsibility for the war, though until the very last moment the Hungarian Government alone opposed the declaration of war. At the discussions and crown councils prior to the declaration of war against Serbia in 1914, it was Count Stephen Tisza, Hungary's premier, who alone opposed the Dual Monarchy's sharp ultimatum to Serbia and had it recorded in the minutes that Hungary protested against any infringement of Serbia's independence as well as against any Austro-Hungarian expansion in the Balkans. Once more before the end of the war did Tisza raise his voice in protest against the politics of the Central Powers, when he opposed the declaration of unrestricted submarine warfare, which, he feared, would give President Wilson the opportunity of bringing the United States into the war. They charged that Hungary oppressed the national minorities by the suppression of their language, literature, and personal liberties. However, there could be no more damning proof of these slanders than the fact that, during the peace negotiations. when Hungary

133

proposed that her nationalities should be allowed to vote freely as to which state they would join, Hungary's neighbors violently protested.

Therefore the Hungarian nation never can and never will submit to the outrageous provisions of the Peace Treaty.

Mr. President, we confidently hope that, if the voice of truth can reach you — and it will be rightly interpreted by the one and a half millions of Magyars who have become faithful citizens of the great American Commonwealth — your sense of justice will be aroused to indignation at the senseless and stupid outrage inflicted upon us by those responsible for the Peace Treaty.(35)

When Hoover was elected President, the League sent a telegram requesting him to consider Hungary's plea for revision. In 1930, on the tenth anniversary of the Trianon Treaty, pleas were sent to Henry Lewis Stimson, at that time Secretary of State, and to other prominent personalities. On that occasion, Senator Borah said that the greatest injustice was committed against Hungary in Versailles and that the Paris peace treaties needed a revision.

Another convinced friend of the Hungarian people and an enthusiastic champion of "Justice for Hungary" was Professor Henry A. Heydt of New York University. During this year, he delivered several speeches at New York University with regard to the injustices of the Treaty of Trianon. He also caused these speeches to be printed and to be distributed to all members of the Congress. Professor Heydt, among others, stated: "If we believe in justice and law, if we believe firmly in Christian morals, we have to destroy Trianon".(36)

---

35 **The Hungarian Nation** (Budapest: Monthly Review, 1921), II, No. 3, p. 1.

36 **U. S., For. Rel., Department of State**, 711.64/12. Some years later, in 1936, Miklós Horthy, Regent of Hungary, conferred on Professor Heydt the Order of the Cross of Merit, 2nd class, for the champion of "Justice for Hungary."

In 1930, Hungary celebrated the nine-hundred years' anniversary of the death of St. Imre, the son of St. Stephen and. the patron of the Hungarian youth. This was a good occasion to have many visitors and receive Church dignitaries. Among them was John Francis Noll, Roman Catholic Bishop of Fort Wayne, Indiana. Bishop Noll was apparently much impressed by what he saw in Hungary. Returning home, he published and circulated a letter in his diocese, stating that Hungary was forced into the war against her own will and, in spite of this, had suffered severely by the terms of the peace treaties. Bishop Noll claimed that Hungary's frontiers were drawn unreasonably, and that apparently only motives of revenge had guided those who had formed the Treaty of Trianon. The letter was published in Hungary too, by the **Uj Nemzedék** (The New Generation), a very popular Catholic daily in Budapest. It was praised and regarded as an effect of Hungarian revisionism.(37)

The nature of Hungarian immigration to the United States changed completely in the inter-war period. The large majority of Hungarian immigrants before World War I came from the rural districts and entered the grand army of unskilled labor in the United States. Under the operation of the post-war quota laws, the ratio of peasants in the small Hungarian quota was insignificant.(38) The majority of the new immigrants were professionals — lawyers, physicians, scientist, artists, and white collar workers in general. Furthermore, most of the intellectuals who left Hungary for the United States were born Jews. They left Hungary to find their careers outside their native land, and, of course, did not forget the anti-Jewish activities of the post-war years.

Hungarian revisionism realized the importance of these immigrants. To win their good will toward the old country, it was necessary to prove that Hungary was not such a Jew-baiting

---

37 U. S., For. Rel., **Department of State, 864.00 P. R./36.**

38 According to the Emergency Immigration Act of 1921, Hungary's annual quota was 869 persons.

country as believed by the left-wing immigrants, mainly socialists and Jews. For that reason, the Hungarian government invited one of the most prominent members of the American Jewish Community, Jacob Landau, President of the Jewish Telegraph Agency, to visit Hungary in 1931. Prime Minister Bethlen received him. After the reception Jacob Landau gave an interview to the **Pester Lloyd**, and he made the following statement with respect to the situation of the Jews in Hungary:

Relations between Christians and Jews are today about the same as they were before the war. The circumstance that Jews played a prominent role in the Bolshevik revolution in 1919 strongly stimulated an anti-Semitic movement at the time. During the course of the last ten years anti-Semitism has steadly declined in influence on public opinion.

The Jews in Hungary are divided into two groups: the majority belong to the neologist branch, a group that has been fully assimilated; the Orthodox group has maintained many of the old forms. Both groups are officially recognized by the State and are subsidized by the Government in the various fields of religious and educational activity.(39)

Jacob Landau stated, furthermore, that the Jews played a prominent role in Hungarian literature, science, industry, and trade.

Every Hungarian newspaper published in the United States after World War I had a permanent column about the "Old Fatherland". The main purpose of these columns was not only to inform their readers about events in Hungary but also to strengthen the patriotic spirit among American-Hungarians. These were informed that all of the miseries of the people in the old country were caused by the Peace Treaty. In 1923, the **Amerikai Magyar Népszava**, published in New York, started a campaign on behalf of the Hungarian refugees from the successor states. The American-Hungarians in New York and New Jersey collected and sent twenty-six carloads of gift packages to Hungary through the

---

39 U. S., **For. Rel., Department of State** 864.4016/80.

agency of Father Joseph Marczinkó, a Hungarian priest residing in Passaic, New Jersey, and David Berkó, Editor-in-Chief of the Amerikai Magyar Népszava. The Uj előre (New Forward), a weekly publication of the American Hungarian Socialist Federation in New York, attacked the campaign furiously. The Socialist paper stated that the campaign was nothing else but a new scheme to rob American-Hungarian workers. The article ended with an appeal to the workers: "Workingmen and working women! Do your best that the plan of the Workman Slayer Government and the Marczinkó-Berkó gang should not succeed."(40) The result was the Uj Előre came to an end for lack of subscription. This fact illustrated the feelings of the Hungarian workers in New York toward the old country.

The Hungarian immigrants really did their best for Hungary's sake. They took every opportunity to declare the injustice of Trianon. During the presidential campaign of 1936, which was also the fifteenth anniversary of Trianon, the Szabadság (Freedom), a Hungarian language daily published in Cleveland, campaigned to collect a million signatures demanding the revision of the Treaty of Trianon. The signatures were collected and given to President Roosevelt on March 4, 1936.(41)

The American-Hungarian organizations increased to over two hundred. It became clear that, for effective work, unity was necessary. On New Year's Day, 1929, a proclamation was issued to the "people of Magyar America" to send representatives to a grand assembly at Buffalo, New York, to establish unity, express everlasting loyalty to America, and lay down the lines along which a just revision of the Treaty of Trianon could be rendered possible.

The grand assembly met on May 29, 1929, in an optimistic but solemn mood. Fraternal organizations, the churches, and the press were well represented. The American Hungarian National

---

40 "Father Marczinkó and Horthy," Uj Előre, April 4, 1923.
41 U. S., For. Rel., Department of State, 711.64/12.

Fedetation was established. After that, this organization represented all Hungarians in America and fought with a united will for Hungary's sake.

In the meantime, a far-reaching plan was worked out by the Hungarian Revisionist League at home. To coordinate all revisionist works, the Hungarian World Alliance was founded, and its first congress met at Budapest from August 22 to August 24, 1929. The congress had a total membership of 746 representatives of which 477 were Hungarians living abroad, and 269 were foreign friends of Hungary. Eighty-eight Hungarian associations located in foreign countries were represented. Count Albert Apponyi, Hungary's grand old man, was elected chairman of the Congress. The Congress opened in the entrance hall of the National Museum with a welcoming speech by Baron Sigismond Perényi, President of the Hungarian Revisionist League. Josika Herczeg, President of the American National Federation, in reply spoke for the foreign citizens of Hungarian origin, declaring that they had come to the mother country with a unity of feeling as regards the work of Hungarian revisionism.

The delegates of the Congress were received by the Regent. He pointed out that the mission of the Hungarians abroad was to develop their talents and abilities. While Hungarians living abroad consider themselves offshoots of the old tree, thriving on foreign soil, they should not forget that they derived their culture from the mother country which expects their support now, more than at any other time in her history. "Be," the Regent declared, "what you must be: good citizens of your new country, and good diplomats of your old fatherland".(42)

The Congress decided, furthermore, that the attention of the whole world was to be called to the Hungarian boundary problem in the most spectacular way. Those were the days of the first trans-Atlantic flights. So it was decided to link the United States

---

42 U. S., For. Rel., Department of State, 864.43/0134

and Hungary by a trans-Oceanic flight. The plan became the most spectacular feat of Hungarian revisionist propaganda. In July, 1931, newspapers all over the world reported on the front page that two Hungarian pilots, Alexander Magyar and George Endresz, had crossed the Atlantic Ocean from the United States to Hungary in a Lockheed-Sirius airplane. The name of the airplane was "Justice for Hungary". According to the original plan, the flight would take place on June 4, 1930, the tenth anniversary of Hungary's signing of the Treaty of Trianon. Technical and financial problems arose, however, and the flight had to be postponed. The two Hungarian pilots flew from Chicago to Harbor-Grace at Newfoundland via Detroit, then to Cleveland and New York. On July 15, 1931, they flew from Harbor-Grace to Budapest on a non-stop flight of twenty-six hours. It was the first time that an airplane crossing the ocean had radio contact both with the starting and landing aerodromes.

The Hungarian World Alliance held its second congress in 1939 at Budapest. The shadows of a new war overclouded the world. It seemed that the war would destroy all the achievements of Hungarian revisionism. Therefore, the new catch-word of the congress was "Justice for Hungary and Peace for the World". Furthermore, the orators of the second congress emphasized that Hungary was not alone. "One and a half million Hungarians see to Hungary's cause all over the world".(43) What Hungary needed at that time, was not so much revision but provision that the new war not end in another Trianon.

When World War II broke out, many American-Hungarians felt that they must speak out. Their country of birth lay along the Nazis' road of conquest. The American Hungarian National Federation, on January 7, 1941, presented a memorandum to President Franklin D. Roosevelt. The federation plegded the loyalty

---

43 Dezső Halácsy, A Világ Magyarságáért, p. 284.

of American citizens of Hungarian birth to the United States, willing and anxious to fulfill their duties of citizenship in the world's greatest democracy. It recalled the services of Colonel Michael Kovats in America's War of Independence. Then it stated:

American citizens of Hungarian origin learned with deep regret that the government of Hungary found it impossible to avoid signing a pact with the Axis powers. By doing so, the Hungarian government had lost its freedom of independent action. The Hungarian people were no longer free to express their will. The Executive Committee of the American Hungarian Federation, therefore, considered it its duty to lead a movement for the preservation of an independent Hungary and for the freedom of its people".(44)

The Federation spoke again a few days before Pearl Harbor. It declared that while it would not accept a Hitler-dominated world, neither would it accept a world, like that of 1920's, in which the seeds of Hitlerism could be planted. This was a reference to the post-World War I peace settlement in which Hungary had lost the largest part of her territory. The Federation claimed that it would feel at liberty to continue its peaceful struggle for Hungary's thousand-year old rights and proposed the fullest autonomy as well as political and economic equality to all Slovak, Ruthenian and Rumanian nationalities within the boundaries of ancient Hungary. Furthermore, the Federation went on record in favor of a Danubian Confederation, in which Hungarians, Austrians, Slovaks, Bulgarians, Serbians, Rumanians, Croatians, Slovenians, Moravians, Bohemians, and Poles would be united for the common good with a view to protect themselves against either German or Russian aggression.(45)

Hungarians, both at home and in America, fought for revision of Trianon with all their might. Had this any effect on America?

---

44 Quoted in Lengyel, **Americans from Hungary**, p. 175.
45 **Ibid.**

From a certain point of view, the answer can be a positive one. Senator Borah's and some other prominent Americans' activities for Hungary's cause were mentioned before. It is also a fact that President Roosevelt dealt with Hungary more leniently than other western statesmen, for instance the British. It seems that the President understood East-Central European problems and was willing to accept some kind of Danubian federation to prevent postwar Russian influence there.

Hungary, to promote this case in the United States, sent over one of the leading Hungarian statesmen, Tibor Eckhardt. There were several suppositions about the object of Eckhardt's American visit. It was said that he had come here as a representative of Regent Horthy. It was also assumed that Eckhardt's object was to prepare an operational basis against the Germans in the United States. Eckhardt maintained many important Washington contacts. (This will be discussed in a later chapter.) However, he met the opposition of the Czechoslovak government-in-exile which did not want Hungary to be recognized as a semi-belligerent and thus reap the harvest of victory after the expected Allied triumph.

Historians, as a general rule, admit that Hungarians were right in fighting for revision of Trianon. It has been argued many times, however, that the desire for revision drove Hungary into the German orbit. As a consequence of this, the second Paris Peace Treaty in 1947 was more severe for Hungary than that of Trianon. Minority protections, for example, for which President Wilson fought so bitterly in 1919 were not mentioned in 1947. Consequently, large Hungarian masses were expelled from the restored Czechoslovakia. And what was more, the mother country itself—with other East-Central European states — ceased to be part of Western European politics. But all of these historical events were beyond the control of Hungarians wherever they might live.

In 1940, in spite of the quota system of the 1920's, Hungarian was spoken in the United States by 453,000 persons, about one-half born in America and the other half abroad. Some of the third-generation Americans spoke Hungarian — 13,800. More than four-fifths of the people of Hungarian descent lived in six great industrial States of the East and Middle West: New York, Pennsylvania, Ohio, New Jersey, Illinois, and Michigan. The Hungarian population of America was growing again after World War II.

CHAPTER VII

THE FOURTH OF JULY AT BUDAPEST:
CULTURAL RELATIONS

A lively interest has always been felt in Hungary for every manifestation of American thought. The American ideal, as seen before, found one of its first and finest interpretations in a Hungarian book by a Transylvanian Unitarian, Alexander Bölöni Farkar, published under the title **Travels in North America.** It contains an almost religiously inspired enthusiastic account of the world of real democracy, the Land of Promise. For the writer of this book, America meant the personification of the highest degree of human happiness, a Paradise on earth. For him, Republicanism, Liberalism, Democracy, were no mere political catchwords, but religious convicitions, as is made evident by his meditations over Washington's tomb.

I have stood at the graves of kings and celebrated men, have admired the memorials of their deeds, but that feeling of reverence which suddenly thrilled through me before this tomb I had only felt in the Pantheon and in Westminster Abbey. There passed through my mind all the sufferings and struggles undergone by America for the rights of man, struggles in which the man whose dust lay at my feet had so large a share, and I felt my heart throb. Had I not been restrained by cold reason, I would willingly have prostrated myself before this tomb".(1)

1 Quoted in Stephen Gál, **Hungary and the Anglo-Saxon World** (Budapest: Published by the Society of the Hungarian Quarterly, 1943), p. 504.

143

Alexander Farkas' book of travels exercised a decisive influence on the course of Hungarian history by directing the interest of public men of the age towards the New World. Tocqueville's work on America was translated into Hungarian within a year of its publication, and it is known that Kossuth read it with lively interest. The example of the American War of Independence was frequently cited in the course of the Hungarian struggle for liberty. "The principles of the American Declaration of Independence", said Francis Pulszky, a leader of the Hungarian revolution in 1848, "were the guiding principles also in the Hungarian war of liberation".(2) In his American speeches Kossuth advocated four fundamental conceptions which have been the guiding ideas of the second half of the twentieth century: 1) the right of every nation to dispose of its own affairs; 2) the abolition of secret diplomacy; 3) America's participation in world affairs, especially in European affairs; and 4) an alliance between Great Birtain and America, which later on might be joined by other states for a concerted defense of the self-determination of the small nations. Kossuth preached the union of the Anglo-Saxon democracies in opposition to the autocratic European powers. "England and America!" he addressed the English-speaking nations, "Do not forget in your proud security those who are oppressed . . . Save those millions of people, and thus become the saviours of Democracy".(3)

Another vehicle for the penetration of American thought into Hungary was the returning emigrants. Besides introducing improved methods of agriculture and industry, they awakened a certain intellectual ambition in their country and introduced a more democratic spirit. They wanted a Hungary more like America. The statue of George Washington in the City Park at Budapest is the best proof of this spirit. This statue, unveiled on September 16,

2 **Ibid.**, p. 507.
3 **Ibid.**

TO THE MEMORY OF
WASHINGTON
THE HUNGARIANS
OF AMERICA
1906

145

1906, was donated by popular subscription on the part of American citizens of Hungarian origin. (4)

Friendly relations were established between the two nations after World War I. During the war, the Hungarians living in the States were treated with consideration, nor was a single American insulted in Hungary. Hungary remembered with no little gratitude the manifold benefits she received at America's hands after the First World War. When, as was mentioned before, the Rumanians tried to carry away the contents of the Hungarian National Museum, it was the American General Bandholtz who prevented them from carrying out this design and thus saved these treasures for Hungary. It was also remembered that during the years of hardship experienced by Hungary in the early 1920's, a large percentage of the children of Budapest were saved through the devoted care of the American Red Cross. Captain James Pedlow, Chief of the American Red Cross Society at Budapest, and Captain George Richardson, Chief of the American Relief Administration at Budapest, organized a child feeding program at Budapest in 1920. With the help of Mrs. Clare Thompson of California, they fed 100,000 children a day in Budapest. Mrs. Thompson had lived in Budapest since the outbreak of the war, and after the war she devoted herself to the support of suffering Hungarians. She herself distributed 15,000 dresses among old ladies. Captain Pedlow also rendered Hungary a great service by furnishing medicines and bandages. From January until August, 1920, the American Relief Action for Hungary distributed 85,962 kgs of coca; 335,200 kgs of sugar; 545,377 boxes of condensed milk; 542,511 kgs of flour; 226,115 kgs of rice; 46,552 kgs of lard; 16,342 kgs of oil; 62,982 tins of fish: a total value of 148,260,475 crowns.

---

4 U. S., **Department of State, 864.43/0165.** According to the best knowledge of the author, Washington's statue is still there and Budapest is the only capital in Eastern Europe which has a statue of George Washington.

Furthermore it distributed 50,000 pairs of shoes and boots; 500,000 stockings; 19,700 overcoats; 17,000 boys' suits; 13,940 girls' frocks: making a grand total value of 42,716,600 crowns.(5)

In reply to this American charity work, the Fourth of July, American Independence Day, was solemnly celebrated by Budapest society in 1920. The municipal schools and the various women's clubs arranged a brilliant festival in the National Museum Gardens where a huge crowd assembled early in the morning. A religious service was held in the large hall of the Museum, richly decorated in Hungarian and American colors. The municipal guard in Hungarian national costume, the cadets of the Military Academy, school children, and the municipal corporations were grouped in the Gardens of the Museum. On the two sides of the altar, the members of the Cabinet and the American Red Cross Mission had their seats. Many prominent figures of Budapest society attended. After the celebration of the Mass by Bishop Zadravecz, hymns and the national anthems were sung. The Bishop concluded the service with a sermon, expressing all Hungary's gratitude to the representatives of American charity.(6)

From that time, it became a custom to celebrate Independence Day at Budapest. In 1921, the Hungarian-American Society was formed at Budapest for the purpose of promoting good relations between the two nations and strengthening the traditional bonds between the two peoples. One of the activities of the Hungarian-American Society was to organize the celebration of Independence Day. Usually the celebration took place at the George

---

5 For details on the work of the American Red Cross and of the American Relief Action, see U. S., State Department, 864.461, and National Archives, Microcopy No. 708, Roll 21.

On the Hungarian side, the American charity work in Hungary is praised in the Hungarian Nation (Budapest monthly review in English), I (April, 1920), 45. "...American charity knows how to work: quietly, zealously, with an exellent organization; where misery is worst there we are sure to find our helpful American friends."

6 The Hungarian Nation, I, No. 8 (1920), 77.

Washington statue in the City Park. Over the years, several United States Senators and Representatives went from Washington to Budapest to participate in the celebration. Outstanding among the American visitors were Senator Borah, Hungary's great advocate in the United States Senate; Senator Elbert D. Thomas; Representative William E. Richardson; Representative Bryant T. Castellow, and Representative Thomas S. McMillan. Robert M. La-Follete, ex-governor of Wisconsin, took part in the celebration in 1922, making some interesting statements against the Versailles Treaties. Prominent Hungarian-born Americans frequently attended, among them George Kende, Editor of the **Amerikai Magyar Népszava**, New York, and Stephen Puky, Editor of **Szabadság**, Cleveland.

The Hungarian government was always officially represented at the celebration. Addresses were delivered by great Hungarian public personalities and by the American Minister at Budapest. Usually, the addresses expressed gratitude for the friendship of the two nations and pointed out that the Budapest monument of George Washington embodied two ideas: the clear recognition of the basic principle on which the greatness of the American nation rested and the feeling of permanent relationship with the American nation. As far as this relationship was concerned, the American conception of freedom was probably different from the Hungarian, but the essential feature was the common ideal in the character of both nations: their love for freedom and independence.(7)

Between the two World Wars, approximately ten thousand American citizens visited Hungary each year. Probably the majority of these visitors were Hungarian-born Americans, but there were many others also. Each year a number of American students went to Hungary. Some were visitors, others studied at the Academy of Music at Budapest. Still others were professional people.

7 For full details of the celebrations of Fourth of July at Budapest, see the annual reports of the American Minister at Budapest. U. S., Department of State, 864.46211/1—17.

Among them were Professor H. A. Heydt of New York University and William Randolph Hearst, the well-known newspaper publisher. On the occasion of the latter's visit, the Hungarian papers recalled that Hearst had proved to be a valuable friend of Hungary. In 1927, a group of American editorial writers visited Hungary under the auspices of the Carnegie Endowment for International Peace. In the next year, sixty American physicians, many with their families, arrived in Budapest on an European tour arranged by the Interstate Post-Graduate Assembly of North America. They visited clinics and hospitals, lectured at the University of Budapest, and were greatly impressed by Hungarian achievements in medicine and surgery.(8)

The most outstanding American who visited Hungary between the two World War was General Douglas MacArthur, Chief of Staff of the United States Army. General MacArthur visited Hungary from September 17 to 20, 1932, as guest of the Hungarian Army. During this time he met many of the leaders of Hungarian civil and military life, including the Regent, Admiral Miklós Horthy, the Prime Minister, Cabinet members, and the chief officers of the Hungarian army, upon all of whom he made a distinctly favorable impression. As the first high American officer to pay a friendly visit to the Hungarian army since World War I, his visit was a source of paricular satisfaction to Hungarians and undoubtedly served to strengthen Hungary's friendly disposition towards the United States. (9)

Another merely cultural event caused some political consequences for Hungary and the United States. Major General Harry Hill Bandholtz, whose activity in Hungary was discussed previously, died peacefully in the sixty-first year of his life in 1925, in Constantine, Michigan. But his name occured again in Hungarian cultural life eleven years after his death. In 1936, the American citizens of Hungarian origin and the Hungarian Revisionist League decided to erect a monument to Bandholtz at Budapest.

8 U. S., **Department of State,** 864.00 P.R./9.
9 **Ibid.,** 864.20111/1—3.

It was decided to erect the mounment on the **Szabadság Tér** (Freedom Square), where there were erected monuments of the Lost Provinces, and where the Flag, in mourning for these provinces, was placed. Appropriately, the Legation of the American Government was also located there. The Organization Committee decided that the dedication ceremony would take place on the Fourth of July, 1936. This was not only Independence Day of the United States but also the day that the Inter-Parliamentary Union held its meeting in the Hungarian Capital. The Organization Committee wanted to give great publicity to the dedication. It was supposed that Senator Barkley, who expected to attend the meeting of the Inter-Parliamentary Union in Budapest, would be invited to deliver a speech. The Committee sent invitations to John N. Garner, President of the Senate; Sam D. McReynolds, Chairman of the Foreign Affairs Committee of the House; and George H. Dern, Secretary of War.

Rumania protested, pointing out that the ceremony was organized by the Revisionist League and claiming that its motive was to shame Rumania. The State Department of the United States wanted to prevent any incident unpleasant either to Hungary or Rumania. It passed a resolution that, since the dedication of the monument was apparently not an official function but a semi-private one, it would be unnecessary for an American citizen to make any remarks and it was to be wished that no high official be there. Baron Sigsmund Perényi, one of the two Presidents of the Organization Committee, pointed out to the American Minister at Budapest that it would be sad indeed to unveil a monument of an American General and not have any American on the program. Furthermore, he promised that nothing would be said to offend Rumania; the addresses would be confined merely to lauding an American General who helped Hungary in a time of great stress.

The negotiations ended in compromise. The Hungarians agreed to hold the unveiling ceremony on the 23rd of August instead of July 4th, and the Department of State permitted the members of the Legation of the United States at Budapest to attend the ceremony. The principal address was delivered by Baron Perényi. He eulogized General Harry Hill Bandholtz as a great soldier, a fearless knight, and an upright man. He did not make mention of Rumania but said that Bandholtz' glory was proclaimed by the invaluable treasures of the Hungarian National Museum, which he saved from destruction; therefore, all honor was due to the American Army which had such blameless and upright officers as Bandholtz; honor was due also the American Commonwealth which breeds gentlemen like Bandholtz, who follow the sublime rules of justice and love of humanity. Finally he stated:

This statue will be companion to another statue which stands in the City Park, to the statue raised by the freedom-loving Hungarian nation to the greatest American. He will be a companion to the statue of George Washington who in his famous farewell message taught his people: Be united, be Americans. Observe Justice and good faith toward all nations.(10)

The statue was accepted in the name of the City of Budapest by the mayor, Dr. Charles Szendy, who spoke as follows: "... I am extremely pleased to accept this monument because it not only expressed the gratitude of Hungary, but at the same time is a model of what we Hungarians should be: upright, strong and brave".(11) The Commander-in-Chief of the Hungarian Army placed a wreath before the statue in the name of the Regent. On the front of the base of the bronze statue there was carved in the stone a quotation from a letter which General Bandholtz wrote to a Hungarian-American in New York:

I simply carried out the instructions of my Government as I understood them as an officer and gentleman of the United States Army.   Harry Hill Bandholtz. (12)

---

10 **U. S., Department of State, 864.413/16.**

11 **Ibid., 864.413/17.**

12 **Ibid., 864.413/18.** Bandholtz' statue was removed by the Communist authorities in 1949.

Besides these social relations, mentioned above, American cultural influences were felt on all levels of Hungarian society in the twenties and thirties. They affected every age group. The writer of this account will simply try to recall his encounters with American culture as he grew up in Hungary.

Hardly any middle class boy reached his teens without reading Indian stories (**Buffalo Bill**) and James Fenimore Cooper's **Leather Stocking**. Together with the works of Karl May who, in spite of being a German who had never left Europe, could spark the imagination with descriptions of the New World, these stories helped to make America and the Wild West very real to Hungarian youngsters. They, of course, were rendered in Hungarian. This streak of substitute adventurism continued to be fed by a host of paperbacks, such as the thrillers of Nick Carter and the cowboy stories of Zane Grey. **Pesti Hirlap**, a prominent Budapest daily, issued a Western in translation each and every Sunday. They sold for 26 fillers (the Hungarian penny), and continued to be published until 1938 when a disapproval of American popular literature began to manifest itself with increasing vigor.

American movies and jazz music influenced the popular mind even more than American literature. Metro-Goldwyn-Mayer and Twentieth Centruy Fox were associated with chains of theaters especially in the capital of Hungary (Royal Apollo, Forum, Capitol, Corvin, etc.) and stood in stiff competition on the novelty market with the German industry (UFA). First showing of American feature films were held in Budapest only a few months or even a few weeks later than in Hollywood. American newsreels reached Budapest with the utmost speed alowed by an age prior to transatlantic flights.

An incessant flow of American motion pictures affected Hungary in those days making very well-known the names of Irene Dunne, Deanna Durbin, Dorothy Lamour, Tyrone Power, Douglas Fairbanks, Fred Astaire, Alice Faye, Hedy Lamar, Bette Davis, and many others. The yearly series of **Broadway Melodies** in the second half of the Thirties, even **Gone with the Wind**, duly reached

Hungary, although the latter was issued when the Second World War was already a reality. Earlier, Charlie Chaplin and the Laurel and Hardy comedies had been equally well known. Indeed, so were all the American classics of the silent movie era. Then came the cartoons: Mickey Mouse, and the early Walt Disneys, such as the **Three Little Pigs** and **Snow White**. **The Wizard of Oz** reached Hungary just before the German occupation. I well remember **King Kong**, not to mention several of the **Tarzan** series, or, of a more serious kind, **Juarez**.

The marketing of records affected a smaller part of the population than paperbacks and motion pictures. Even so, practically no middle class household was without American records, especially if the household included young people. Among the classics, Gershwin; among the popular songs, Irving Berlin — these one could find all over. Gershwin's **Rhapsody in Blue** was played continuously and his **Porgy and Bess** received great recognition when an American company of Negro singers staged it in Budapest in 1935.

If Hungary ever had an influence on American cultural life, it was in the world of music. Every music student in America knows the name of Ferenc (Franz) Liszt, the greatly celebrated Hungarian pianist and composer who introduced a new composition of harmony and melody that presaged the development of modern music in the twentieth century. Between the two wars, many of Hungary's best musicians came to the United States. Among them was Béla Bartók, Hungary's great composer of the century and one of the great composers of the age, who made his first tour in the United States in 1927-28, playing with orchestras and in concerts from coast to coast. Upon his return to Hungary he continued to teach and compose in Budapest. In the fall of 1940 he came to America again, where he remained until his death. The influence of Bartók music on young composers in Hungary and in the United States was very great, and still has continued to increase since his death. Some of Bartók's music was used on the stage. **Prince Bluebeard's Castle**, a one-act opera, and **The**

Wooden Prince and **The Miraculous Mandarin** ballets, all had great success in New York.(13)

Imre Kálmán, one of the most famous composers of Viennese music, also came to the United States preceding the outbreak of the Second World War. In the United States millions were familiar with the melodies of "Countess Maritza" and "Sári", though they might not know the name of the composer. His first success was with **The Gay Hussars**, performed in New York just before World War I. Between the two wars, many of Kálmán's light operas had their first performances in the United States, such as **Her Soldier Boy, Golden Dawn,** and **Marinka**, the romantic story of crown Prince Rudolph of Austria and Hungary and Baroness Marie Vetsera.(14)

Sigmund Romberg, another Hungarian, became one of the most successful composers of popular operetta music in the United States. Romberg composed over seventy operettas, including **The Midnight Girl, The Blue Paradise, The Rose of Stanboul, The Student Prince, The Desert Song, My Maryland, The New Moon, Up in Central Park,** and many others.(15)

Albert Szirmay has also enriched American musical life. Szirmay arranged the music of the **Songs of the Rivers of America**, edited by Carl Carmer, and a collection of more than a hundred songs from Gilbert and Sullivan operettas. Among the more notable compositions of his own was **Mézeskalács** (Gingerbread).

Another Hungarian-born musician in the United States was Tibor Serly, composer and conductor. Serly was taken to America as a child but studied at the Royal Academy in Budapest. After graduating, he returned to the United States and played viola in the Cincinnati Symphony Orchestra, the Philadelphia Orchestra, and the N.B.C. Symphony Orchestra. In 1937 he settled in New

---

13 Nicolas Slominsky, **Baker's Biographical Dictionary of Musicians** (New York: G. Schirmer, 1958), p. 93.

14 **Ibid.**, p. 802.

15 **Ibid.**, p. 1364.

154

York as a music teacher. Besides being a violinist and conductor, Serly was a composer of symphonies, a ballet for orchestra, suites, chamber music, and orchestral music.(16)

It would be out of the question to enumerate all the noted singers Hungary has given to the United States, so that again selections must be made at random. One of the most promising Hungarian-born opera singers was Lajos Rózsa. He came to the United States after World War I and appeared on the Metropolitan Operate stage with success. His son, Miklós Rózsa, carried on the family's musical tradition as a successful film music composer.

One of America's recognized Wagnerian singers was also Hungarian-born, Friedrich Schorr. His operatic career began in the Austrian city of Graz. The New York Metropolitan Opera House first saw him in 1924 and he was strong in Wagnerian roles for two decades.

Among many other Hungarian singers who appeared in the United States the most famous was Alexander Svéd. He made his Hungarian Royal Opera debut in Il Trovatore in 1927, sang in State operas in Vienna, Berlin, and Munich at Covent Garden, the Paris Opera Comique, the Teatro della Scala of Milan, at the Teatro Reale of Rome, in the festivals of Firenze, Salzburg and Bayreuth, at Buenos Aires and Rio de Janeiro, at the Chicago Civic Opera, winding up at the Metropolitan of New York, with a repertory of thirty-four roles, singing in English, Italian, German, French, and Hungarian.

Another Hungarian-born singer to earn high praise in the United States was Enid Szántó. She had her musical education at the Royal Academy of Music at Budapest, her debut at the Vienna Opera in 1928, and her American debut with the New York Philharmonic in 1936. Also she appeared at the Bayreuth Wagner Festivals, Covent Garden, the City Center, and Metropolitan Opera in New York.

---

16 **Ibid.**, p. 1498.

Several Hungarian-born conductors have become household words in the United States. The success story of Eugene Ormándy should be compulsory reading for gifted children to show that child prodigies may make good. Ormandy entered the Royal Academy of Music in Budapest at the age of five. He received an artist's diploma for violin when he was fifteen. At the age of seventeen he was appointed professor of the State Conservatory of Budapest, which was no mean achievement in such a highly musical city. He sailed to America in 1921 and obtained the position of concertmaster of the Capitol Theatre Orchestra, New York. In 1929, he conducted the New York Philharmonic at Lewisohn Stadium. Ormándy was invited to head the Minneapolis Symphony Orchestra which became one of the best in the country. From that post he became in 1936 the associate conductor of the Philadelphia Symphony Orchestra and traveled with it on transcontinental tours.(17)

Budapest-born George Szell began his musical career at the age of eleven, and at eighteen he was already assistant conductor of the Royal Opera of Berlin. From that post he was called to the Prague Opera as director and became professor of the Prague Academy of Music. In 1930 he conducted for the first time in America, with the St. Louis Symphony. He then became conductor of the Scottish Orchestra in Glasgow. The outbreak of World War II caused its suspension, and Szell accepted a position as teacher at the opera workshop of the New School for Social Research in New York. He also taught theory at the Mannes School of Music.(18)

Aladár Szendrei (in the United States he changed his name to Alfred Sendrey) conducted opera in Chicago and New York, settling in 1940 in Los Angeles as a music teacher. Joseph Szigeti, famous violinist, in 1926 made his home in the United States. His tours covered every part of the world. Each year New York heard him in Carnegie Hall and gave him the name of "The Musicians'

---

17 Hope Stoddar, **Symphony Conductors of the United States of America** (New York: n. p., 1957), pp. 147—59.

18 **Ibid.**, pp. 236—43.

Musician". Among those who became famous with their violins only a few can be mentioned here. Edward Kilinyi, Sr., was born in Hungary and studied in Budapest at the Conservatory. In 1908 he settled in the United States, took courses at Columbia University with Rybner and Daniel Gredory Mason. In 1930 he went to Hollywood, where he remained as a film composer and music teacher. He was for five years the teacher of George Gershwin. His son, Edward Kilinyi, Jr., was born in Philadelphia and went to Budapest to study with Dohnányi at the Conservatory of Budapest. After graduating in 1930, he made a concert tour of Europe, then returned to America where he continued his career as concert pianist.

Hungarian artists who made their names as cellists in the United States were Gábor Rejtő, János Scholz, and Ottó Déri. The best known quartets from Hungary were the Roth Quartet and the Budapest String Quartet. Indeed, with the best opera house, the best symphony orchestras, and the best artists, the United States became the musical center of the world, and Hungary was the birthplace of many great musicians who appeared in America. While these Hunarian artists fitted into the American scheme and followed American taste, the special flavor of the Hungarian cultural background lingered on in America's musical life.

After the First World War, painters from Hungary also began to come to the United States. Many of them had a distinguished career in America. Andrew Károly and Lajos Szántó did their most notable works on large murals. Their best known work is the "Freedom of Speech" mural at Poughkeepsie, New York, depicting the history of the American press. Both of them did etchings and painted portraits. Lajos Jámbor was also a muralist, with works in auditoriums and churches of several cities of the United States, particularly Philadelphia and Atlantic City. Frank Imrey painted the mural in Convention Hall, Atlantic City; the cyclorama "Little America" in Syracuse, New York; and murals for the United States War Department. Sándor Vágó's "Old Tom", the picture of a Negro, became the best-known painting of the Cleveland Museum of Art, and Lily Füredi's painting, "The New York Subway", hangs in the White House in Washington.

Among the sculptors, Alexander Finta had a name before he came to the United States, having created monuments in Europe and in Brazil. Among his numerous other works are a bronze portrait relief of Michael Kováts, whose name was mentioned above, exhibited in the museum of the New York Historical Society; a marble portrait of St. Stephen, King of Hungary, for the Catholic Church of St. Stephen, New York; and a portrait of Cardinal Patrick Joseph Hayes, exhibited at the Metropolitan Museum of Art, New York.

Paintings and sculptures by contemporary American artists were shown at Budapest during the inter-war period in several American art exhibitions. The Royal Hungarian Ministry of Public Worship and Education and the Hungarian Council of Arts worked always in close collaboration with the American Legation at Budapest in connection with these exhibitions which daily attracted a large number of visitors. The paintings of a number of prominent American contemporary artists were much admired in Budapest during these years. Hungary had no less success in New York with her art exhibitions, and Hungarian art earned the unstinted prise of the American artistic public.(19)

The theater has long been one of Hungary's most favored arts. After World War I, the New York stage was practically swamped by Hungarian plays. Almost any play by a Hungarian writer had a more than fair chance of being performed. The best known among these playwrights was Ferenc Molnár, the most successful author of the sophisticated comedy. He wrote indulgent, polite plays on manners and human frailties. This was not the social criticism of an Ibsen or the social satire of Shaw. But it was first-class theater, and America loved it. Particularly, this country knew his **Liliom**, a tender tale of crime and punishment, the story of a Budapest thief who wanted to do a good deed for his child and stole a star.

---

19 U. S., **Department of State**, 864.00 P.R./26.

The play was performed in countless variations on stage, screen, and music hall. America was far ahead of the author's own Budapest in its appreciation of Liliom. Molnár seemed to have a magic touch as success followed success, with the presentation of The Guardsman, The Swan, The Wolf, and The Play's the Thing. In New York, Molnár was treated with respect as a benefactor of mankind, a man who made millions laugh.

Hungary has not given many stars to the American stage, no doubt due to language difficulties. Paul Lukas and Lili Darvas, wife of Ferenc Molnár, were among the few Hungarians who had success on the Brodway stage. The dancing Dolly Sisters gained an international trade-mark. Among American theatrical producers of Hungarian origin the names of Martin Beck and All Wood stand out. As a final remark concerning the artistic relations between the two countries, it may be said that the artistic life of Hollywood would have been less colorful without the two Hungarian-born pioneers of the film industry: Adolph Zukor and William Fox.

In Hungary, serious American literature continued to be translated and published up to the very day of German occupation on March 19, 1944. In consequence, the bookshelves of the typical middle and upper class Hungarian family were quite well stocked with American authors. In the 1930's, two Hungarian poets, Michael Babits and Dezső Kosztolányi, did much towards the propagation of American poetry in Hungary. By their translations, two American poets, Edgar Allan Poe and Walt Whitman, gained great fame in Hungary. Joseph Reményi, a Hungarian professor at Cleveland University, set himself the task of acquainting Hungarians with the American novel. In his American Decameron, Professor Reményi endeavored to acquaint the Hungarian public with such American authors as Sherwood Andersen, Ernest Hemingway, and William Faulkner. Furthermore, Sinclair Lewis, Theodor Dreiser, Pearl S. Buck, Thornton Wilder, Margaret Mitchell, Ralph Waldo Emerson, Washington Irving, Jack London, and, to a lesser degree, Upton Sinclair attained the greatest popularity in Hungarian literary circles. Their works, like Anderson's **Dark Laughter**, Faulkner's **The Sound and the Fury**, Hemingway's **The Sun Also Rises** and **A Farewell to Arms**, and many others, were translated into Hungarian soon after their English publication and were read by sophisticated Hungarians. Perhaps every Hungarian junior-high and high-school student read Mark Twain's **The Adventures of Huckleberry Finn** and **Life on the Mississippi**. With his **The Innocents Abroad**, Twain probably influenced such great Hungarian novelists as Géza Gárdonyi and Kálmán Mikszáth.

Professor Reményi also made an attempt to introduce America's scholars to some of Hungary's most influential writers, especially Endre Ady who is considered Hungary's greatest poet in the twentieth century. He also tried to create a Hungarian-American literature. He published a collection of stories dealing with the life of the Hungarian immigrant in the United States. His best known work **Emberek ne Sirjatok** (Thou Shalt Not Cry) had four editions, his **Élni Kell** (You Must Live) two.

Ferenc Molnár, the playwright mentioned before, was many-talented. He also wrote novels and several of them were translated into English, such as **The Prisoners, Eva and the Derelict Boat**, and above all **The Boys of Paul Street**, a story that made many eyes grow misty all over the world.

Another Hungarian author with an international reputation was Rene Fülöp-Miller. After a journalistic career in Berlin, Paris, and Vienna, he settled down to write a large number of noted books in English, such as **The Mind and Face of Bolshevism, Lenin and Ghandi, Rasputin the Holy Devil**, and **Leaders, Dreamers and Rebels**. The last is an account of the great mass movements of history and the dreams that inspired them.

Pál Kelemen, a Hungarian historian, became a leading authority on the pre-Columbian art and civilization of America. His two volume **Medieval American Art** was a pioneering venture. In this study Kelemen covered the Maya, Aztec, and Inca arts, approaching his subject from the point of view of art history, combining it with the study of archeology, anthropology, and ethnology.

He also wrote **Battlefield of the Gods**, devoted to Yucatan and Aztec history, art, and exploration.

International law also found a prominent Hungarian in Francis Deák, author of numerous important works in the field, including one about Turkey and the Straits question. His other publication **Hungary at the Paris Peace Conference** is one of the best works in this field.

The most influential Hungarian historian in the United States between the two World Wars was Dr. Oscar Jászi, Minister of Nationalities in the Károlyi government. Jászi, as was mentioned before, went into exile after the downfall of the Károlyi regime and was preceded by his high reputation in scholarly circles in the United States. He became professor of political science at Oberlin College in 1925 and taught there for seventeen years. His two standard books, **The Dissolution of the Habsburg Monarchy** and **Revolution and Counter-Revolution in Hungary,** reached several publications and influenced American scholarly circles — an influence by no means favorable to the Habsburgs or to postwar Hungary.(20)

The name of Charles Feleky deserves a special notice in any discussion of American-Hungarian cultural relations. As a Hungarian immigrant in New York, he devoted much of his time to building up a unique library of **Hungariana**, English-language books about Hungary. He collected books written by Hungarians or by foreigners on Hungary, as well as rare documents by great Hungarians. Between the two World Wars the Hungarian government used the Feleky library as the nucleus of its information service in the United States. Mainly from these collections, the Hungarian Reference Library was established at 19 West 44th Street, New York, on April 20, 1938. The library was under the supervision of the Royal Hungarian Ministry of Public Worship and Education. (21) After World War II, the Hungarian Reference Library was

---

20 For full details on Hungarian literature in the United States, see Leslie Könnyü, **A History of American Hungarian Literature.**

21 **U. S., Department of State,** 864.01 B 11/14.

placed under the supervision of Columbia University and is still one of the best libraries for research on Hungary.

Contemporary Hungary has produced some of the great scientists of the age, and the United States has absorbed many of them. In the life stories of several great Hungarian scientists there is a pattern. They were born in Hungary and had their technical education there — Hungarian technical education was good. In many cases they could not find the right occupation in postwar Hungary and were forced to leave their native country, going to the West. Many went to Weimar Germany, which was extremely hospitable to scientific talent. Many of these stayed in Germany until Hitler took power. Then a great number came to the United States.

Among American scientists of Hungarian origin, one of the greatest names was Theodor von Karman. He matriculated at the Royal Hungarian Technical University at Budapest at the turn of the century. He was a very young man when his own alma mater gave him an appointment as an instructor and one of Hungary's largest industrial establishments, the Ganz Machine Manufacturing Company, employed him as a research engineer. During World War I, Karman became head of the research department of the Austro-Hungarian Aviation Corps. He held this position until the end of the war. In 1930, he came over to America, settled in Pasadena, California, and became director of the Daniel Guggenheim Graduate School of Aeronautics at the California Institute of Technology. Theodor von Karman wrote a two-volume book in general aerodynamic theory and a standard work on methematical method in engineering. He had more than sixty important publications. They included papers on applied mathematics, physics, strength of materials, stress analysis, theory of elasticity and vibrations, the mechanics of compressible and viscous fluids, turbulence, aerodynamic of aircraft, hydro-dynamics of planing surfaces, and heat transfer.(22) Karman became a major general of

_____

22 See **Theodor von Karman's Anniversary Volume** (New York: Clark B. Millikan for friends of Theodor von Karman, 1941).

the United States Air Force, a distinction no other contemporary Hungarian-born citizen of America shared.

In another field of science, psychiatrist and phychologist Ferenc Alexander gained a large measure of public recognition. During World War I he was in charge of an Austro-Hungarian bacteriological field laboratory and malaria prophylaxis station on the Italian front. He was one of the young Hungarians fascinated by the teachings of Sigmund Freud. Alexander was especially interested in the connection of mental and brain processes, and in 1921 he received the Freud Award of the International Psychoanalytic Association for the best research work in the field. In 1930 he was invited to the University of Chicago as a visiting professor. The following year the Judge Baker Foundation at Boston invited him to undertake a research project in criminal psychology. His book **Roots of Crime** was the result of his work.(23)

Among the small group of atomic scientists in the United States one can find three Hungarians: Eugene P. Wigner, professor of physics at Princeton University; Edward Teller, professor at the University of Chicago; and Leo Szilárd, professor at Columbia University. The application of atomic energy to explosives was introduced to the United States by Hungarian-born scientists, as the official record of atomic energy for military purposes clearly shows. Dr. Leo Szilárd was the first to think of the application of the atom to bombs.(24)

Hungarian scientists, attracted to the United States, played a part out of all proportion to the size of their native country. Here we have mentioned only a few of the great. Among the smaller nations, Hungary ranks with Austria, Sweden, and Switzerland as having made the largest contributions to American science. Sixty Hungarian professors taught in American colleges just prior

23 Lengyel, **Americans from Hungary**, p. 243.

24 For details see Henry De Wolf Smyth, **Atomic Energy for Military Purposes** (Princeton: Princeton University Press, 1945).

to the Second World War.(25) Furthermore, the fellowships of the Rockefeller Institute enabled a great number of Hungarian students to gain expert knowledge in their own special branches of study in American laboratories. No less valuable for Hungary was the Jeremiah Smith Foundation, formed out of the honorarium offered to Jeremiah Smith by the Hungarian Government for the financial supervision imposed by the League of nations. For two years, Jeremiah Smith, a distinguished Boston lawyer, served as Commissioner General of Hungary and he performed the job to the satisfaction of all concerned. His character was well illustrated by his refusal to accept the 100,000 dollars which represented his two years' salary. The Hungarian Government then devoted the sum to the establishment of a scholarship fund to enable two Hungarian technical students each year to study in America. "The only compensation I desire for my work", Jeremiah Smith said, "is the appreciation and friendship of the Hungarian people".(26) And this he had in large measure.

The average man both in Hungary and in the United States heard about each other's life from the press. The permanent political topics covered by the American press on Hungary were: the stability of the Hungarian government; the Treaty of Trianon; the possibility of a Habsburg restoration; the relations between Hungary and the Little Entente; political matters concerning Hungary, Austria, Italy, and Germany. Concerning the stability of the government, the American press was impressed in general by the fact that in spite of several years of severe depression, during which Hungary was struggling for her economic existence, there was a stable government and an absence of unrest.(27)

A journalist needed to be in Hungary but a few hours to realize that the whole nation was in mourning for its lost territories.

25 For details see Maurice R. Davie, **American Men of Science** (New York: Harper & Brothers, 1947).

26 T. J. C. Martyn in the New York **Times Magazine,** July 11, 1926.

27 U. S., **Department of State,** 864.00/806.

This being so, it was easy to understand that Hungary instinctively drew close to those who symphathized with her in her plight and held aloof from those who did not. For those neighboring countries which were given Hungarian territories after World War I (Czechoslovakia, Yugoslavia, and Rumania), there was openly manifested bitterness.

After the revision of the Treaty of Trianon came the question of the restoration of a monarch. This question was not active in the 1930's. At that time, the main problem was Germany, for what happened in Germany was a matter of great importance to Hungary and the other Danubian States.(28)

Besides political events, the American press reported every important cultural, social, and economic fact concerning Hungary. The cultural and scientific successes of the Hungarians in America also had colorful coverage in the press.

Accusations of feudalism in Hungary, however, often arose in the American newspapers. Stories about feudal Hungary were planted incessantly in the American press after World War I, probably by the Little Entente States, in order to calm America's conscience, which was a little troubled by the fact that in the name of national self-determination more than three million Hungarians had been put under foreign rule. The authors of these articles, in all probability, had never set foot on Hungarians soil. The Hungarian government protested against these news reports each time they appeared. In answer, the American ministers at Budapest pointed out that the press was not the business of the government in the United States. They tried to assure the Hungarians that the freedom of the press did not at all mean that American public opinion agreed with tendentious reports on Hungary.(29)

Those American reporters who visited Hungary usually wrote in a different tone about Hungarian social conditions. They observed that industrial labor was organized in Hungary preceding

---

28 Ibid.
29 Ibid.

World War I and had obtained there in the 1930's a similar status to that of American labor gained through the New Deal.(30) While industrial labor enjoyed in Hungary all the social security which a poor country could afford to provide, the situation was different with agricultural labor. Real poverty could be observed among agricultural labor mainly because there were not enough jobs for them. In general Hungary impressed the reporters with the fine character of its people. The man in public life were impressive in their personalities, strength, and democratic outlook. Usually they resented the appelllation of "democracy" as they associated it with "strikes, bomb outrages, and demagogues", but they were distinctly liberal and democratic in their outlook and aspirations.(31)

Hungarians were always interested in news from America. The volume of American news published in the Hungarian press increased during the 1930's. The beginning of the increase of the American news material in the Hungarian press coincided with the beginning of the economic crisis. Aware of the intra-dependence of national economics and greatly interested in welfare and employment problems, the Hungarian press avidly watched American production in general as well as developments in social welfare and employment.

The Hungarian press was greatly interested in the New Deal. It carefully registered, generally without comment, all measures and events of importance of the Roosevelt administration, especially those which might have an effect on financial and other world markets. The Hungarian press likewise registered, without comment, opposition to the Roosevelt administration. It did not take sides with or against the American government. It did not express views of its own. It reported whether the government had succeeded or failed and described the activities of the various elements which were in opposition to the government.(32)

---

30 Montgomery, **Hungary, The Unwilling Satellite**, p. 28.
31 **U. S., Department of State**, 864.00/873.
32 **Ibid.**, 864.911/16.

President Franklin D. Roosevelt was of special interest to the Hungarian press, not only because of his position but also from the human point of view. His infirmity, combined with his courage and cheerfulness, were impressed on the Hungarian public in non-political articles. Human interest articles also made Mrs. Roosevelt better known in Hungary than were most of her predecessors. The Hungarian press kept fairly well informed regarding all things which the President and Mrs. Roosevelt did or said.(33)

The concrete political events given considerable publicity by the Hungarian press were the 1932 Presidential election, the "Brain Trust", Dollar depreciation, Budgets, New Deal laws and decrees, Court decisions against the New Deal, Huey Long's and Father Coughlin's political activities. As regards the "Share-Our-Wealth Society" of Huey P. Long, United States Senator from Louisiana, and the "Social Justice Movement" of Father Charles E. Coughlin, Royal Oak, Michigan, the Hungarian press took over some American press comments criticizing or making fun of the persons involved. With regard to the rest of the subjects, the Hungarian press showed its customary interest combined with impartiality.(34)

The permanent non-political topics covered by the Hungarian press included sports, aviation, inventions, science, literature, art and philosophy. Charles A. Lindbergh, the youthful aviator, was the American about whom the Hungarian press wrote more than about any of his compatriots. Apart from the news material connected with his child's murder, the Hungarian press watched with attention his flights, his activity as an expert, his marriage and private life, and his scientific experiments. As far as philosophy is concerned, the less serious-minded Hungarian papers occasionally had a laugh at the expense of the new American religions and their followers.

---

33 Ibid.
34 Ibid.

Film news was the type most often met in the Hungarian press. Apart from natural interest in the accomplishment of the American film production, the Hungarian theatres which showed American films included interesting news items which served as advertisements, such as Hollywood scandal stories and news verging on the grotesque.

The Hungarian press showed the natural human interest toward occurrences in which loss of life was involved. Nevertheless, floods of the Mississippi claimed more interest than those of China or India, and the coverage was proportionately larger. Weather in general, however, was of great interest inasmuch as Hungary was an agricultural country. The Hungarian press watched the wheat crop figures of the United States on account of their effect on the international wheat market and also reported on the maize and cotton crops.

The Hungarian press very readily reported success of Hungarians in America, such as appointments and tours of musicians, lecturers, and artists. It kept track of anything interesting happening to, or among, Hungarians living in America. Statements and articles on Hungary or Hungarian affairs formed an essential part of the American news material in the Hungarian press. If they favored Hungary's case for revision, the Hungarian press gave them the widest possible publicity.

Realizing the seriousness of the case, the Hungarian press generally refrained from expressing any view regarding the Negro problem. Nevertheless, one might read between the lines that the Hungarian press was sympathetic to the Negroes. The Hungarian press was also interested in strike movements or social disturbances in the United States, not because of the subject itself but because of the dimensions they usually assumed. Thus the veterans' marches, the farmers' strikes, and the San Francisco strike of 1934 were given considerable publicity. Gangster warfare during the period of Prohibition was a favorite topic of the lower-grade press. Serious papers limited themselves to the recording of events with a positive news value, such as cases where many or well-known persons were killed, large consignments were confiscated, and large robberies took place.

During World War II, Hungary was the only country in southeastern Europe which permitted its newspapers to publish news from neutral and Allied sources. Until the Nazis occupied Hungary on March 19, 1944, some Hungarian newspapers published at least as many items coming from neutral, British, or American sources as from German sources, and often Allied news received better play than German items. The writer saw Budapest newspapers during World War II with full texts of speeches of President Roosevelt, Vice-President Henry A. Wallace, and Wendell Willkie, Republican nominee for President in 1940. Hungaran publishers, as we have seen before, were permitted to publish translations of current American books, which were sold openly in Budapest book stores during the years of the war. This fact was a political paradox. But it reveals that in spite of political hostilities, cultural relations did not come to an end between the two nations.

CHAPTER VIII

BETHLEN'S HUNGARY:
RECONSTRUCTION AND DEPRESSION
1921—1932

From the early Middle Ages, Hungary had evolved as a constitutional monarchy based on the royal recognition of the rights of the nation.(1) The whole Hungarian constitutional development was based on the doctrine of the Holy Crown of Hungary. According to this doctrine, the source of every right is vested in the Holy Crown of St. Stephen, which became not only a sacred relic used at the coronation and other solemn ceremonies but the symbol of national sovereignty and unity. The head of this entity (**caput Sacri Regni Coronae**) was the King, who attained this position only through the coronation performed by the nation (**membra Sacri Regni Coronae**). The duly crowned King and the nation together form the entire body of the Holy Crown (**totum corpus Sacri Regni Coronae**). A decision may become law only with the consent of these two components. As a consequence, without a crowned King the nation is not a perfect entity.(2) So, in Hungary's case, the re-

---

1 For full and good Hungarian history in Englist, see: Carlile Aylmer Macartney, **Hungary** (Chicago: Aldine Publishing Company, 1962; reprinted 1966, 1968), or see Denis Sinor, **History of Hungary** (London: Allen & Unwin, 1959.

2 For further details see William Solyom-Fekete, "The Hungarian Constitutional Compact of 1867," **The Quarterly Journal of the Library of Congress**, XXIV, No. 4 (October, 1967), 287.

turn to the old monarchical form meant an unbroken allegiance to the principles of liberty and self-government in a world seething with ideas of state omnipotence and totalitarian authority.

Because of the Rumanian occupation, it was not until January, 1920, that the work of reconstruction could begin. It was universally recognized that constitutionalism must be restored, but it was at the same time clear to everyone that this could not be achieved simply by declaring the resumption of the old constitutional life at the point where it had been interrupted by war and revolution. The fact that the union with Austria had ceased to exist and the crowned king was unable to return necessitated the introduction of new measures and arrangements which, however, should not do away with old institutions and traditions.

After the collapse of the proletarian government, there followed a bourgeois administration. In the absence of a king the old legislative power could not function, and the government decided to convene a "National Assembly". General elections were ordered for January 25, 1920, on the basis of an equal, obligatory franchise by secret ballot. The largest party to emerge was the "United Agrarian Laborers' and Smallholders' Party", which got seventy-one mandates. This party, with sixteen other Liberals and Independents, represented the "Left". The "Christian National Union" gained sixty-eight seats and with nine other sympathizers represented the "Right".(3) The Assembly was elected for the limited period of two years. It confined itself to the task of finding a provisional solution for the existing constitutional situation.

In Law I, which was enacted in February, 1920, the Assembly declared itself to be the depository of national sovereignty which entitled it to provide for the "restitution of the Constitution and for the organization of the sovereign power". It further declared that the laws and decrees of the Károlyi and Communist republics and Law XII of 1867, on which the vanished Monarchy had been

---

3 C. A. Macartney, October Fifteenth (2 vols; Edinburgh: University Press, 1956), I. 24.

based, should be null and void, and that, until such time as the sovereign power could be definitely regulated, the Assembly should elect by ballot a Regent who, within certain limitations, should exercise the rights pertaining to the royal power.

The monarchy was thus maintained, but an interregnum set in. On the first of March, 1920, Admiral Horthy, at the time Commander-in-Chief of the national army, was elected Regent of Hungary. Twice King Charles attempted to regain his throne. He went to Hungary from Switzerland, where he lived in exile, in March and in October, 1921, but he failed in both cases. As a result, he was taken out of Hungary on a British gunboat in October, 1921. He died in Madeira Island, the next year where the English authorities had banished him. The heir to the throne, the Archduke Otto, was still a child.

Hungary's post-war era began with short-lived and ineffective governments. However, a change occured in 1921, when a new government was formed under the leadership of Count Stephen Bethlen. Since he served as Prime Minister for ten years, the first decade of Hungary's inter-war history was generally called the Bethlen era.

Count Stephen Bethlen came from a historic Transylvanian family.(4) He had the same family roots as Gabriel Bethlen, the

---

4 Transylvania sometimes played a significant role in international relations. Stephen Báthory, prince of Transylvania (1572—1581) was elected king of Poland in 1575 and defeated the Russian Czar, Ivan the Terrible. Several of the Transylvanian princes, chiefly Gabriel Bethlen (1613—1629) and George Rákóczi (1630—1648) maintained close relations and often negotiated alliances with Western European Protestant powers and with France, in order to strengthen their position against the Habsburgs. In the second half of the seventeenth century, Transylvania was ravaged by Turkish and Tartar hordes. Thus she gradually withered away from the European scene as a power factor. In 1691, the **Diploma Leopoldinum** declared Transylvania a Habsburg province.

For the history of Transylvania, see Ladislaus Makkai, **Histoire de Transylvania** (Paris: Presses Universitaites de France, 1946); and C. A. Macartney, **Hungary and Her Successors** (New York: Oxford University Press,, 1937), pp. 254—70.

172

Protestant ruling prince of Transylvania in the seventeenth century. His studies had taken him to Vienna and England. Bethlen was a Calvinist in faith and, like many Hungarian magnates, admired England, where he had received his education. He entered Parliament in 1901, and in politics he was a conservative. He distrusted all forms of revolutionary ideologies and extremisms whether they came from the country's socialists or from the right-radical groups. He began his term of office by declaring that the revolutions and counter-revolutions were over.

Bethlen's chief aim was undoubtedly the restoration of Hungary to pre-1918 territorial form. He did not put it first on his timetable, for he was convinced that any such adventure would be futile until Hungary had consolidated her internal position and gained powerful friends abroad. He looked on the problems of Hungary as those which local and short-term devices could not solve. Only a comprehensive and long-term plan could be successful, a plan which took into account the realities of the world forces. Hungary's first step must therefore be a general process of consolidation and reconstruction.

Hungary's immediate need was for investment capital. The resources of Hungary's native capitalists were insufficient; Hungary had never been rich in capital of her own, since many of her industries had been owned by holding banks outside the country.(5) Thus capital was needed from aboard, but investors would not risk it in a country in which revolution was a possibility. Political and social stability were prerequisites to economic and financial reconstruction; for both, foreign help was needed. From this it followed that until reconstruction had successfully gotten under way, Hungary would have to adopt a political orientation satisfactory to those circles which could supply the financial help. This applied both to internal and external policy. First Hungary must

---

5 For details on Hungarian social and economic history, see Béla Kovrig, **Hungarian Social Policies, 1920—1945** (New York: Published by Committee for Culture and Education of the Hungarian National Council, 1954).

gather sufficient strength in order to make herself again a factor to be reckoned with in world politics. Only then could she hope to secure friends, and only after this would she be in a position to advance toward her national objectives.

Bethlen's first diplomatic success was the treaty between the United States and Hungary. On July 2, 1921, President Harding asked Congress to establish peace between the two countries. The message stated: "Considering that the former Austro-Hungarian Monarchy ceased to exist and was replaced in Hungary by a national Hungarian Government, considering that the Treaty of Trianon has not been ratified by the United States, it is necessary to establish peace and friendly relations between the two nations".(6) Congress approved the presidential message on the same day. President Harding reposed authority to negotiate peace with Hungary on Ulysses Grant-Smith and Hugh Frazer, American Commissioners at Budapest.

The negotiations started on July 9, 1921, in Budapest. The commissioners of the two countries had no difficulty. During the war, the armies of the two countries had not fought each other. The Hungarians living in the States were treated with consideration, nor was a single American interned at that time in Hungary. There was such a great understanding between the delegations that the first draft was approved both by the President of the United States and by the Hungarian Government. The treaty was signed on August 29, 1921.(7) This historic act, the first treaty signed between the two states, took place at Budapest in the Building of Parliament. Ulysses Grant-Smith and Hugh Frazer, plenipotentiaries, accompanied by Colonel Edwin C. Kemp, the military charge d'affaires, and the secretaries, Wallace Smith Murray and Warrington Dawson, represented the government of the United States. The chief representatives of the Hungarian government were the Foreign Minister, Count Nicholas Bánffy, and the head of the po-

---

6 U. S. For. Rel., Department of State, 711.64119/9 B.
7 Ibid., 711.64119/37.

174

litical section of the Foreign Ministry, Count Alexander Khuen-Hédervary. Ambassador Grant-Smith welcomed the peace restored between the two countries with the following words: "I believe in Hungary's future and prosperity. Hungary will live for a long time to come, will live and thrive".(8) On that occasion, as the Hungarian news-media pointed out, there were no references to the territorial changes of Trianon in the separate peace treaty. The Hungarian Nation, a monthly official periodical of the Foreign Ministry, wrote:

Mr. Ulysses Grant-Smith, during his nearly three years' stay at Budapest, has repeatedly proved his sympathy and valued friendship for our afflicted land. All this time he has been one of the unnamed actual factors in the American charity movement in Hungary. In this third year he witnesses the peace between America and Hungary. The conclusion of this peace is that the United States of America does not recognize the territorial provision of the Trianon Treaty.(9)

In any case, the peace treaty between the United States and Hungary meant that ordinary diplomacy was set up between the two states. The following month, Nicholas Roosevelt, the newly appointed American Minister to Hungary, arrived at Budapest. He held his office there for more than ten years and in doing so became the most permanent ambassador at Budapest. His reports to the State Department show that nothing disturbed the good relations between the two states during his term.

Another significant diplomatic event occurred between the two states in 1929, when Hungary joined the Kellogg Pact which condemned war as a means for the solution of international controversies. First, Hungarian public opinion looked upon the pact with suspicion. The Kellogg-Briand Pact was interpreted by the French press as a formal blessing on the Paris Peace Treaties, up to then withheld by America.(10) The Pester Lloyd, in discuss-

---

8 Ibid.
9 II, No. 9 (1921), 85.
10 U. S., For. Rel., 711.6412/27.

ing these remarks of the French press, stated on October 18, 1928 "Hungary is ready to condemn war, but must leave the door open to the revision of unjust and unnatural conditions".(11) Another paper, the **Pesti Napló** (Diary), protested that the Central Powers had never dreamed of fighting the United States and stated that the grievances which led America into World War I could have been settled according to international law by the compensation usual to neutrals suffering from war. The paper stated furthermore that the United States, on the basis of the Monroe Doctrine, should have refrained from entering a war which was entirely the concern of Europe. The unlimited submarine campaign, the paper stated, was a pleasing pretext for the commencement of hostilities and concluded that "America, after playing a leading part in the breaking up of old Europe, would have nothing to do with the creation of the new Europe".(12)

The Hungarian Government really was in trouble. If it joined the Kellogg Pact, it could mean accepting the status quo. If Hungary did not join the Pact, it could be interpreted that she was on the side of the war. The eyes of her neighbors were watching her. The **Echo de Paris,** for instance, stated: "Hungary only feigns to preach peace as she attacks at the same time one of the most important guaranties of European peace: the Trianon Treaty".(13)

Hungary's hope regarding the Kellogg Pact, that the United States would take some future interest in remedying injustices to Hungary, aroused unfavorable comments in Czechoslovakia, Rumania, and Yugoslavia. Before she joined the Pact, however, Hungary sent Tibor Eckhardt, one of her best diplomats, to Washington with a memorandum of the effects of the pact in Europe. The memorandum called attention to the fact that Hungary was of all the most cruelly ill-treated by the peace treaties and asked the United States not to concur in any legal stabilization of the pres-

11 **Ibid.**
12 **U. S., Nat. Arch., Micr.** No. 708, Roll No. 11.
13 U S., For. Rel., 711.6412/25.

ent territorial status quo in Europe. Kellogg, the Secretary of State, assured Hungary that the Pact did not have that intention. What was more, Senator Borah, during the debate in the Senate on the Kellogg Pact, stated regarding Central Europe: "It is quite clear to me that very much is wrong in that part of the world".(14)

Hungary joined the Kellogg Pact and the **Budapesti Hírlap** published an article entitled "The Ways of Hungarian Foreign Policy", which was more than usually inspired by government sources. The article stated:

> The Hungarian Government emphasized the fact that it joined the Kellogg Pact with the assumption that the Government of the United States would try to find ways and means for ensuring, in the future, the remedying of injustices by peaceful ways. The United States cannot consider the root of its intervention in European politics to be closed by the Kellogg Pact. There is the fact that the United States, which had rejected the Treaty of Trianon and concluded a separate peace, ought to try to find ways and means to remedy injustices. The Hungarian government was very wise to seize the opportunity to remind America to go on with her mission for the sake of world peace and to open before her the closed book of revision, telling her to look and read that book which is full of serious injustices.(15)

At a session of the Committee on Foreign Affairs of the Upper House of Parliament on the same date, Dr. Lajos Walkó, the Minister of Foreign Affairs, referring to the Kellog Pact, informed the Committee of the reasons which influenced his government to join the Pact. He stated that in its note the government intended not only to emphasize the final aim of Hungarian political life, but also to voice the principle that international life in general needs effective means by which unjust and unnatural relations may be peacefully remedied.(16)

---

14 **Ibid.**
15 **Ibid.**, 711.6412/26.
16 **Ibid.**

Ultimately, sixty-two nations signed the Kellogg Pact, but the futility of all such declarations was demonstrated by the attack of Japan on China. Nevertheless, European statesman saw significance in the willingness of the United States to cooperate in the effort to maintain world peace. For her part, Hungary hoped that American public opinion could be allied with that of Hungary in an endeavor to modify the Covenant of the League of Nations, and in creating a new spirit which would eliminate the one-sided privileges of the victorious states.

Far more important during this period were the economic relations between the United States and Hungary. As noted above, the economic development of Central Europe had been different from that of the West. Most of the large industry in Central Europe, and nearly all in Hungary, was directly owned or controlled by holding banks. The structure of Hungarian big business was even more oligarchic than that of the landed interests. It was controlled to an overwhelming degree by a relatively small number of persons, nearly all of them closely related by blood or marriage. (17) Hungary could never have achieved the economic results which she did during the Reconstruction period without the active cooperation of these citizens and without foreign capital.

On September 18, 1922, Bethlen scored his first success when Hungary secured admission to the League. The next spring she applied for a loan. The Little Entente announced that it would waive its rights only if it received serious guarantees that the loan would not be used by Hungary either to increase her armaments or to finance irredentist propaganda. More discussions followed, and at last it was possible to sign, on March 14, 1924, two Protocols. By the first Protocol, Britain, France, Italy, Czechoslovakia, Rumania, and Yugoslavia promised to respect Hungary's territorial integrity, sovereignty, and political independence, while Hungary undertook, in accordance with the stipulations of the Treaty of Trianon, strictly and loyally to fulfill the obligations contained in

---

17 See Kovrig, **Hungarian Social Policies, 1920—1945**, p. 32.

the Treaty, and in particular the military clauses. The second Protocol laid down what guarantees Hungary was to give for a loan and fixed her total reparations. She was to pay two hundred million gold crowns, in installments rising from five million gold crowns in 1927—28 to an annual maximum of fourteen million to be reached in 1942.

This settlement provided the negotiation of a loan for two hundred fifty million gold crowns.(18) The operation was an immediate success. As previously noted, the reconstruction loan was oversubscribed, and this proved only the first trickle of what soon turned into a flood of capital. Domestic capital repatriated itself, and foreign capital found remarkably favorable opportunities in Hungary. According to figures quoted by B. Kovrig,(19) the capital imported into Hungary between 1920 and 1931 totalled 488,856,928 dollar. The currency at once became stable, and the new independent Bank of Issue replaced the old crown with a new unit, the "pengö" based on gold. That unit in its turn remained for years among Europe's most stable currencies. By July, 1924, the budget had been brought back into equilibrium, so effectively that every year thereafter it showed a surplus of revenue over expenditures. Two new universities, many high schools and thousands of elementary schools were built. New factories were founded to replace those lost at Trianon; new sources of raw materials were developed or foreign sources found, and new markets were opened abroad. The number of establishments ranking as factories rose from 2,124 in 1921 to 3,553 in 1928, while the index of industrial production rose from 100 to 294.(20) Agriculture flourished. The year 1929 found Hungary with a prosperous ownership class, both urban and rural. The former included not only the major financiers and industrialists but also many shopkeepers and artisans. The well-being of these classes was shared by the state employees of the higher and

---

18 It was issued at 8 percent and bore interest at 7—1/2 percent.

19 Kovrig, **Hungarian Social Policies, 1920—1945**, p. 37.

20 **Ibid.**, p. 38.

medium grade. Bethlen had also succeeded in establishing a large degree of social and political harmony between these classes and in finding solutions for many of the problems. The skilled industrial workers lived in relatively good conditions. The average standard of living of a worker in factory industries was up to the general Central European level and above that prevailing in much of Eastern Europe.(21)

Of all the financially reconstructed countries Hungary was the most interesting and attractive to the financial world. When the League of Nations Reconstruction Loan was being negotiated in 1923 and 1924, international bankers were unanimous in expressing apprehensions as to Hungary's political stability. After two revolutions, two Habsburg "putsches", and the occupation of the country by a foreign army, it was scarcely surprising that foreign financiers were nervous when asked to loan money. Yet of all the countries of Europe, Hungary had proved herself one of the most politically stable. Count Bethlen had been in power far longer than any other Eastern European Premier and social order had been maintained during the whole reconstruction period. Count Bethlen's prestige was so strong that people spoke of him as the Per-

---

21 A formal written agreement was concluded with the Social Democrats on December 22, 1921. This agreement enabled the workers to retain a complete system of vocational representation and a modicum of political representation. For the text of the agreement, see C. A. Macartney, **October Fifteenth**, I. 43—44.

Furthermore, probably because of the work of the political refugees, the leaders of counter-revolution were anxious to demonstrate to the Hungarian workers and to the outer world that their hostility to Marxism did not imply hostility to the workers. As proof of this, they kept in being the Ministry of Social Welfare, first established towards the close of World War I, which by convention was allocated to a member of the Christian Party. Msgr. Joseph Wass, who held this ministerial post for nearly a decade, exercised a considerable influence on the government, and considerable improvements in working conditions were made when state finances were available. The most important advance was the introduction in 1927 of an excellent social insurance system both for workers and for salaried employees. In addition, the average working day and week were shortened substantially, while many other less important reforms were introduced.

manent Premier. The **London Times**(22) compared him to Montague Norman, who was at that time, the permanent Governor of the Bank of England. This continuity of policy and its guidance by a statesman of real ability were probably responsible as much as anything for the success of the reconstruction plan. Bethlen's respect for a Parliamentary form of government and his desire to guide rather than dictate, combined with an undisputed sway over the mass of the people, constituted excellent assurance against rash political ventures on the part of Hungary. Agitation at home or abroad was not in the least likely to influence him in the direction of a policy that could endanger the prospects of improving his country for the sake of uncertain political advantages in the future. For proper understanding of the financial and economic position of Hungary, it is essential that this phase of Hungarian politics be studied.

Since the year of the Reconstruction Loan, 1924, Hungary had more than fulfilled what was expected of her by those who had formulated the League of Nations plan. Her budget had not only been in equilibrium but there had been relatively large surpluses. These had been employed for useful capital investment. All foreign obligations had been fulfilled. Hungary was paying England 1,500,000 dollars every year for the liquidation of the pre-war debts. In 1928, from the purely economic point of view, Hungary was somewhat in the position of the "Good Boy" waiting to have her merits recognized. All agreements had dutifully been made in accordance with the highest principles of the Geneva Economic Conference. In 1928, the metal reserve of the National Bank was more than four times larger than in 1924.(23)

When Bethlen applied for the League of Nations loan, it was clear that such a loan would bring with it political obligations. He wanted the minimum obligations and therefore he, by no means, wanted continental money. Instead, he borrowed from American

---

22 May 5, 1928.
23 U. S., Nat. Arch., Micr. No. 708, Roll No. 30.

and English banks because this would mean no political obligations other than those cited in the Protocol of the League of Nations. Although the loan was under the auspices of the League of Nations and issued in England, the United States, Italy, Switzerland, Holland, and Sweden, it was in reality financed by the House of Morgan.(24) Unlike the Austrian Reconstruction Loan, it was not guaranteed by foreign states. Being so, it was proposed that a General Commissioner of the League of Nations be named to Hungary and, furthermore, that an American fill this post. The **New York Times** reported on February 9, 1924, that the post had been offered to and accepted by an American and mentioned two names: Charles G. Dawes and P. G. Harding, the Governor of the Federal Reserve Bank of Boston. In fact, the Secretariat of the League of Nations had proposed Harding. Harding was unable to go to Hungary and suggested the name of Jeremiah Smith, who accepted the invitation.

Jeremiah Smith was a Boston banker and an expert on the American peace delegation in Versailles. He had been one of Thomas W. Lamont's assistants in recent financial negotiations with China and Mexico. Royall Tyler, Representative of the Trustees of the Reconstruction Loan, also an American, was principal assistant to Jeremiah Smith. Certainly there were other circumstances which helped Hungary's economic recovery, but the fact remains that Jeremiah Smith rendered great service in a work considered difficult and unpleasant by all right-thinking Hungarians.

It is believed that, after General Bandholtz, it was Jeremiah Smith who gave the greatest aid to Hungary. When he ended his work in Hungary on June 25, 1926, Dorsey Richardson, Acting Chief, Division of European Affairs of the State Department, sent the following telegram to the American Minister at Budapest:

I understand that a dinner is to be given by the Hungarian Government on June 26, in honor of Jeremiah Smith. I hope you will express the satisfaction of the Government of the

---

24 For further details, see **ibid.**, Micr. No. 708, Roll No. 30.

United States and of the people of this country at the successful termination of Mr. Smith's work. Americans who have followed it are glad that it should have been an American citizen who has been able to give this important aid to the Hungarian Government and people.(25)

Smith was possibly no more successful than Zimmerman was in Austria, but he did his work modestly and unobtrusively and in such a way that, instead of being detested as Zimmerman was in Austria, he was really loved. Jeremiah Smith won the esteem of the Hungarian people by his simple mode of life. He lived without extravagance or ostentation and steadily declined any kind of reward. His virtuous and upright character raised the credit of America among Hungarians of all classes. Of his ability as an economist, nothing but praise can be said. Colijn, ex-Prime Minister and Minister of Finance of the Netherlands, paid a warm tribute to the ability and to the character of Smith when he visited Hungary in 1926. He said to the American Minister at Budapest: "Zimmerman undoubtedly accomplished very useful work as financial adviser to the Austrian Government. But your compatriot has made his name even more illustrous than my countryman".(26)

As we have seen, under the direction of Jeremiah Smith, rapid progress was made in the fiscal reconstruction of Hungary. In summary, the budget was balanced in less than one year, leaving the greater part of the proceeds of the Reconstruction Loan unused; in the year ending June 30, 1925, there was a surplus over expenses; the currency had been stabilized and a new monetary unit, the "pengö", was established. The reserves of the National Bank of Hungary in gold and foreign exchanges were equal to about 55 percent of the circulation. All obligations of Hungary towards the United States had been paid or funded.

Though Hungary was principally an agricultural nation, large amounts of capital were invested in Hungary by American ban-

---

25 U. S., National Archives, Micr. No. 708, Roll. No. 30.
26 Ibid.

kers and corporations. In June, 1925, the Bauer, Pogue, Pond and Vivian Company, New York, invested $3,400,000 into the Hungarian Discount and Exchange Bank of Budapest. On January 23, 1925, Harnblower, Miller and Garrison of New York invested $3,000,000 into the Rima Steel Corporation of Budapest. On May 20, 1926, the Itnernational Acceptance Bank, New York, loaned $2,000,000 to the City of Budapest. On April 29, 1926, the Guaranty Company of New York loaned $3,000,000 to the Hungarian Land Mortgage Institute. On July 20, 1926, Speyer and Company gave a $10,000,000 loan to the Hungarian Counties. On September 17, 1927, a deposit of $1,500,000 was made to the British-Hungarian Bank, Limited, of Budapest. On March 3, 1927, Hornblower, Miller and Garrison of New York made a deposit of $1,000,000 to the Hungarian-Italian Bank of Budapest. Some months earlier, Olehn and Ganter of New York made a $2,700,000 deposit in the same Budapest Bank. On April 27, 1927, the Hines, Rearick, Dorr, Travis and Marshall Company of New York gave a loan of $2,000,000 to the National Central Savings Bank of Hungary. Besides these there were many other business activities. Far more important was the Budapest City Loan on May 10, an issue of $20,000,000 of Thirty Five Year 6.5 percent Gold Bonds, of which $10,000,000 were intended to be sold in American Market. The loan was concluded between the City of Budapest and the Bankers' Trust Company of New York. The proceeds of the loan were to be used for a variety of productive works, including extension of electric power, water works, central and other markets, slaughter-houses, the development of bus transportation, and the construction of public buildings and dwelling houses. (27) As a result of these business matters it became necessary to initiate direct telephone communication between Hungary and the United States on November 12, 1928.

---

27 For city-owned tenement houses and public medical facilities, $9,000,000; for completion of electric works, $5,500,000;; for reconstruction of water works, $2,500,000; for development of bus transportation, $700,000; for slaughter-houses, $1,000,000; for enlargement of market halls, $800,000; for building new market halls and open markets, $1,200.000. **U. S. Nat. Arch.**, 708—30.

Another factor of importance was the agreement with the Swedish-American Match Trust, on July 6, 1928. This agreement provided that, in return for concessions to be granted for match production in Hungary, the Trust granted a loan of $36,000,000 at 92 percent, bearing 5.5 percent interest. The Trust agreed that not more than twenty foreign workmen would be employed by it in Hungary.(28)

American small business was also involved in Hungarian economic activity. On August 24, 1927, the Joint Security Corporation of New York offered for public subscription 100,000 American shares of the United Metropolitan Savings Bank of Budapest. Each share had a value of $7.00, and the stock was paid in dollars. The Joint Security Corporation gave the following survey of Hungary on that occasion:

> Hungary is the most fertile land in Central Europe, producing wheat, rye, corn, flour, sugar, beef, cattle, swine, fowl and game, all kinds of vegetables, wine and mineral waters. The production of sugar-beets and of potatoes is also considerable. For generations Hungary has been known universally as the granary of Europe, or at least Central Europe, which it still is and will remain for the time being, particularly as Russia has to be practically counted out as a wheat and grain exporting country.(29)

Up to 1929 everything went well with the reconstruction, Hungary's prosperity increased year by year and, with its increase, Bethlen's prestige rose to extraordinary heights. It must also be admitted, however, that the Reconstruction Era failed to carry out many political and social reforms. Bethlen was not totalitarian, nor tyrannical. Personal and political freedoms in Bethlen's Hungary were far more restricted than in the real democracies of the day, but generous compared with conditions prevailing in Yugoslavia, Rumania, and Poland, or even in Italy.

---

28 U. S., Nat Arch., Micr. No. 708, Roll No. 30.
29 Ibid.

Nevertheless, Bethlen's Hungary was emphatically a class state in a Europe which then believed itself to be advancing towards democracy. In spite of prosperity, Bethlen's Hungary included grievous unsolved social problems. First of all it failed to carry out land reform. The census of 1935 showed that nearly three million people — 60 percent of those employed in agriculture — were either totally landless or occupying holdings insufficient to support life in decency. The condition of the rural poor was bad. Although industrialization was proceeding, it could not absorb all of the unemployed rural workers and, unfortunately for them, the American legislation had closed the main outlet of emigration. Moreover, the universities were beginning to produce a large new intellectual proletariat.

Many of these problems might ultimately have vanished if prosperity had continued, but the whole structure of Bethlen's system rested on two pillars: the maintenance of international credit, until such time as Hungary no longer needed to borrow, and the continuance of high prices on the world market for her exports, particularly wheat. In 1929 both of these were shaken by the collapse of world wheat prices, started by overproduction in Canada, and by the Stock Exchange crash on Wall Street. In 1930 the government had already supported the price of wheat, but the consequences for Hungary did not become really serious until the collapse of the Austrian Creditanstalt in May, 1931. Even this did not shake Bethlen's position; a month after it, he held elections which returned the Government Party to power with the usual large majority. But in the next weeks the full impact of the financial crisis hit the country. Unable to meet the demands of her foreign creditors, who were trying hurriedly to withdraw their funds, she had to appeal to the League of Nations. American capital, which had sustained the Hungarian economy in the 1920's, was no longer available. Hungary then, through the channels of the League, turned to the one large country in Europe which was still financially stable, France. On August 13, 1931, after feverish negotiations, a contract was signed for a new international loan of

$20,000,000 mainly subscribed in France. With this the worst of the immediate financial crisis seemed to be over. The League of Nations, however, prescribed a policy of ruthless financial orthodoxy, including the balancing of Hungary's budget by increasing revenue by heavier taxation and reducing expenditure by salary cuts and dismissals in the public services, and balancing of Hungary's balance of payments by the throttling of imports. The Financial Committee of the League of Nations appointed Royal Tyler, formerly the Assistant League Commissioner General for Hungary, to carry out this financial policy, and Henry J. Bruce, a London banker, was nominated to be the adviser of the Hungarian National Bank.(30)

The fantastic severity of the depression not only wiped out the economic gains of the previous decade but also threatened the political and social consolidation. The opposition accused the regime in general of following a policy beneficial to a few individuals but not in the wide national interest. Bethlen was held responsible for the system. His political opponents accused him of having betrayed the nation's cause for gold. Count Stephen Bethlen resigned in August, 1931. This was, however, an unexpected event, considering the absolute majority of the Government Party in the Parliament. Rumors were that France had made the dismissal of Bethlen a condition for the granting of the loan of the League.(31)

----

30 For full details on Hungary's financial situation, see **League of Nations** (the official journal of the League of Nations, Geneva), October 22, 1931, Report 10.

31 See the report of the American Minister at Prague to the State Department on September 1, 1931:

"The consensus of opinion seems to be that Bethlen resigned in order to placate the French Government and make possible the conclusion of the French loan to Hungary. It is felt that France demanded greater securities before granting the loan, particularly in the line of Hungarian foreign policy and that Bethlen, unable to secure the loan elsewhere, and confronted with a severe economic crisis, resigned rather than face the alternative disaster for his country. It is also stated that the particular demand of the French is the cessation of Hungary's revisionist policy and the maintenance of more friendly relations with the countries of the Little Entante." U. S., **For. Rel., Department of State,** 864.00/9

Bethlen's successor, Count Julius Károlyi,(32) set himself with determination to carry out the League's recommendations. But as one severe measure followed another, unrest grew. There were strikes and demonstrations among the workers, but more dangerous to the system was the revolt of the medium and small farmers, crushed under the weight of their indebtedness to the banks, the fired civil servants and the officers, and the jobless young university graduates. These events caused a new revival of Right Radicalism.

In September 1932 Count Julius Károlyi declared himself unable to solve Hungary's social and financial problems and resigned. Regent Horthy had to yield to the demand of the Right and appointed to the Minister Presidency, General Julius Gömbös, the leader of the Right Radicals. With this, a new era began in Hungary's history.

---

32 Count Julius Károlyi was a cousin of Michael Károlyi, but a very different man. He was a member of one of Hungary's wealthiest and most famous families. He was a man of the most rigid honor, and an ascetic person. In character, he was a "Puritan". He also had a strong social sense toward the employees of his own big estates. He was a model landlord, having exacted low rents, paying high wages, and spending not only money but time and conscious thought on providing them with good welfare institutions. He advocated the same course to others. In politics, he was conservative.

CHAPTER IX

IN SEARCH OF NEW ROUTES:
THE REFORM GENERATION
1932—1939

Between the two world wars Hungary was a small country. As a result of Hitler's rise to power in 1933, however, Hungary suddenly attained great importance for international politics. The uniqueness of her geographical position (being in the very heart of East-Central Europe) and her people (neither German nor Slav, and endangered by the two fires of Teuton and Slav imperialism) made her capital, Budapest, an important post of diplomatic observation. President Franklin D. Roosevelt became aware of her unique situation soon after his election and sent his envoy, John Flournoy Montgomery, to Budapest with special instructions: besides his ordinary diplomatic duties, he was to send reports from time to time directly to the President himself.

Before going to Hungary in July of 1933, Montgomery spent thirty days of preparatory study in the State Department, where he learned that the Hungary of that time was a puppet of Italy with no independence of action. Arriving in Budapest, however, he found out that in foreign affairs nothing is more misleading than oversimplification. On many occasions, Hungary's inclination was to side with western democracies, but circumstances made it not so much a question of what the people would like but what they knew they had to do.(1)

The regime of the reconstruction period, as we have seen before, left many unsolved problems. It failed to carry out political, economic, and social reforms. As a result, the Bethlen regime had lost the younger generation. This new generation, growing up after World War I, broke with the old outlook of the traditional ruling class, with which it was no longer willing to identify itself. Furthermore, as a consequence of a good educational system, Hungary, within her straitened frontiers, turned out as many university graduates as historic Hungary had produced before her dismemberment — perhaps more.(2) This jobless but strongly patriotic intellectual group was a natural leader of any reform movements. In other circumstances most of them would have gravitated to the Left, as indeed, a few of them did. But the Left bore the stigma of having betrayed the national cause and brought about the ruin of Hungary, and Western democracy that of having imposed the unjust peace. Thus, the younger generation turned inevitably to the Right.

There is no doubt that the Reform Generation was seeking for true social and political reforms, genuine remedies for real grievances. But doing so in the circumstances described, it was attracted toward Nazism. It must be remembered that Nazism, as preached in East-Central Europe, was not merely an anti-Semitic movement but one of social reform. To ignore this is to distort the whole political picture of the period.

While industrial labor enjoyed all the social security which a poor country could afford to provide, the situation was very

---

1 John Flournoy Montgomery was Minister of the United States in Hungary from 1933 to 1941. He became a great friend of Hungary and published his diplomatic experiences in a book entitled **Hungary, The Unwilling Satellite** (New York: Devin-Adair Company, 1947).

2 In 1914 the total number of students graduating in historic Hungary was 11,000. From 1925 onward the annual average of Trianon Hungary was 12,000, Macartney, **October Fifteenth**, I, n.1, p. 78.

different with agricultural labor. Real poverty could be observed among agricultural labor mainly because Hungary had a badly balanced distribution of its arable land. While many magnates and the Church owned large estates which were legally entailed and could neither be sold nor mortgaged, nearly three million people (two-thirds of Hungary's total rural population and one-third of her total national population) possessed almost nothing which could be regarded as providing a living for a family.

The general spirit of the Hungarian employer was certainly not anti-labor. For instance, when living conditions became bad and jobs hard to find during the depression, the landowners voluntarily put a considerable part of their agricultural machinery out of use in order to provide more jobs to manual labor. All of this, however, did not change the fact that the land distribution was unhealthy and this landless, jobless agrarian proletariat turned to the Right for social justice, the Left being taboo in Hungary.

Furthermore, among countries having appreciable Jewish populations, Hungary ranked fourth, being exceeded only by Poland, Lithuania, and Rumania. The 1930 census figures show that the number of Jews increased from the year of 1920 from 5 percent to 7 percent. Their position in the national life was, moreover, far stronger than even these figures would suggest.(3) Among the Jewish element of Hungary, one in four belonged to the middle class, whereas only one in fifteen Gentiles belonged to this class. In the pre-war years, 290 Jewish families were elevated to the nobility and 25 were given the title of Baron, and 70 marriages occurred between Jews and members of the oldest families of Hungary. Of the large Hungarian estates in 1916, Jews owned 1.5 million catastral yokes (one catastral yoke equals 1.45 American acres) out of a total of 10.8 million yokes. During the war they bought another 100,000 yokes, bringing the percentage up to fifteen. Fifty percent

3 The figures of this paragraph and of those which follow are based on the dispatch of the American legation. "The Jewish Problem in Hungary", **Department of State**, 864.4016/92 (Budapest, February 6, 1937).

of the Gentile population were agriculturists, and only 3 percent of the Jews belonged to this classification. However, 13 percent of the owners of large estates (200 to 1,000 yokes) and 37 percent of lessees of very large estates (over 1,000 yokes) were Jews. Approximately 18 percent of the estate bailiffs and clerks were Jews, and only 0.9 percent of agricultural workers were Jews.

Of industrial enterprises employing more than twenty workers, 361 out of 783 (46 percent) were owned by Jews, divided according to industry as follows:

Sugar refineries — — — — — — — — 10 out of 12
Iron and Metal Industry — — — — — — 23 out of 61
Machine and Vehicle Industry — — — — — 26 out of 76
Stoneware, pottery, glass industry — — — — 18 out of 33
Spinning and Weaving — — — — — — — 35 out of 53
Clothing — — — — — — — — — — 77 out of 113
Paper — — — — — — — — — — 10 out of 15
Starch Manufacturing — — — — — — — 2 out of 2

The Stock exchange Year Book showed that in the twenty largest industrial enterprises of Hungary, 235 board members out of 336 were Jews (70 percent), and only one of these enterprises did not have a majority of Jewish directors. Of privately owned medium sized enterprises, 78 percent were owned by Jews, including the entire asphalt and tar industry, the three largest poultry companies, the ten largest transportation companies, and three largest wine shops. To the State services, the Jews supplied only 1.6 percent. On the other hand, 53 percent of the independent persons engaged in commerce, 80 percent of those in finance, 50.6 percent of the advocates, 59.9 percent of the doctors in private practice, 27.3 percent of the authors, 23.6 percent of the musicians, and 22.7 percent of the actors were Jewish.

Of taxpayers who have declared fortunes in excess of one million Pengö (four pengö equal $1), 83.2 percent were Jews (not including land owners). Of persons declaring an annual income above 100,000 pengö, 84.3 percent were Jews, and of those declaring incomes from 30,000 to 100,000 pengö, 85.6 percent were Jews. The total income of Jews in Hungary was estimated at 750 million pengö in 1936, and the per capita income of Jews averages 2,506 pengö against 427 pengö for Gentiles.

Figures from the 1936 Press Year Book showed 306 out of 418 professional journalists (73 percent) to be Jews. In nine of the largest newspapers of Hungary, the percentage of Jewish journalists ranged from 77 percent to 97.5 percent. The proportion in the publishing industry was about the same. The part played by Jews in the ownership and control of theaters, films, radio, sports, and other lucrative enterprises of Hungary was equally important.

Accusations against Regent Horthy's Hungary, being a Nazi anti-Jewish regime, often arose abroad. The truth is that the extremist excesses ceased after 1922, and thereafter the regime set its face strongly against anti-Semitism, even in its non-violent form. The figures quoted above show that the Jews had become an urban and bourgeois element in Hungary and illustrate the degree of control exercised by them over the industry, banking, and resources of Hungary. Furthermore, these figures explain why any attempt to regulate the large industries and estates or any attack on the privileges of industrialists may appear to be anti-Semitic in character; and, indeed, a large number of the younger generation, searching for social reform, became more anti-Semitic.

The situation became more complex for Hungary as Hitler's power grew. The country was faced with a political dilemma: Germany was the only power capable and willing to break the iron ring of the Little Entente and its French support; but the accomplishment of this would place Germany in a dominant position in Europe, a position also dangerous to Hungary. This political dilemma shadowed the whole Hungarian political spectrum of the 1930's and, complicated by Hungary's social and economic problems mentioned above, drew the country step by step into Hitler's net until she fought World War II on Germany's side.

In spite of the common desire for reforms, the younger generation was not totally of one accord. A great majority of the youth herself completely into Germany's arms. Mostly due to their work, Hungary's policy during this period was a sort of permanent hesitation both in foreign and domestic affairs and, despite the strong German pressure, she was able to maintain a more decent, human, and civilized policy longer than some of her neighbors could.

One movement of the time cannot be classified as belonging either to the Left or to the Right. A group of young men, most of them sons of landless agricultural laborers, who by their talents had won scholarships to universities, together with some sympathizers from other circles, founded a little group known as the "Village Explorers" with the purpose of making known the conditions prevailing among the rural poor. They published a series of studies which were often exceedingly radical. They tended to be Hungarian radicals, attacking both German and Jewish influences impartially. This was a standpoint difficult to maintain for long, and, as time went on, most of them tended to drift into other camps: some joined various Right Radical movements, some became crypto-Communists. The movement gained its significance, however, by the fact that Professor Gyula Szekfü, the most famous Hungarian historian of that time and Professor at Peter Pázmány University at Budapest, was sympathetic to it. Professor Szekfü had been led by his studies to realize how small was the genuine Magyar element in the Hungarian ruling class. He regarded the Jews as a separate element, which could never be assimilated, and had observed the movement of dissimilation which had been taking place among the Swabians (the German minority in Hungary) since about 1930. He also had a feeling for social justice, and the effect of all this made him a patron of the Village Explorers, some of whom had been his pupils.

During the late 1930's this intellectual movement of the Village Explorers had come to the fore, participated in by some of the best writers, poets, and politicians of the younger generation. It was a passionate movement, a popularism, for the liberation of the abandoned small peasantry and agricultural proletariat. The fact that most of its representatives were immediate descendants

rejected any revolutionary and alien ideas, Communist or Fascist, and wanted true national reforms based on national traditions and on disciplined Christian aims. They worked out a program which consisted of the following eight points: land reforms; reform of taxation; regulation of agricultural indebtedness; credits for agriculture and industry; development of foreign trade, especially with British, French, and Scandinavian markets; a balanced budget; and, once these were achieved, introduction of secret and general franchise; and a foreign political orientation on Italy.(4) Their movement, officially known as "Reform Generation", wanted to follow the policies of Count Stephen Széchenyi, the great Hungarian reform politician of the first half of the nineteenth century.(5) This meant that they hoped to achieve their ends by parliamentary evolutionary policy, by pure Hungarian patriotism, and through a more or less English type democracy. This group came into power in 1932 and carried out its program with partial success during the coming years.

The forces which had governed Hungary through the reconstruction era were now in the opposition, of which they formed, for all practical purposes, the ultra-Conservative wing. Their recognized leader during the whole period remained Count Bethlen. The other parties — the Legitimists, the Liberals, the Social Democrats, and above all the Jews — found themselves also in opposition to the government, not because of its social program but because the reform movement meant to link up with Germany, according to them Hungary's hereditary enemy. Moreover, it was not just Germany; it was Nazi Germany. To these parties, of course, Nazism was a touch of horror. They argued that Nazism in Hungary was not only abominable itself but the greatest threat to the nation's independence, since the Nazi-minded Hungarians

---

4 U. S., For. Rel., Department of State, 864.00/827.

5 Count Stephen Széchenyi (1791—1860) is often called "the Greatest Hungarian". He was a political opponent of Louis Kossuth. Széchenyi wanted reforms by evolution and not by revolution.

were Germany's "Fifth Column". In addition, they were convinced (as were such men as Bethlen and Regent Horthy himself, the one man in Hungary who understood the importance of sea power) that Germany's methods would end in provoking a war in which she would be defeated. Thus, they were extremely anxious to avoid any too-close link with Germany; no fate could be worse, they argued, than to again suffer defeat and dismemberment as Germany's ally.

The Opposition Front, as they called themselves, was of course an exceedingly heterogeneous body, whose various components held very different views on social problems and on the extent to which resistance to Germany could or should be carried. By the autumn of 1937, an attempt was being made to find a common basis for opposition to Hitler. The last hope was some kind of a restoration of the vanished Austro-Hungarian Monarchy. It seemed that Western democracies also favored the plan. The leader of the Legitimist Party, Count Antal Sigray, organized a rally in a little city in West Hungary. The leaders of all the bourgeois opposition parties attended, and all of them came out openly in favor of Legitimism. The Social Democrats could hardly participate openly in the rally, but at a meeting of theirs a week later their leaders made an unmistakable reference to it when they said that "if the Socialists were confronted with the choice between dictatorship and constitutional freedom, we should unhesitatingly choose the latter, whatever the name which the form of Government guaranteeing it might bear".(6)

As a general rule the opposition parties became more and more conservative and although some of them had been fighting for social justice earlier, they now seemed to be trying to prevent the government from carrying on the much needed reforms. As a consequence of this policy, their popularity decreased. Yet their work was not useless: since there were many influential politicians among them, they were able to prevent Hungary from throwing

6 Macartney, October Fifteenth, I, 183.

of the racially purest classes of the country gave their struggle additional momentum. Although they did not form a united political party, they called themselves the "March Front" (an allusion to the revolution of 1848) and agreed in their conviction that without the liquidation of the feudal system there was no hope for Hungary. They produced an astonishingly large, many-sided, and enthusiastic literature, which is worthy of careful consideration even from an international point of view.(7)

This literature can best be characterized as the expression of Hungarian **narodniki**, because it had a striking resemblance to the more moderate wing of those Russian agrarian socialist who "went to the people" in the second half of the nineteenth century in order to rebuild the old Tsarist structure on a popular basis. They regarded the Russian peasantry as the only source of salvation in a society where there was no conscious bourgeois class or enlightened intelligentia. Race, soil, and the anti-capitalistic traditions of Russia's genuinely popular forces were preponderant factors in the formulation of their doctrine. The characteristic at-

---

7 In this note the author of this study can refer only from memory to the most influential works, all of them published in Budapest during the 1930's: Ödön Málnási, A Magyar Menzet Öszinte Története (A Sincere History of the Hungarian Nation); Gyula Illyés, Puszták Népe (The People of the Prairies); Imre Kovács, A Néma Forradalom (The Silent Revolution); Géza Féja, A Viharsarok (The Tempest Corner); Mátyás Matolcsy, Uj Élet a Magyar Földön (New Life on the Hungarian Soul); Zoltán Szabó, A Tardi Helyzet (Situation at Tard); Ferenc Erdei, Futóhomok (Flying Sand); Péter Veres, Számadás (My Account); Joseph Darvas, A Legynagyobb Magyar Falú (The Biggest Hungarian Village); L. Lipták, Egy Veszedelmes Nép (A Dangerous People); A. Németh, A Naposabb Oldalon (On the More Sunny Side); Gyula Ortutay, Parasztságunk Élete (Life of Our Peasantry); A Viharsarok a Biróság Elött (The Tempest Corner before the Court), edited by the "March Front"; A Néma Forradalom a Biróság és a Parlament Elött (The Silent Revolution before the Court and Parliament), edited by the Brotherhood of Service and Writing.

197

titude of the Hungarian Village Explorers was similar. They believed in the Messianic role of the Hungarian peasantry. Their whole literature was a flaming protest against existing conditions.(8)

Besides these movements described above, there were the extreme Right Radicals, generally known as the "Arrow Cross".(9) This movement claimed to draw much of its inspiration from either German Nazism or Italian Fascism. Of these two, Nazism was by far the more popular model because of the anti-Semitic ingredient in its doctrine. But it should be emphasized that the whole strength and appeal of Right Radical extremism did not consist exclusively in anti-Semitism. Their objection to the Government Party was not that it was insufficiently anti-Semitic but that it was insufficiently radical in social matters. It had proclamed war on the big estates and on big capital, but it had not lived up to its promises on land reform and on the secret franchise; and even had it fulfilled all its pledges, it was still a middle-class party, still the embodiment of the old ruling clique. These far-rightists would have been Communists had Communism not been taboo in Hungary.(10)

---

8 For details see Oscar Jászi, "Feudal Agrarianism in Hungary", **Foreign Affaires**, XVI, No. 4 (1938), 714—18.

9 Some of these groups had begin by adopting as a symbol the German Hakenkreuz. When the government forbade the use of foreign political symbols, the device was changed to one of two crossed arrows, each barbed at both ends.

10 For instance, the program of the Hungarian National Socialist Party, founded by Zoltán Meskó in 1934, held clearly Marxist ideas in its program. It demanded among other things: the introduction of compulsory labor for all and the right to work for all who want to work; limitation of private property and the abolition and prosecution of all revenue not derived from work and labor; the sharing by workers (employees) in the profits of enterprises; nationalization of the credit system; nationalization of all big enterprises and mines; nationalization of exports and imports; planed production for the whole country; a general and national economic organization under State control; ownership of land by those who actually cultivated it. The Hungarian National Socialist Party was one of the so-called "Arrow Cross' parties. **U. S., For. Rel., Department of State**, GRC 864.00/798.

The extreme Right Radicals were not united even among themselves. They tended to form separate little political parties under various leaders, the most important of whom, in the late 1930's and early 1940's was Major Ferenc Szálasy. Their members comprised only some 5 to 6 percent of the lower house until October 15, 1944, when they took over the country in a **coup d'etat** supported by German troops.

The real struggle for power which went on in Hungary during the early 1930's was the struggle between the two great groups of the Government Party — Bethlen's Conservative-Liberals and the "Reform Generation". An agricultural crisis, industrial unemployment, the dismissal of large numbers of government and civilian employees, and the hopeless situation in which the country's youth found itself had all created a revolutionary intellectual atmosphere. This situation caused the fall of Bethlen's Conservative-Liberals; the government was assumed by the Reform Generation, whose acknowledged leader was General Julius Gömbös.(11)

Gömbös' Prime Ministership had been awaited with many sanguine hopes and many anxious fears. Both hopes and fears were to prove unfounded. It was Gömbös humanly tragic destiny never to see the effects of his work. Nevertheless, if Gömbös could not build, he could plan and lay foundations by which the whole future course of Hungarian policy, both international and domestic, was irrevocably decided. His enemies afterwards accused Gömbös of having delivered over Hungary to the German power. So far as his own intentions were concerned, nothing is more untrue! If that was the ultimate effect of his policy, it was the result of the dilemma of the inter-war Hungarian policy, described above. No Hungarian in the inter-war period was more intractably hostile to any hint of danger to Hungary's independence than was Gömbös,

---

11 Julius Gömbös, 1886—1936, one of the most prominent leaders of the counter-revolution in 1919 and a convinced anti-Habsburg, served as minister of defense in the cabinets of Bethlen (1921—1931) and Julius Károlyi (1913—1932). He was appointed premier in September, 1932; he died in office in October, 1936.

and interference by Germany was no more welcome to him than interference by anyone else.(12)

Gömbös definitely rejected any compromise with the Successor States, terming it defeatist policy. He also rejected the alternative solution of Habsburg Legitimism, which he believed to be more dangerous to Hungary than Pan-Germanism could ever become.

Gömbös' political creed was centered around two main points: anti-Habsburgism and racialism. Around these two poles he found room for a genuine wish to improve the social conditions of his people, whom he regarded as the exploited victims of Jewish financiers and Habsburg-tainted landlords. His foreign political program was a surprising theory at that time, and made him the father of the "Berlin-Rome Axis".(13) In 1927, under the imminent effect of the Italo-Hungarian Treaty of Friendship and of Mussolini's consequent public sponsoring of Hungarian revisionism, Gömbös had conceived a vision of an "Axis" which was to consist of a new semi-Fascist Hungary, Fascist Italy, and Nazi Germany. These three states, linked by kindred ideologies, were to help each other to realize their national objectives and thereafter to exercise a sort of joint leadership of Europe, a better Europe, purged of Bolshevism and its shadows. Germany was to annex Austria (except for the Burgenland, which she would restore to Hungary), allaying Italy's fears by guaranteeing the Brenner frontier. "If that can be brought about, Italian and German nationalism will change the map of Europe".(14)

---

12 This unorthodox interpretation of Gömbös' character and policy is based on Macartney's **October Fifteenth**. However the author of this study found the same, or an even more favorable interpretation of Gömbös' character and policy in the contemporary reports of the Legation of the United States at Budapest. See **U. S., For. Rel., Department of State**, documents 864.00/320 — 864.00/366, 864.00/775 — 864.00/803, 864.00/943.

13 For details, see Macartney, **October Fifteenth**, I, 75—78 and 136—54.

14 Lajos Marschalkó, **Gömbös Gyula, a fajvédő vezér** (Julius Gömbös, the race-protecting Leader) (Budapest: n.p., n.d.), p. 39.

The basic idea of this plan was that the three like-minded States should make such small adjustments between themselves as would eliminate all possible causes of friction, and then form a common front to realize their respective ambitions against the other world. According to Gömbös' calculation, history proved that the status quo camp would not yield except to force. Making such an alliance, Hungary, as a third party, would keep the balance against Germany for Italy's sake.

The tragic fallacy in Gömbös' ideas is that it never once occured to him that either Germany or even Italy might have ideas of their own about East-Central Europe. He believed that a common interest in overthrowing the Peace Treaties was all that was required for such an alliance.

When Gömbös came into office, one member of the proposed Axis was in any case lacking, for Hitler was not yet in power in Germany. But Mussolini was there, and Gömbös took the opportunity in the autumn of 1932 to visit Rome. But it did not bring the Axis nearer, for when Hitler did come into power, the only early move which he made in East-Central Europe was to start an agitation in Austria. As Mussolini by no means accepted Gömbös' Axis doctrine but regarded Austrian idependence as a vital interest of Italy's, the first result of Gömbös' policy was that Hungary was drawn into a bloc, composed of Italy, Hungary, and Austria, the chief reason for which was precisely to thwart Hitler's ambitions. If, in the negotiations which began at the end of 1934 between Italy and France, France had been able to persuade her allies of the Little Entente to make any concessions of substance to Hungary, Hungary might yet have found herself a member of a new European combination directed against Germany. The Franco-Italian negotiations of 1934 failed, however, leaving behind them, as their first fruit, the Franco-Soviet and Czechoslovak-Soviet Packs of Mutual Assistance, and were followed by Mussolini's quarrel with the West and his announcement of the formation of the "Rome-Berlin Axis". (15)

By this time Hitler had occupied the Rhineland and it was clear that Germany would soon be able, if she were willing, to perform the role which Gömbös had assigned to her. But by now it was also clear that the situation created by Germany's emergence was nothing as simple as Gömbös had imagined. Hitler made it clear that he had no intention of restoring Hungary's historic frontiers. He told Gömbös, when Gömbös visited the Führer in June, 1933, that nothing should stop him from annexing Austria; sooner or later he meant to dismember Czechoslovakia; Hungary might, if she would, take her share in the partition of Czehoslovakia. That was all Hungary would get out of Germany. As regards Yugoslavia and Rumania, Hiter's instructions to Hungary were to keep her hands off.

---

15 The failure of the Franco-Italian negotiations ruined the last hope of a Danubian unification. What Laval and Mussolini were after was an anti-German front on the Danube. It would be done by some frontier readjustment and some kind of a Habsburg restoration. The Little Entente, however, refused to hear any mention of the revision of the Versailles Treaties and was strongly against a Habsburg restoration. Instead of this, it demanded that both Italy and Hungary should join with it in a Pact of Mutual Assistance on the status quo of Versailles. Hungary rejected this plan. She was afterwards widely accused of having torpedoed the plan of the anti-German front. It may, however be remarked that if she sinned, she did not sin alone. Austria also would not accept an anti-German combination and in the next year negotiated her Pack with Germany based on Austria's acknowledging herself to be a "German State". Yugoslavia and Rumania also were taking steps toward Germany. They made it clear that while the Little Entente held against Hungary, it did not bind them to any action against Germany, with which they desired good relations.

The Franco—Soviet and the Czechoslovak—Soviet Pacts of Mutual Assistance were signed in May, 1935.

Mussolini annouced the formation of the "Berlin—Rome Axis", using the word, on November 1, 1936. Gömbös had died three weeks earlier.

202

It seems that Gömbös did not accept Hitler's plan in full. He said that Hungarian revisionist policy must aim at three objectives: the unification of all Magyars, the safeguarding of the nation's economic interests, and the strategic security. He showed Hitler a line on a map which took in all the preponderantly Magyar areas adjacent to the Trianon frontier, plus the Székely districts (Hungarians in East Transylvania) with a corridor through Central Transylvania.(16)

In spite of this, Gömbös seems to have scored a considerable personal success with Hitler, who liked him as he liked few Hungarians and was prepared to help him where he could do so without detriment to his own plans. He promised him not to make his position difficult at home by stirring up the extreme Right Radicals or the German minorities, to supply him with arms, and to give favorable treatment to Hungarian exports.

Germany's trade with Hungary now rose rapidly. Germany began to take a high proportion of Hungary's agricultural produce, especially livestock and industrial plants, and almost monopolized the exports of the newly-developing bauxite industry of which she was taking 96 percent in 1937. She exported to Hungary chiefly finished products, but also coal, coke, and tar derivatives. It was not only quantitatively that Germany thus occupied a dominant position in Hungary's economy. She interlocked Hungary's economy with her own in such fashion that many Hungarian factories would simply have been unable to carry on production without German raw materials, machines, or machine tools. The Hungarian factories carried out certain processes which had to be either begun or finished in Germany.(17)

Germany's financial and economic relations with Hungary, as with other countries in East Europe, now added powerfully to her

---

16 See the map, U. S., For. Rel., Department of State, 711.64119/73 GC. The line closely resembled that proposed by Lord Rothermere.

17 For details see Antonin Bach, The Danube Basin and the German Economic Sphere (New York: Columbia University Press, 1943).

influence, political as well as economic. But the Hungarians could not altogether reject this opportunity of trade relations which brought them many advantages: a regular and assured market for Hungary's most important exports and, in return, cheap goods of reasonable quality adapted to her needs. The decrease in unemployment and the revival of industrial production was related to the trade with Germany and increased the popularity of Germany among the workmen. Germany was even more popular among the agricultural laborers, many of whom now began to go to Germany for seasonal work. They were well treated and well paid, and often returned ardent Nazis.(18)

Gömbös certainly never gave up his aspiration to create a one-party corporate State. Nevertheless, those who expected him to become a dictator were disappointed. His freedom of action was strongly limited, and his time in office was too short to justify either the hopes or the fears which the news of his appointment evoked. First, Regent Horthy tied Gömbös' hands on appointing him: Gömbös was not to dissolve Parliament, which meant that he had to work with a body made by Bethlen, his conservative predecessor. The Regent also made Gömbös promise not to introduce either a drastic land reform or anti-Semitic legislation. Besides this, the world depression, which had swept him into office and had seemed to him to call for revolutionary action, turned out to make any such action impossible. For the crisis, as it affected Hungary, was one of credit. No Hungarian Government could have followed any policy to which its creditors objected strongly. And the financial powers to be placated were the City of London, Wall Street, and France. The pressures exerted by these various factors outside the country limited Hungary's freedom of action at home, since Hungary's creditors were not going to relax their claims against a Government which allowed itself to imitate Nazism. Furthermore, the Government was also indebted to the big

18 See "Report on the Hungarian Arrow Cross Movement", U. S., For. Rel., Department of State, 864.00/867.

Hungarian banks, and the banks, which were almost purely under Jewish control, were not going to make things easy for anyone who played with anti-Semitism.

This situation placed the whole Hungarian internal development on a path quite different from that expected by many of Gömbös followers. After his appointment, Gömbös started secret negotiations with the leaders of the Jewish community, and a protocol was signed between the leaders of that community and the Government, under which the Jews recognized and approved Gömbös' progressive policy, while the Government promised to carry that policy through without violence and without detriment to the Jews' material interests. The agreement did not kill anti-Semitism in Hungary. But it should be recorded that both parties to the agreement kept it punctiliously. During his time in office Gömbös abstained from any government measure injuring the Jews directly or indirectly. Even the Government press never wrote in an anti-Semitic vein. On the other hand, the Jewish community realized that the best way to kill the dangerous spread of Nazism was to introduce social reforms. The dignitaries of the Masonic Lodges, which had been officially dissolved in 1919, held the same opinion.(19)

Having made these agreements, Gömbös launched a far-reaching political and social program, recapitulating it in a statement of ninety-five points. Each point dealt with a different aspect of Hungary's problems. It was apparent that he wanted a gradual reform not only of the Hungarian political organization but also of the social and moral forces of the nation. Not only had he ignored the aristocracy in the formation of his cabinet (Gömbös' cabinet was the first one of the entire Hungarian history, except Béla Kun's, which had not a single count among its members), but he appealed directly to the people of Hungary as a mass: "Nowadays

---

19 See Legation's dispatch: "Conversation with Dr. Kiss, the foreign editor of Pester Lloyd, one of the leading Jewish papers in Budapest," U. S., For. Rel., Department of State, 864.00/366.

it is the worker who belong to the 'historic class' of the country".(20) His speeches, furthermore, made it plain that even though he believed in a strongly centralized government under firm guidance he was opposed to unnecessary political restrictions and favored giving the people power. He took up the cause of the working classes and orders were issued authorizing the introduction of the eight-hour day and forty-eight hour week and the establishment of a system of minimum wages in industry. Furthermore, the general improvement in the world situation did not exclude Hungary. Employment was better and production was improving. Agriculture was prosperous and the national income was rising again.(21)

With respect to agricultural problems, the government advocated a greater diversification of crops and made specific suggestions with a view to facilitating this work by experiment stations and marketing organizations. The government accomplished, furthermore, a large amount of useful work in many other fields, including rural housing and health, afforestation and irrigation. In addition, the Land Settlement Bill provided for the settlement of 37,000 landless families on about 600,000 acres, to be taken from large estates.(22)

Gömbös appeared to be democratizing the government by removal of some of the higher permanent officials in various government departments. These changes strengthened the impression that he wished to end the old system of government by the privileged classes in Hungary and planned instead to give power to representatives chosen from the people at large — particularly the small farmers and townsmen who heretofore had had but little voice in governmental affairs. He introduced three constitutional bills on the extension of the power of the Regent and the Upper House and a franchise reform claiming: "Parliamentarism must continue to live. I stand for the secret ballot. I consider my own

---

20 Ibid., 864.00/320.
21 Ibid., 864.00/778.
22 Ibid.

nation to be mature enough to be given rights which it may freely use because a right which is not freely used is no right at all".(23)

With regard to the German question Gömbös stated that a nation of seventy million would always have a decisive influence upon the problems of the Danubian valley. He stated, furthermore, that Germany's internal policy was not Hungary's concern, but "should a similar regime or political tendency assert itself in Hungary, it is the duty of the government to oppose this tendency".(24)

No wonder such a program conquered many hearts at home and caused a leniency of policy toward Hungary in some foreign countries. Even the American Minister at Budapest enthusiastically reported to his government that "Hungary will in the not too distant future have a government that is truly representative instead of as in the past a government of the nobles, by the nobles, and for the nobles".(25) The American press also showed a lively interest in Hungarian affairs.(26)

The opposition parties at home could hardly object to the reforms, as noted before, but they feared for the future. They strongly believed that Gömbös was only playing for time and, when the moment came, would simply proclaim himself dictator and set up a Fascist State. They even suggested that if the Regent died, Gömbös would proclaim himself Regent and Premier at once, with unlimited power. This moment did not come, however, even if Gömbös had wanted it, for he left Hungary to go to a sanatorium in Munich in September, 1936, and a month later he was dead.

---

23 **Ibid.**, 864.00/803.

24 **Ibid.**

25 **Ibid.**, 864.00/785.

26 See, for instance, **New York Times,** November 19, 1934; December 7, 1934; December 8, 1934; and so on.

The Regent appointed as Gömbös successor Koloman Darányi, who was much more of a conservative than a radical. The opinion generally held both inside and outside Hungary was that his appointment represented an act of resistance to the increasing pressure of Germany in both the foreign and the domestic fields. The Germans chose to great Darányi's appointment with open hostility and the German press attacked mercilessly every weakness of the Hungarian social and political system and her revisionist claims.(27) On the other hand, in spite of all discouraging experiences, Hungary continued, during this period, her pursuit of the friendship of Great Britain and her appeal to the justice of her cause. Repeated statements on these points were made by the Prime Minister and by the Minister for Foreign Affairs; and the Revision League and a newly founded Anglo-Hungarian Society made strenuous efforts to create in England good will towards Hungary and understanding for her cause. A new literature arose in Hungary, published in English, and a political periodical in English, the **Hungarian Quarterly**, was started for the cause of a better understanding of Hungary's problems by the English-speaking world. Even in the United States books appeared to capture more Americans' good will towards Hungarians: books like Edmund Vasváry's **Lincoln's Hungarian Heroes**, dedicated to the President himself.(28)

Hungary at this time refused to leave the League of Nations (although requested by Italy to do so) and, while not pretending to renounce revision against either Czechoslovakia or Rumania, made almost passionate appeals to the United States through diplomatic channels to push England toward Hungary and to bring about an equitable settlement of the Danubian problem by peace-

---

27 See Alfred Rosenberg, "Unterdückte Volker und Revision," **Völkischer Beobachter** (Berlin Daily), November 17, 1936.

28 See Appendix II

ful means.(29) Hungarian diplomats pointed out the central difficulty of Hungarian foreign policy: she had no contrepoints for Germany, and therefore had to submit ultimately to the latter in
everything.(30)

Meantime, an increasing pressure was exercised by Germany
in both the foreign and the domestic fields. The German Government officially took up the cause of the German minority and of
the Right Radicals. Innumerable newspapers and brochures were
produced in Germany and distributed in Hungary via newsvendors.
Lecturers, students, commercial travelers, and an extraordinary
number of tourists overran the country. It was whispered
that the Arrow Cross planned to overthrow the Government. The
Anschluss had further strengthened Germany's hold in Hungary.
It had made the two countries contiguous, thus immensely facilitating German penetration of every kind. It had cut Hungary's
direct line of communications to the West via Austria and Switzerland. It had put Germany in charge of the Austrian economy and

---

29 See the Hungarian diplomatic note to the Secretary of State. It says
among other things:

"...Unfortunately while generally admitted that Hungary received a
'raw deal' at Trianon she had not received in her peaceful efforts to
remedy it any encouragement by the Western Powers.

The latter seemed to have lost sight also of the fact that the ancient
parliamentary form of Government in Hungary has become of late a true
modern democracy and is engaged in a life and death struggle for its
survival.

If the Western democracies helped Hungary to obtain satisfaction of
her reasonable and legitimate aspirations, Hungary would be indebted to
England and France to which she is drawn also by her traditions and
feelings.

If they fail to do so, if they fail to lend a helping hand to this little
country of Hungary struggling to maintain its independence and its popular form of Government as well as its legitimate rights, then it will be
they who have thrown Hungary into the very current against which she
has manfully struggled."

U. S., For. Rel., Department of State, Strictly Confidential File 864.00/920 I/2.
30 Ibid., 864.00/943.

had even transferred to Germany's hands the Austrian economic and financial interests in Hungary. In the spring of 1938 Darányi finally succumbed to the temptation of negotiating secretly with the Arrow Cross and introduced a measure of anti-Jewish legislation. The Regent dismissed nim in favor of Béla Imrédy.

Béla Imrédy was avowedly appointed because he enjoyed the status of being a particular friend of the West, and especially to the City of London. He was named with the specific mission, on the one hand, to strengthen those links, and on the other to take drastic action against the Arrow Cross. Imrédy began well enough. He dissolved the Arrow Cross and arrested its leader, Francis Szálasi, accusing him of conspiracy against the Government. During his term of office came the Munich crisis. While Hungary vehemently pressed her claim to ethnic revision at the expense of Czechoslovakia, she also made every effort, even at the risk of grievously affronting Hitler, to get her demands satisfied peacefully, with the assent and approval of the West. Unfortunately for the Western-minded Hungarian politicians, England and France showed little understanding for their cause, and although they eventually sanctioned in principle the settlement of Hungary's claims, they washed their hands of the details, leaving Germany and Italy to arbitrate when difficulties arose. This convinced Imrédy that it was futile to appeal to the West against Germany, and when Hitler seemed inclined to take the Czechs' side, he rushed to bid for his favor by promising him international cooperation and a right-wing program in Hungary; he promised Hungary's adherence to the Anti-Comintern pact and her resignation from the League of Nations. At home, Imrédy introduced a new and more drastic anti-Jewish law. Hungary slipped a stage rightward. This slide was quickly checked when the anti-Radical forces succeeded in bringing about Imrédy's fall in February of 1939 and his replacement by Count Paul Teleki, who was an anti-Nazi and a convinced Westerner in international politics.

During this period, as was mentioned before, the United States was nothing more than an observer on the political field of Europe and, consequently, in Hungarian affairs too. The economic relations between the two countiies, however, were beyond expectation. The Standard Electric Company of Budapest, for instance, was the largest of I. T. and T.'s manufacturing subsidiaries in Eastern Europe. Standard Budapest employed some 3,000 workers in the manufacture of telephone, telegraph, and radio equipment. In turn it controlled a company known as **Telefongyár**, which employed some 1,400 workers in the manufacture of cables, air brakes, railroad signals, and electrical components, and a small company known as **Dial**, which rented and maintained private telephone exchanges.(31)

Far more important was the discovery of oil in Hungary. The presence of oil and natural gas in western Hungary was known for many years before European Gas and Electric Company (Eurogasco), an affiliate of Standard Oil Company (New Jersey), commenced exploration and development there in 1934. Surface seepages similar to those which led to the discovery of oil in Rumania were prevalent. However, the Anglo-Persian Oil Company had spent a good deal of money on surveys and borings in the 1920's but had never found petroleum in paying quantities and had retired from the field after serious financial losses, claiming that oil in worthwhile amounts did not exist in Hungary. American and Hungarian petroleum geologists did not agree with this view and their opinion was shared by experts of the European Gas and Electric Company, an American company incorporated in the state of Delaware.

Eurogasco's Hungarian concessions, as stipulated in the contract between it and the Hungarian Minister of Finance dated June 8, 1933, comprised about 8,000,000 acres and covered all of Hungary west and south of the Danube River (that part of the country known as Trans-Danubia), an equal area in size to the states of Connecticut and Massachusetts combined. This contract covered exploration rights, and in addition provided that, in case oil was

---

31 Robert Vogeler, **I Was Stalin's Prisoner** (New York: Columbia Press, 1951), p. 23.

discovered, Eurogasco would form a new company under Hungarian law to handle production, transportation, and marketing.(32)

The contract clearly stipulated the rate at which wells should be drilled and required drilling to be increased, in case of discovery, until the oil requirements of Hungary were met. Other clauses in the contract provided for the employment of Hungarian nationals and the payment to the Hungarian government of a 15 percent royalty on all crude oil, natural gasoline, butane, and propane, and a 12 percent royalty on all natural gas produced. The contract was to run for forty years, beginning with the formation of the new company, and it contained a provision for extension.(33)

Upon the conclusion of the contract negotiations Eurogasco began an energetic oil exploration program. In 1937 these efforts resulted in the discovery of Hungary's first commercial oil well, at Lispe in the southwest section of the concession near the Yugoslav border. In accordance with the contract a new company was thereupon incorporated in Hungary to produce, transport, and market the production. This company, **Magyar Amerikai Olajpari Részvénytársaság** (Hungarian-American Oil Company, Limited), better known as "MAORT", was entirely owned by the Standard Oil Company of New Jersey.

With the incorporation of MAORT by Standard, a fullscale drilling program was inaugurated. A new and more promising producing field was discovered, and intensive exploration of the producing strata revealed an extremely important oil property. Between 1937 and December, 1941, MAORT produced 6,595,862 barrels (851, 720 tons) of crude. Production increased from 288,423 barrels (37, 254 tons) in 1938 to 3,258,977 barrels (421,661 tons) in 1941. In those four years MAORT became one of the largest and most important industrial undertakings in Hungary. The MAORT-owned wells produced 5,117,155 barrels (665,201 tons) of crude oil in 1942; 6,425,718

---

32 **Standard Oil Company** (New Jersey) and **Oil Production in Hungary by MAORT** (U.S.A.: European Gas & Electric Company, 1949) p. 1.
33 **Ibid.**, p. 2.

barrels (837,711 tons) in 1943; and 6,204,065 barrels (809,969 tons) in 1944.(34)

The Standard Oil Company sought to obtain as much labor and machinery as possible from Hungary. In 1939, only nine of some seven hundred employees were Americans. Those Americans were specialists for whom Hungarian substitutes of sufficient experience were not available. However, the Company was constantly training Hungarians to do even the most technical work and two engineers were sent to the United States for training with the Standard Oil Company. (One of these was stated by Standard to be the best engineer who had ever been sent to them from any part of the world.) The Company also started a school, in order to improve the theoretical and technical knowledge of its personnel. Wages of employees were higher than those paid generally in Hungary. The Company ordered machinery from Hungarian concerns, several of which had benefitted extensively from this policy. The Company also paid about $250,000 for railroad transportation per month in 1939, and this figure grew with the production.

The Company, besides improving the country's economic standard, did a good deal for the social and cultural benefits of its employees. Many houses, a sports club, a swiming pool, and a sports field were built for the workers just before World War II started. The Company had also undertaken medical service for the employees and their families, transportation to and from the nearest town, the construction of schools for the children of employees, and other such services which one finds so often in large American works of this nature.(35)

The carbon dioxide well which was discovered by the Company near the Hungarian German border was used for the manufacture of dry ice, which was sold by the Company to a Hungarian

34 Ibid., p. 3.

35 The standard of living of the MAORT's workers was certainly higher than that of workers on similar large projects in Hungary. The author, born and raised in that part of Hungary, can state this from his own experience.

agricultural cooperative organization which had been developing the exportation of frozen agricultural products to England and other countries.

Up to World War II, there had been no difficulties with the Hungarian authorities, and the Company was well pleased with the cooperation which it received. When the war came in 1939 (Hungary was neutral until 1941), the question of protection of the oil fields was raised. As all wells were flowing wells, the derricks could be dismounted when the flow began. The wellhead was then placed underground in a bomb-proof cellar and nothing was visible from the surface or from the air. Bombing from airplanes was virtually impossible, as the pipelines and wells were invisible and were spread over a considerable area.

When World War II broke out, the New York office of the Company was somewhat in the dark regarding the exact situation of MAORT. The uncertainty of the European situation made long-time planning difficult. The discovery and large production of high-grade oil in Hungary indicated to the United States that perhaps this discovery would be comparable to one of the most important American fields. Budapest became more than just a listening post of diplomacy, since Hungary was now one of the most important business-partners of the United States in Eastern Europe.

For Hungary, the acquisition of wealth afforded the economic prosperity essential to a successful Government. Possession of petroleum itself made possible the advance of industry, so assiduously developed since World War I, by providing cheaper industrial fuel, surfacing for much-needed roads, motive power for transportation by air, water, rail, and highway; exportation of oil and products permitted the purchase of essential raw materials. The resulting prosperity permitted the Government to draw the vitality necessary to surmount its insistent problem of accumulating capital and maintaining credit in order that she might gain economic solidity and to pay her national debt.

From an international point of view, the vision of possibility broadened. Hungary became a petroleum competitor of Poland

and Rumania, and she became of much greater interest to European countries which had little or no petroleum production. Furthermore, the Hungarian fields were nearer by rail to the great European Powers requiring oil for maritime and naval purposes than were the Eastern Galician and Rumanian fields. In general, the possession of petroleum made Hungary a vastly more important country both to its friends and its foes. The country's situation was rendered more dangerous with added treasure to defend. Next to possessing oil within its boundaries, a nation's best advantage is to obtain control of production elsewhere. During World War II, neither Hungary nor the United States were able to defend the Hungarian oil deposit, the first being too weak, the second being too far away to perform this job. First German, later Russian troops, occupied and controlled MAORT's oil fields.(36)

---

36 In 1948, the Rusian controlled Hungarian Government seized the Standard Oil Company's whole property, the MAORT, bringing an accusation of sabotage against it. The book value of the MAORT properties, calculated at the time of seizure and including plant facilities and money owed by the Hungarian government, was approximately $20,000,000. This does not include the value of crude oil and other related products which MAORT had discovered but had not yet produced.

In the ten years 1937—1948, the Hungarian government received free of charge under the terms of the contract about 6,000,000 barrels of oil worth millions of dollars. During that time the government also received about $6,000,000 in royalties, taxes, and direct charges from the American company. MAORT's payroll in 1947 was $3,041,000. In 1948 it employed 3,800 Hungarian nationals, whose jobs ranged from laborers to vice-president and general manager.

Although the Hungarian government received millions in revenue, MAORT's stockholders received dividends of only $206,000. All profits except the single dividend mentioned here were invested in the expansion of the properties. For details see MAORT, **Standard Oil Company and Oil Production in Hungary.**

CHAPTER X

THE LOST GAME:
THE DIPLOMACY OF WORLD WAR II
1939—1944

The replacement of Béla Imrédy by Count Paul Teleki as Minister President of Hungary on February 16, 1939, meant that Hungarian policy was going to alter its course once more. Furthermore, as Minister President, Count Paul Teleki became one of the most important and memorable persons of inter-war Hungarian history.

Count Teleki was a member of a famous and historic Transylvanian family, many of whose members had played a large part in Hungarian history.(1) Teleki's own interests were always primarily academic. Although he had entered Parliament as early as 1905 (when he was only twenty-six years of age), he had even then devoted most of his time to his special study of geography, and particularly cartography, in which fields he earned an international reputation. In 1920 he devoted himself to preparing Hungary's case for the peace negotiations, in the form of a series of maps, statistics, and treatises which were in a class by themselves, from the point of view of learning, among all the material

---

1 One member of the family, Michael Teleki, played an important role in the history of Transylvania in the seventeenth century; another, Ladislas Teleki, during the revolution of 1848.

216

submitted to the Peace Conference in any of its phases. In 1920 he was asked to serve as his country's Foreign Minister and soon after as Minister President; but he resigned in 1921, devoting the next eighteen years primarily to teaching at the University as Professor of Geography but also to a number of public activities. He was founder and President of the Hungarian Sociographical Institute, Director of the Cartographical Institute, Rector of the University of Economics, President of a score of societies, and — the occupation nearest his heart — Chief Scout of Hungary. With all these interests he found time to travel widely in Europe, America, and Asia. Among other things, he served on the League of Nations Commission for determining the frontiers between Turkey and Iraq.

Count Teleki was a man of very wide and deep culture. Besides an acknowledged master of his own profession he was also deeply read in the history and sociography of many lands. He spoke half a dozen languages fluently and was an extremely brilliant lecturer. He was a very devout Catholic and quite indifferent to riches, living on his professional stipend. It was among his students and his Scouts that Teleki was at his happiest and best. And it was, perhaps, only here that he found complete spiritual satisfaction; for believing as he did in the powers of reason and of the spirit, and having a strong faith in the efficacy of personal contact and example, he held that the most direct and effective way in which he could serve his country was by communicating his vision to the younger generation and inspiring them with it.

Teleki loved his country and his fellow-countrymen with a deep and sincere passion and lived only for their service. In his social and political philosophy he held history to teach that no political formation could survive in the Middle Danube Basin unless its frontiers coincided with the natural frontiers of that area. Nature, by creating that area a geographical unity, had imposed on it the necessity of political unity, and any attempt to give it any other form of political organization, being contrary to nature, carried the seeds of its own destruction within it.

Although holding the view that Hungary must be a politically unitary state, he was absolutely and sincerely opposed to any aggressive or unjust treatment of the non-Magyar population, or any attempt to Magyarise them forcibly. He took great pains to ensure that the treatment of the national minorities should be as he wished it, personally selecting enlightened officials for the minorities areas, instructing them most carefully in their duties, making tours of inspection and even organizing a network of independent private observers, most often priests and Scouts, who had orders to report to him secretly and directly any cases in which the conduct of the authorities was such as to give the minorities cause for complaint.(2)

More idealistic than many of his contemporaries, Teleki saw that the problem of existence for Hungary, and for the Hungarian people, was not simply one of recovering lost territories but also of defending what remained against further dangers. He seemed to have been relatively little impressed by the fear of Pan-Slav imperialism. He abhorred Bolshevism, mainly on account of its Godless character; yet he does not seem to have regarded Russia as seriously threatening Hungary's national existence. But he was impressed by the fear of the danger presented to Hungary by the expansive force of Germany. While he saw that only Germany could or would break the Little Entente, he also regarded Germany as a danger to the very existence of the Hungarian peope, a danger which was ultimately more formidable than that presented by any other state. He had a peculiar dread of seeing Hungary encircled by Germany and squeezed to death between the two arms of German expansion—the one running north, the other south. He thought it essential, if Hungary was to live, to cut these lines, or keep them cut. It was largely this consideration which made him press so strongly for a new policy for Central Europe. He saw a solution to the problems of that area in the formation of a Central European and Balkan bloc guaranteed by Britain,

---

2 Kovrig, **Hungrian Social Policies, 1920—1945**, p. 177.

France, and the United States and stretching from Finland to Turkey. This bloc, he thought, must be anti-Bolshevik; and yet it would be to Russia's interest that it should be formed, for it was the only means of defending the small states from German aggression, and it would be Russia's best protection against German attack.

For the purpose of a Central European and Balkan bloc, Teleki strongly advocated a policy of friendship with Poland and Yugoslavia, even at the cost of sacrificing part of Hungary's revisionist claims. It was his hope to link Hungary with these two states in a North-South "Axis" which would form a barrier at once against Germany and against Russia. Furthermore, he believed Hungary could very easily come to agreement with the Bulgars and the Turks. Teleki was even prepared to offer Rumania a reasonable compromise. Teleki left out Czechoslovakia because he was confident that time would bring about the collapse of the Czechoslovak state. Furthermore, he would never trust Eduard Benes. Once he told one of his friends: "Everything that man touched became a source of catastrophe".(3)

Besides fearing Germany, Teleki detested Nazism, which he regarded as only one degree less satanic than Bolshevism, and far more dangerous to Hungary, since the attraction exerted by it on the politically significant elements in Hungary was so much stronger.

Not all aspects of Western culture were to his taste, but he saw in the West the main repository of that Christian culture to which Hungary also was an heir. He also shared Horthy's view that in a conflict between Germany and the West, Germany would be defeated. Both sympathy and calculation therefore made him an "Anglophile", and he was logical enough to apply his conclusions to the question of the revision of the Peace Treaty. He was convinced that it would be fatal for Hungary to associate herself with Germany for revision's sake, since any gains which could be represen-

3 Nicholas Kállay, **Hungarian Premier** (New York: Columbia University Press, 1954), p. 251.

ted as acquired by German help would only be taken away a few years later as a gift from the Axis. In his revisionist campaigns he therefore concentrated on appealing to the West, and when the crisis came he sought, in fact, to claim no more than he thought the West would approve.

Immediately on taking office, Teleki sent a telegram to London to assure the Foreign Office that "although Hungary's geographical and political situation compelled her to cooperate loyally with Germany up to a point, the Hungarian Government attached great importance to the understanding and support of the British Government and would never do anything to injure the interests of Great Britain".(4)

Early in Teleki's period of office came the completion of the dismemberment of Czechoslovakia and, during this period, Hungary's foreign political activities consisted of diplomatic preparations for the recovery of Carpatho-Ruthenia. Teleki attached the utmost importance to the recovery of that area because a common Hungarian-Polish border was an essential link in his guiding political concept of a North-South Axis. Although he was anxious to keep the good will of the Western Powers and to give them no excuse to brand Hungary as Germany's accomplice, yet not even for the sake of their good will was he prepared to renounce Ruthenia. Nevertheless, the difficult position of the Hungarian minority in Ruthenia and the impossible geographical and economic effects for both Hungary and Ruthenia were explained to London, Paris, and Washington, all of which showed understanding. The British parliamentary Undersecretary of State for Foreign Affairs, R. A. Butler, explained on February 17, 1939, to the Hungarian envoy, George Barcza, that, in his opinion, Great Britain and France had committed a mistake in not supporting the establishment of a common Hungarian-Polish frontier at the Munich conference. Czechoslovakia, he said, became a German colony after Munich. Thus the attachment of Ruthenia to Hungary would have been in accord-

---

4 Macartney, **October Fifteenth**, I, 331.

ance with British interests. By the same act German expansion toward the Ukraine and the Rumanian oil fields would have been checked. Butler pointed out that it was difficult for him to understand the political blindness which had overlooked these facts. A few days later Sir Alexander Cadogan, permanent Undersecretary of State for Foreign Affairs, stated to Barcza that he had recently studied the Ruthenian problem and had become convinced that the vital interest of the Ruthenian people demanded their re-attachment to Hungary; irrespective of such local interests, the interest of the great powers and European peace demanded that the German push to the East should be barred by a common Hungarian-Polish frontier. He recognized that it would have been to the French-British interest to attach Ruthenia to Hungary and that this interest still existed.(5)

The first American reaction was hostile toward Hungary. William C. Bullitt, Undersecretary of State, sent a sharply formulated telegram to the American Minister at Budapest instructing him: "Find a way to inform the Regent, Teleki, and other Hungarian leaders regarding the evolution of thought in the United States concerning acts of aggression as well as to express the personal hope of the President that Hungary will not again be so unfortunate as to find herself on the side which wins the early battles but loses the war".(6) Having been informed by the Hungarian Government that the occupation of Ruthenia was against Germany's will, the Department of State showed a better understanding and heeded the warnings of the event. Bullitt's message even offered some help against German pressure. "I believe that the best elements of the country (Hungary) will strongly resist being dragged into war by Germany. I am of the opinion that anything that can be done to strengthen them in this determination would prove helpful in the general interest".(7)

---

5 Stephen D. Kertész, **Diplomacy in a Whirlpool** (Notre Dame: University of Notre Dame Press, 1953), p. 44.

6 U. S., **For. Rel., Department of State,** 864.00/954.

7 **Ibid.,** 864.00/954, Sec. I.

The occupation of Ruthenia (now a part of the Soviet Union) on March 15, 1939, was carried out without the knowledge and counsel of Germany and very much against her wishes. It was Poland which urged the establishment of a common Hungarian-Polish frontier, partly in order to prevent the German army, which had entered Slovakia, from moving far east into the back of endangered Poland, and partly because she realized the importance of Teleki's North-South Axis plan. Teleki's plan could never become fact. Nevertheless, the usefulness and importance of this Hungarian move was fully justified by subsequent events when, after the German attack against Poland, Hungary prevented the German troops from crossing this strategic territory and opened up the Ruthenian frontier to more than a hundred thousand soldiers of the Polish Army. These men were well received in Hungary and all but some thirty thousand clandestinely joined the armies of the Western democracies. Polish flyers participated in comparatively large numbers in the famous Battle of Britain in the autumn of 1940, a battle which saved England from German invasion.[8]

After the outbreak of the Second World War, the Hungarian Government issued a proclamation which amounted to a declaration of neutrality. Prime Minister Teleki sought to maintain a non-belligerent status and, in the face of the growing German influence, some measure of independence for Hungary. But German-Russian collaboration gradually reduced the possibility of an independent Hungarian policy. The situation was aggravated by the gradual disappearance of Western influence in Eastern Europe. The Western powers ceased to exist as power factors along the Danube, and Hungary was squeezed between overwhelming German and Russian forces.

The occupation of the smaller Western European states by Germany and the unexpected collapse of France caused general

---

8 For details on Ruthenia, see P. G. Stercho, "Carpatho-Ukraine in International Affairs, 1938—1939" (unpublshed Ph. D. dissertation, Indiana University, 1959). On the treatment of Polish refugees in Hungary, see Kállay, **Hungarian Premier**, pp. 232—44.

consternation to the Hungarian public. The press manifested a dignified reserve and, when Italy declared war on France and England, Hungary continued her nonbelligerent status.

The Soviet Union reacted to the German victories in the West by the incorporation of the Baltic states, and following a Russian ultimatum Rumania evacuated Bessarabia and Bukovina and ceded these territories to the Soviet Union. After these events Hungary and Bulgaria demanded the settlement of their territorial issues. In August, 1940, the Rumanian Government agreed with Bulgaria concerning the retrocession of Dobrudja, but declined to entertain seriously the Hungarian claims.

But now the situation became more serious due to the possibility of intervention by Soviet Russia. Molotov declared to the Hungarian Envoy, Joseph Kristoffy, that the Soviet government considered the Hungarian claims well-founded and would support them at the peace table. "The Hungarian Government", stated Molotov, "may rest assured that the Soviet Government never regarded Rumania of Versailles as realistic, and that it was equally objectionable to Russia, Bulgaria and Hungary".(9) Even Stalin invited the Hungarian minister, whom he had never seen before, to call upon him.(10)

Meanwhile the Rumanian Government received reports of concentrations of Soviet troops on the Rumanian frontier. Both Rumania and Germany believed that Russia was deliberately fomenting the Hungarian-Rumanian dispute with the intention of then marching into Moldavia and Wallachia, perhaps to wipe out the Rumanian State altogether, seize her all-important oil wells and then

---

9 Macartney, **October Fifteenth,** I, 418.
10 In Stalin's studio the following conversation took place:
Stalin: Has Hungary given up her claim to Transylvania?
Kristóffy: No, she has not.
Stalin: Why then don't you attack Rumania? Now is the time.
Kristéffy: I shall inform my government.
Stalin: All right. Do.
Quoted in Montgomery, **Hungary: The Unwilling Satellite,** p. 138.

march on Istanbul. If Hungary did not move, the Soviet troops might cross the Carpathians and themselves occupy Transylvania; or they might foment a revolution, resulting in Rumania's turning herself into a Soviet Republic and placing herself under the protection of the Soviet Union.

To prevent such a possibility, Hungary had insisted that negotiations be conducted directly between Hungary and Rumania. King Carol of Rumania, however, requested arbitration from Hitler in order thus to obtain Germany's guarantee of Rumania's new frontiers. Hitler himself could do nothing else but impose a solution which would avert a complete collapse of the whole Rumania and his Balkan politics. On August 28, 1940, an Axis conference was held at Berchtensgaden, attended by Ciano, Ribbentrop, and the German and Italian envoys to Rome, Berlin, Budapest, and Bucharest. Two days later, the Hungarian and Rumanian prime ministers were summoned to Vienna, where another Vienna Award awaited them, this time concerning Rumania. There was a German ultimatum; neither the Rumanian nor the Hungarian delegates were allowed to say a word. Hungary received somewhat less than half of Transylvania and the new frontiers of Rumania were guaranteed by Germany and Italy.(11)

---

11 The First Vienna Award on November 2, 1938, restored to Hungary 12,103 square kilometers of territory with over one million population from Czechoslovakia. The British Minister in Budapest, Geoffrey Knox, submitted to the British Government the following population data of the returned area: Hungarians — 830,000; Slovaks — 140,000; Germans — 20,000; Ruthenes and others — 40,000.

Hungary occupied Carpatho-Ruthenia by force on March 15, 1939. Ruthenia had a territory of 12,171 square kilometers and a population of 700,000, the majority of which was Ruthenian. According to the 1930 Czechoslovak census, the number of the Hungarian minority was 121,000.

The Second Vienna Award on August 30, 1940, restored to Hungary an area of 43,492 square kilometers from Rumania with a population of 2,600,000. According to the Hungarian censuses of 1910 and 1941, the number of Hungarians exeeded the Rumanians in this territory, while the Rumanian census of 1930 indicated a slight Rumanian majority.

The new frontiers were unsatisfactory to both Rumania and Hungary. Rumania thought that Hungary had received more than she had ever dreamed of getting. The Hungarians believed the same about Rumania. Furthermore, the new frontier neglected all geographical and economic considerations and, most of all, those of communication. By drafting an impossible new frontier, Germany wished permanently to divide and rule both Hungary and Rumania.

Meanwhile the Western powers indicated their understanding of Hungary's attitude. In July, 1940, Rumania renounced the Anglo-French guarantee of Rumania's political independence. Subsequently, the permanent Undersecretary of the British Foreign Office declared to Barcza, the Hungarian Minister, that the British Government fully understood that Hungary was pressing her territorial demands but hoped that these would be realized by peaceful settlement. The Hungarian minister to the United States, John Perényi, reported that the head of the European division in the Department of State showed an understanding toward Hungary's attitude in the Transylvanian problem and disapproved of the delaying tactics of the Rumanians.(12)

Hungary's position nonetheless was made more difficult after the Second Vienna Award by the pro-Axis reorientation of Rumania's foreign policy. This had been achieved with amazing speed. Rumania resigned from the League of Nations and from the Balkan Entente and began to transform the internal structure of the country according to National Socialist principles. The most dangerous step, however, was the invitation extended by Rumania in early October, 1940, to the German "instructor corps". An entire German panzer division was transferred to Rumania, manifestly as a training unit but in fact for the purpose of preparing the Rumanian army for war. It became clear soon that Rumania as Germany's client was, in the situation of the time, far more dangerous to Hungary than was Rumania as her enemy in the one-time Little

---

12 Kertész, **Diplomacy in a Whirlpool**, p. 51.

Entente. The situation produced a race for Germany's favor, for which Rumania bid in the hope of securing the reversal of the Award, and Hungary to ensure its maintenance. This rivalry led to Hungary's signing the Anti-Comintern Pact in November, 1940.

A secondary effect of the developments which brought about the Second Vienna Award was that Yugoslavia would accept Hungary's friendship. With Czechoslovakia off the map, France out of the picture, and Rumania in the Axis camp, Yugoslavia was almost isolated diplomatically. Yugoslavia could no longer afford to despise an offer of friendship from Hungary, a Hungary which was now very considerably enlarged and strengthened. As for the Hungarians, one of the motives which had first led them to seek a rapprochement was the need for support against Germany and for keeping open a window to the West through Yugoslavia's Western connections. In December, 1940, Hungary signed a "Pact of Eternal Friendship" with Yugoslavia, and although this was sincerely meant as reinsurance against Germany, to give Hungary a "window to the West", it was also concluded on the assumption that Yugoslavia would follow a policy similar to Hungary's own: passively resisting Axis pressure from inside but not actively opposing it.(13)

But Hitler pressed Yugoslavia too hard; the Opposition revolted, and on March 26, 1941, deposed its government. Hitler in fury prepared to invade Yugoslavia and asked permission to send his troops across Hungarian territory to attack Yugoslavia. Hungary had to choose between complying with or resisting this German request. Teleki sent a special emissary to Mussolini to ask whether Hungary could count on his help. Mussolini, however, refused any assistance. Finding resistance impossible, Count Paul Teleki sought escape from the problem in death, hoping thereby to make the nation aware of the gravity of the situation and the world aware of the tragedy in which the small nations were becoming involved. Teleki committed suicide in the early morning of April

---

13 For details, see Macartney, **October Fifteenth,** I, 446—54.

4, 1941. Winston Churchill noted in his memories that "his suicide was a sacrifice to absolve himself and his people from guilt in the German attack upon Yugoslavia. It clears his name before history. It could not stop the march of the German armies nor the consequences".(14)

Teleki's successor was his Foreign Minister, Ladislav Bárdossy, a professional diplomat. Under Bárdossy, Hungaryy's international position rapidly grew worse. It has often been said that the day when Bárdossy succeeded Teleki marked a turning point in Hungarian policy: the change from resistance to eager cooperation. There is some truth in this as a long-term judgment. But the view that he was a Nazi is unjust. Bárdossy was no Right Radical. He was no devotee either of Germany or Nazism and no anti-Westerner. He was indeed, very attached to England, where he had served and had developed many lasting friendships. But precisely his English experience had convinced him that Britain was bound ultimately to support the re-establishment of that treaty system of 1919 which she had helped to construct. In his view, Hungary could never hope to outbid the Little Entente states in the competition for the favor of the West. Hungary's only course was therefore to cooperate with Germany.

Meanwhile Croatia proclaimed its independence. Hungary, claiming that Yugoslavia no longer existed, was ready to occupy former Hungarian areas assigned to Yugoslavia in 1919. Bárdossy sent telegrams to London and Washington insisting that Hungary had no aggressive intentions but was interested only in the fate of the Hungarian minorities in Yugoslavia. He still seems to have hoped that the Western Powers would understand Hungary's policy and not take it amiss. But before the Hungarian Minister in London could pass on the message to the British Government, British aircraft bombed some Hungarian cities and on the same day, April 7, 1941, Sir Owen O'Malley, British Minister in Budapest, notified the Hungarian Government that Britain was breaking diplo-

---

14 Winston S. Churchill, The Great Alliance (Boston: Mifflin, 1950), p. 168.

matic relations with Hungary. On the next day, the Hungarian Minister in London received the same notification from Mr. Eden, who told him:

It would be an eternal shame on Hungary that she had attacked a country with which only a few months previously, she had concluded a Treaty of Eternal Friendship. If a State was not master of its will and its actions, let it at least not conclude treaties which it then breaks. Teleki was the last Hungarian whom Britain had trusted. His successors should know that Britain would win the war and would remember this conduct of Hungary's at the Peace Conference.(15)

The United States showed more understanding of the position than Great Britain. On April 7, 1941, the Secretary of State told the Hungarian Minister that he wished to speak quite openly and in the strictest confidence. He fully understood Hungary's difficult situation. But nothing was at present more important from the point of view of later developments than the formal attitude adopted by Hungary. It was understandable if the Hungarian Government did everything possible to defend its territory but very important that it should not appear formally as the aggressor.(16)

Meanwhile, the day of Hitler's planned attack on Soviet Russia was approaching. Following the outbreak of the German-Russian war, on June 21, 1941, the Eastern European states entered

---

15 Macartney, **October Fifteenth**, II, 8. Churchill's judgment, however, was not so severe. He said on the same day:

"The Hungarian Minister is really right; we English have been guilty of serious faults and omissions in the past. Hungary, after all, always openly maintained her claims to revision, and now, if the Hungarian troops confine themselves to occupying the territories which were formerly Hungary, that is, humanly speaking, understandable. I regret that politically it is impossible for me to do otherwise than break off diplomatic relations, but so long as Hungarian troops do not find themselves opposed in the field by British forces, there is really no need for a declaration of war. The Hungarians, incidentally, are very sympathetic people." **Ibid.**

16 **Ibid.**, II, 9.

a new phase of their history. Italy, Rumania, and Slovakia declared war on Russia on June 22. Croatia followed with a declaration during the night. Finland, however, did not enter the war until the 25th; Hungary, not until the 27th. The Hungarian towns Kassa and Munkács were bombed allegedly by Soviet planes on the preceding day, and Bárdossy considered this action a casus belli and declared war on Russia without consulting parliament.(17)

Hungary's participation in the Russian war was, however, very limited. Hungary sent only a light armored division, a few infantry battalions, and labor cadres to the Russian front. The light armored division operated in the central Ukraine; the rest of the Hungarian forces were employed in construction work and policing behind the lines. At the end of 1941, the armored division returned to Hungary, and only a very small number of troops remained in Russia.

The most fearful event of the Russian war was, however, that it got Hungary involved in war with England and with the United States. This fact was not without dramatic incidents. When the American Minister to Hungary, Herbert Pell, representing British interests in Hungary, handed over, on November 29, 1941, the British ultimatum,(18) Bárdossy replied as follows:

17 For details on Hungary's declaration of war on Russia, see among many others, Macartney, October Fifteenth, II, 16—60.

18 The British ultimatum read as follows:

"The Hungarian Government has for many months been pursuing aggressive military operations on the territory of the Union of Soviet Republic, ally of Great Britain, in closest collaboration with Germany, thus participating in the general European war and making substantial contribution to the German war effort. In these circumstances His Majesty's Government in the United Kingdom finds it necessary to inform the Hungarian Government that unless by December five the Hungarian Government has ceased military operations and has withdrawn from all active participation in hostilities, His Majesty's Government will have no choice but to declare the existence of a state of war between the two countries." The text is given by Kertész, Diplomacy in a Whirlpool, p. 208.

Your information comes as a surprise. I never believed it would go that far, not that England could help the Soviets only by declaring war on us... There are no Hungarian forces fighting in Russia now. We have withdrawn our forces from the front. The Hungarian Government is not participating in any direct military action. . . Most of the Hungarians placed their faith in English fairness to judge the present situation. They will feel hurt by such a decision of the British Government.(19)

Minister Pell showed a most understanding attitude toward Hungary. Pell said that he considered the decision of the British Government as his own defeat. Counselor Howard K. Travers stated that the American Legation tried every means of preventing a declaration of war by England on Hungary after the first rumors of such a decision. Pell said that his country and he himself, on his own initiative, had done all they could to stop the British declaration; he (Pell) sent three messages to Washington (one of them directly to Roosevelt) urging that the British note was "most unwise". Another attempt at intervention was made through Vatican channels. Justinian Serédi, Cardinal of Hungary, wrote to the Holy See asking for its intervention. Cardinal Magliône, on receiving Serédi's message (transmitted via the Nunciature in Budapest), had spoken to the British Minister in Rome who gladly agreed to pass the message on, saying that "Hungary enjoyed much sympathy in England". But the news that war was declared came the next day.(20)

The whole nation heard with profound indignation the British Government's decision. On December 5, the Minister President made a statement in Parliament saying that the British decision, which was "contrary alike to law and justice, was directed not only against us, and those States in a position similar to ours, but against all Europe".(21) The Hungarian Press

---

19 Kertész, **Diplomacy in a Whirlpool**, p. 55.
20 Macartney, **October Fifteenth**, II. n. 4, p. 61.
21 **Ibid.**

commented in the same vein. The **Pester Lloyd** wrote that Hungary was the poorer by an illusion, but the richer by an experience. She would preserve her dignity and "perhaps our example will teach the English what being a gentleman means".(22)

On the very day that the Hungarian public learned of the British declaration of war there came also the news of the Japanese attack on Pearl Harbor, and four days after that Germany's declaration of war on the United States. Bárdossy convoked an extraordinary Minister Council to discuss the situation arising out of Germany's declaration of war. He said that Hungary was under strong German pressure, but there were still two possibilities: the one, to break off diplomatic relations with the United States, the other to register the fact that Hungary was in a state of war with the United States.(23)

None of the ministers was keen on war. The Minister of Defense, Charles Bartha, said that in view of the disparity between the strengths of the two countries, war might look ridiculous. Francis Keresztes-Fischer, Minister of Interior, argued that Japan had undoubtedly been the aggressor. The Council accepted the first formula, expressing the hope that the rupture of diplomatic relations would prove sufficient for Germany. That evening Bárdossy informed Minister Pell of the rupture of relations and when asked "Does it mean war?" answered categorically, "No!" But on the same night Rumania and Bulgaria declared war on the United States and the two Axis Powers informed Budapest that the Hungarian rupture of diplomatic relations was not enough: the German and Italian Governments wanted a state of war declared. Bárdossy told them what his Government had decided: they could not be expected in practice to give military support

---

22 **Ibid.**

23 According to the Hungarian Constitutional Law, a declaration of war had to be approved by the Parliament and signed by the Regent. A declaration of the Minister President that a state of war existed meant a little more than to break of diplomatic relations, but not actual war between two nations at all.

against the United States; Hungary could gain nothing, even if the United States was defeated. Moreover, further action would seriously endanger the interests of the millions of Hungarians of the United States.

Italy and Germany, however, did not accept Bárdossy's arguments. They insisted on declaring war on the United States, pointing out that all the others (Rumania, Bulgaria, Slovakia, and Croatia) already had declared the state of war, and "higher political interests necessitated an unanimous attitude of the European states. Hungary can either choose solidarity or be treated as an enemy." In such a situation, Bárdossy could not but choose to ring up Minister Pell and inform him that his formula of the previous day had after all meant that a state of war now existed between Hungary and the United States of America. Minister Pell showed the greatest possible patience and understanding and said: "I know that you are doing this under heavy pressure from Germany, and that the declaration reflects no hostility on the part of the Hungarian people towards the people of the United States".(24)

Indeed, the Hungarians had no hostility towards America. When the first secretary of the American Legation, Howard Travers, made his goodby call on the Regent, the latter said to him: "Remember that this so-called declaration of war is not legal; not approved by parliament, not signed by me".(25) Before the American diplomats left Hungary, they were the objects of stormy proofs of friendship. One of them was invited to dinner by a friend who belonged to one of the leading families of Hungary. When he arrived he was astonished to find a large number of prominent people assembled there: members of parliament, members of the cabinet, and so forth. When they sat down, he was seated on his hostess' right. During the course of the dinner, the hostess arose and said:

24 Macartney, October Fifteenth, II, 63.
25 Montgomery, Hungary: The Unwilling Satellite, p. 153.

I am not accustomed to making speeches, but since our guest of honor tonight is an enemy, I feel that I must explain this. I am not pro-German; I am not pro-English; I am not pro-American; I am just pro-Hungarian and as a pro-Hungarian, I ask that you all rise and drink a toast to a speedy American victory.(26)

The reluctance of Hungary to declare war on the United States reflected the fact that the free will of small nations was very limited in a world conflagration. Bárdossy well described the tragic dilemma of Hungarian statesmen when he told Mussolini's representative in Budapest, Filippo Anfuso that "God confronted us with Hitler. If the Germans demand something, I always give a quarter of it. If I refused categorically, they would take everything, which would be worse." Bárdossy expressed the same idea even more strongly before the people's court in 1945 when in his last speech he explained that half of his audience would not have been present for his trial but would have perished on the battlefield had he refused to declare war on Russia and on the United States in 1941. In that case, said Bárdossy, the German occupation of Hungary would have taken place three years earlier and a government installed by Hitler would have carried out a total mobilization of Hungary.(27)

President Roosevelt evaluated this situation correctly. He knew that war declarations coming from the small countries of Central Europe were forced by Hitler; and he was, therefore, inclined to ignore them. On June 2, 1942, that is, after six months of Soviet insistence, the President sent a message to Congress stating that Rumania, Hungary, and Bulgaria had declared war on the United States, but he added: "I realize that those three gov-

---

26 Ibid., p. 154.

27 Quoted by Kertész, Diplomacy in a Whirlpool, p. 56. After the war the American authorities extradited Bárdossy to the new Hungarian regime. He was sentenced to death by the people's court in Budapest and was executed.

ernments took that action not upon their own iniative or in response to the wishes of their peoples, but as instruments of Hitler.(28) Not before July 18, 1942, after a strong Russian request, did Congress declare that there was a state of war between the United States and these nations.

When America entered the war, Hungarian public opinion began seriously to envisage the possibility of defeat for Hungary and her allies, and logical conclusions were that Germany's defeat could mean that Russia would be let into Central Europe. They argued that there was no changing Hungary's course now. The fall of Germany and Italy would mean the tragic fall of Hungary; a defeat more fatal from the national point of view than that of Trianon. The **Magyarország** (Hungary), a Budapest conservative daily, gave utterance to the opinion of many in writing:

> We know Benes' and Stalin's ideas, we know what awaits us . . . If we are defeated, there are only two possibilities: either a resurrection of Little Entente aggression, much greater, much more frightful than before, or Bolshevism. . . England and America are bound, as things stand, to back Benes against us and to help Bolshevism. There is no changing this — no recriminations, false optimism or self-deception can help. . . If Germany does not win, we fall with her, and perhaps deeper than she, as we are weaker than she is . . . There is no changing the fact that if Germany is defeated, we too shall finish on the list of defeated enemies. That was decided in the first World War and at Trianon.(29)

Regent Horthy, and many others, saw the situation differently. Horthy was quite convinced that the war would end in an Allied victory, but he also believed that the West did not want the Bolshevisation of Europe. He also could not bring himself to believe that Britain and America would sacrifice Hungary to Bol-

---

28 Montgomery, **Hungary: The Unwilling Satellite**, p. 153.
29 The Christmas number of 1941.

234

shevism unless she herself absolutely forced them to do so. In March, 1942, he therefore dismissed Bárdossy in favor of Nicholas Kállay, who shared these hopes, and one more attempt was made to recover the good will of the Western democracies. For two years Kállay conducted a remarkable policy. He afforded to Hungary's Jews a protection then unparalleled on the Continent; (30) allowed almost complete freedom to all anti-Nazi and non-Communist elements, whom he allowed to build up an "Independence Front" which openly speculated on an Allied victory, and opened secret conversations with the Western Powers, with whom, in August, 1943, he actually concluded a secret agreement to surrender to them when their troops should reach the frontiers of Hungary.

So once again Hungary had an "Anglophile" premier who set his hopes on the victory of the Western Powers and refused to believe that they would not somehow come to see the justice of Hungary's case and the force of the argument that a big and strong Hungary would be a factor of order in Europe and a bulwark against both tyrannies. An absolute postulate of this policy was that Hungary must be defended from Bolshevism, buying the protection of the West at the price of dissociation of Hungary from Germany.

To appreciate this Hungarian policy it is necessary, first of all, to consider the military and political situation of that time. Early in 1942, there was only one power on the European Continent: Germany. The whole Continent from the Iberian Peninsula to the Caucasus lay within the German sphere of power.

---

30 A Jewish writer dealing with the fate of Hungarian Jewry and with the annihilation of Jews in adjacent countries wrote: "While the Germans had practically annihilated Central European Jewry, roughly one million Jews lived in Hungary. They all had to thank the protection afforded them by Régent Horthy and the Kállay Government for their physical existence in what the Nazis called the "Central European Jewish Island." Eugene Lévai, **Black Book on the Martyrdom of Hungarian Jewry (Zürich and Vienna: n.p., 1948), p. 73.**

Switzerland was the only Continental state that had preserved its complete independence. Sweden had made a great many concessions and was wavering between neutrality and nonbelligerency; the same held true for Spain and Portugal. Russia was still fighting for her life. The German and Italian troops were advancing victoriously in North Africa, and Allied naval casualties in the Mediterranean were severe. Considerable portions of the American and British fleets had been destroyed in the Pacific. American and British soldiers were surrendering one position after another. Nearly all the Western strongholds in Asia had fallen into Japanese hands.

In such a situation, Hungary could not even hope for any kind of military assistance from any quarter whatsoever. This fact determined whether any resistance was possible, useful, or sensible. Germany would occupy Hungary if she made a false step and the fate of Poland and Yugoslavia clearly showed what a German occupation could mean. The Germans would eliminate the patriotic government and set their Quisling in its place. Hungary's military, political, and administrative system would crumble away. A condition of chaos would exist at the end of the war; and then, when the German army was beaten and the Russian troops entered, there would be no organized force in the country to take over the power except the Communist movement. Moreover, it would not be only the Germans who occupied Hungary, but the Rumanians, the Slovaks, and even the Croats would join them, and it was sufficient for Hungarians to recall the few months of Rumanian occupation in 1919 to realize what would happen in such a case.

It seemed that there was only one possible way out of this dilemma: at all costs to defend, preserve, and restore the complete independence of Hungary. That is, as regards Germany, to develop the highest measure of moral resistance and to confine concessions to the minimum short of provoking an occupation. At the same time, as to the West, to seek contact, diverting Germany's attention by emphasizing an anti-Russian policy. This policy could show to the West that the anti-Bolshevik peoples of East-Central Europe were its natural allies and perhaps the West would therefore not revenge Hungary for having participated in the war against Russia. The Hungarian army, too, was to be kept as intact as possible, so that when the Allies won the war, they would not be tempted to treat Hungary as a satellite of Germany's and might even enlist her help as a factor of order in Southeastern Europe.(31)

This Hungarian policy was founded on the supposition that British and American forces would reach Hungary's frontiers by the beginning of 1944, possibly at an earlier date. Such a development would have opened the way for Hungary to join the Allies against Germany. With the intent of making contacts with the British, Hungary made her first overtures to the Poles. The Polish Government in London was recognized secretly in early 1942, and the Hungarian minister in Lisbon tried to send information to London through Polish channels. Consequently Hungary succeeded in establishing direct contacts with the British in the summer of 1942. The Stockholm, Berne, and Constantinople Hungarian legation staffs were recognized to facilitate strictly confidential parlays. In the course of these contacts with Greatbritain Hungary obtained little positive encouragement as to her future position in Danubian Europe but instead was threatened with a variety of unattractive possibilities in case she failed to turn in time against Germany. While the leading Hungarian diplomats were willing to take all risks and were eager to make all possible preparatory steps for an Anglo-American occupation (which was the basis of their policy), for the British, talks with Hungarian emissaries were only part of the Allied psychological warfare. Their interest was mostly concentrated on matters of military intelligence and sabotage.

---

31 In 1942, Hungary possessed almost 1,000,000 trained soldiers and a fully equipped army of about 300,000. Kállay, **Hungarian Premier**, p. 322.

One of the fundamental and catastrophic anomalies of the situation was that Hungary was seeking the protection of the British, not only against Germany but also against their allies, against Russia. Allied unity, however, seemed to be so perfect that the British could hardly recognize that the anti-Nazi resistance in Hungary could be an official operation undertaken by an anti-Communist government. Consequently, the only circles which British policy was willing to regard as representative of the true Hungary were the Left emigrees of 1919, Count Michael Károlyi, and his friends. As a result of this, the B.B.C. (and the Voice of America too) ceaselessly and abusively denounced the Hungarian Government as Quisling and left all Hungary under the impression that the only element in the country which the West was not determined to destroy was the extreme Left. The strange thing, as it turned out, was that the two minorities in Hungary, the pro-German and the pro-Russian, could always be assured of the support of their patrons, while the pro-Anglo-Americans, who were the great majority of population and were headed by their legal government, could not be assured of support.

In spite of these facts, on August 17, 1943, Hungary was ready to accept the Casablanca formula for unconditional surrender, should the forces of the Allies reach the frontiers of Hungary. The only Hungarian request was that Czechoslovak, Rumanian, and Yugoslav troops should not take part in the occupation of Hungary. The capitulation of Hungary was to be kept secret and regarded as practicable only if the military situation made it possible. The Allied forces were still at a great distance from the boundaries of Hungary.(32)

Secret radio connections had been established between Budapest and the Allies. A shortwave transmitter and receiver had been placed in the basement of the Budapest police headquarters building and at certain hours of the day regular and direct com-

---

32 For the full text of the surrender, see Kertész, **Diplomacy in Whirlpool**, p. 68.

munication was maintained with an Allied agency. Allied flying units, in passing over Hungary, were not fired upon or chased by Hungarian fighter planes. On the contrary, their flights were facilitated by information about air defense. The important practical result of this attitude was that, until German troops occupied Hungary on March 19, 1944, Hungarian territory was not bombed by the British and Americans.

Simultaneously with the British negotiations, parlays started with the United States and after a while Hungarians were forced to realize that the Americans handled matters with more courage behind their convictions and with less prejudice than the British. The United States did not feel bound to pay so much regard to the 1919 Treaties, or to the Little Entente. The Americans were easier to deal with. This was principally because of the work of Archduke Otto, the Hungarian crown prince, who succeeded in awakening the interest of President Roosevelt, with whom he had several conversations and who showed distinct good will towards the Hungarian question. Furthermore, while the British agents usually were Hungarian Left radical emigrées of 1919, like Wilhelm Böhm in Stockholm, the ex-Commissary of Béla Kun, and George Pálóczy-Horváth in Constantinople, a left-wing Socialist and a spy of Moscow, the American agents were diplomats who had served in Hungary before and knew the Hungarian problems well. In spite of the opinion of many historians, the United States planned ahead for peace. The White House, the State and War Departments bristled with plans, committees, and experts' papers· Within the State Department a "special sub-committee on problems of European Organization" examined regional federation plans, a European customs' union, a Balkan federation, and a Habsburg restoration. The functioning of multi-national states such as Yugoslavia and Czechoslovakia was examined in connection with the foreseeable problems. The sub-committee also appraised possible Soviet programs and attitudes with respect to Eastern Europe so far as they were then known or could be conjectured.(33) All of these facts led to a better understanding on the part of Americans and the good will of President Roosevelt. On the other hand in England the Hungarians, apart from the matters mentioned above, had to fight the antipathy of Eden (at that time Minister of Foreign Affairs) towards Hungary.

The Hungarians did their best to capture America's good will and understanding. In 1940, during the Teleki regime, it was decided that the opposition leader, Tibor Eckhardt, would go to the United States and start a Hungarian emigré movement there. Eckhardt arrived in New York in 1941. Before his suicide, Count Teleki also sent a number of young Hungarian scholars to the United States.

Contacts were now established between Hungary and the United States through Eckhardt in New York via Lisbon, which was an active center for the intelligence work of America. At first Eckhardt met with success in America, but soon the combined forces of the Czechoslovak emigration and the Hungarian-born Left in New York opened a concentric and coordinated attack on Eckhardt's mission and his person.(34) Following this, the representative leaders of Hungarian Jewry addressed a memorandum to influential Jews in the United States defending the attitude of the Hungarian Government and the Hungarian people

---

33 John A. Lukács, The Great Powers and Eastern Europe (New York: American Book Company, 1953), p. 425.

34 The Czechoslovak emigration was split into two groups: pro-Benes and anti-Benes. Benes was anti-Habsburg and wished to restore the Little Entente system, leaning rather on Russia. Benes envisaged Czechoslovakia as playing the role of a great European power after the war, a great "bridge" between the East, Soviet Russia, and the Western world, the Anglo-Saxon Powers. Many Czechoslovak patriots rallied, however, around Milan Hodza, the former Premier of Czechoslovakia, and Dr. Stefan Osusky, the former Czechoslovak Minister to Paris. These two statesmen regarded Benes as one of the authors of the Czechoslovak catastrope. Osusky and Hodza put their faith in plans for a great Austrian-Hungarian-Polish-Czechoslovak federation and maintained contacts with various emigre leaders of these countries. Lukács, The Great Powers, pp. 392—94.

towards the Jews and pleading strongly that it was a vital interest of the 800,000 Jews of Hungary that there should be nothing done which might provoke a German occupation of Hungary.

Another important fact of the American Hungarian relations was the activity of Archduke Otto von Habsburg, who lived at that time in the United States as the personal guest of the President and as his advisor in Central European affairs. As early as 1940, President Roosevelt had remarked that he favored the Archduke's ideas and could help the plans for a Habsburg restoration. Furthermore, a plan of a Central European bloc was considered, including South Germany, Austria, Czechoslovakia, Poland, and Hungary under Otto von Habsburg. Archduke Otto made his headquarters in Washington, where he was in touch with many of the most influential members of the Administration and of the Senate.

In January, 1942, the Archduke set out his ideas on the future cooperation of the nations of the Danubian Basin in an article published by him in **Foreign Affairs** under the title "Danubian Reconstruction". Many people in Hungary considered the article as the suggestions of President Roosevelt for the solutions of East-Central European problems after the war and the ideas, written in the article, were acceptable to them. So the Hungarian Minister President sent a message to the Archduke Otto in America asking him if he would establish contact between the Hungarian Government and the Government of the United States and authorized the Archduke to act in the name of the Hungarian Government.(35)

From that time Archduke Otto and Eckhardt were in close cooperation and they made perceptible progress. Otto had several conversations with President Roosevelt, who showed distinct good will towards the Hungarian question and offered the Archduke and Eckhardt the use of the American Navy code to facil-

---

35 Archduke Otto Habsburg received the credentials on January 15, 1944, and took them to President Roosevelt. Macartney, **October Fifteenth**, II, 205.

itate the sending of their messages to Lisbon.(36) The Archduke's and Eckhardt's reports raised great hopes in Hungary. Otto von Habsburg sent his younger brother, Archduke Louis Charles, to talk to the Hungarians in Lisbon, and soon after Colonel Fracis Deák, an American citizen of Hungarian origin, was sent to Lisbon and attached to the American Legation with a special mission to talk to the Hungarians officially. Deák had a dual commission from the State Department and the High Command and his mission was a direct link between the Roosevelt-Otto Conversations and the Hungarian Government.

Deák's messages were very satisfactory to Hungary. According to these messages, the Americans wanted to save Hungary from being occupied by Russia or assigned to the Russian sphere of interest. They wanted to avoid revolutions in the Danube basin and hoped that a Hungary which had not been disarmed would be the central focus of consolidation. They hoped also to find a territorial settlement satisfactory to Hungary; most likely they could get her Transylvania, and they were not committed to the Trianon frontiers to the north or south. Nor did they want Hungary to commit sabotage or provoke a German occupation as the interests of Hungary would be better served if this did not happen.(37)

Archduke Otto had seen Roosevelt and Churchill together at the time of the First Quebec Conference in August, 1943. Both men had said that they believed in a conservative solution for Central Europe and had advised Hungary to reach agreement with the Allies in good time. Then, on October 1, 1943, Roosevelt had received Otto alone and had gone much further. Roosevelt said at that meeting that if Hungary would now settle her relationship with the Allies, they would be prepared to accept her as a cobelligerent and not insist on her unconditional surrender. Moreover, said the President, if Hungary changed hands

---

36 Lukács, **The Great Powers,** p. 803.
37 Macartney, **October Fifteenth,** II, 204.

while Rumania remained with the Axis and Hungary then occupied South Transylvania, he was willing to support her claim to that area, since the present proposals were that Rumania and Bulgaria were to be left to the Russian sphere of influence, but not Hungary. To give Transylvania to Hungary would thus be to save it from Russia.(38)

The Hungarian answer reached Lisbon on November 28, 1943. The Hungarian Government ordered its minister to Portugal to get into contact with Archduke Otto at once if contact with Budapest were to be interrupted or broken. A further document authorized Otto von Habsburg to act as Head of the Hungarian State if the Germans invaded Hungary and the Regent abdicated or was deposed. The Hungarian memorandum again reiterated willingness to surrender to the Allies and said that the occupation of Hungary by Russian armies should be avoided, while American, British, and Polish troops would be most welcomed. The Hungarian Government also asked that Benes must not be allowed to learn about the negotiations, or he would betray everything to the Russians. News from America showed that Benes and his circle were violently anti-Hungarian, ready to sabotage any secret Hungarian secession efforts. This indicated that the Czechs might inform the Russians and the Russians might let the Germans know indirectly.(39)

---

38 **Ibid.**, II, 192. For more details on the political activity of Archduke Otto in the United States during World War II see also Emil Csonka, **Habsburg Otto** (Munich: Uj Európa, 1972) pp. 316—390.

39 Benes' journey to Moscow and the signature of the Soviet-Czechoslovak Treaty on December 12, 1943, seemed to the Hungarians to prove that the Soviets had assigned to Czechoslovakia the role in which Hungarians had always seen their northern neighbor, the outpost of Slav expansion and Bolshevik thought. Benes always denied this. However, he confessed later: "Since 1922 our effort has been oriented towards the Slav East (Russia) . . . We never changed our ideas or our plans . . . We worked methodically. Our endeavors to maintain this 'Eastern' and 'Slav' line were conscious and premeditated; they were based on a new conception of Europe's future." Eduard Benes, **Ou vont les Slaves?** (Paris: Edition Notre Temps, 1946), p. 18.

243

Preparations were made now both on the political and military fields to Hungary's leaving the Axis camp. The Hungarian diplomats who had been contacts with the Allies formed an organization of "dissident diplomats". A group of some thirty ex-Ministers and Consuls-General took form, with the purpose of providing some sort of machinery for the continuation of the diplomatic contacts with the Western Powers if Hungary was occupied by the Germans. Furthermore, if the Regent could be persuaded to take refuge abroad, a Government in exile might be formed. It also proved possible to secure the consent of the Hungarian Government and the National Bank for transfer to Switzerland of substantial sums in gold to cover expenses. At the end of February, 1944, 35 kg. of gold was deposited in the Swiss National Bank.

Meanwhile, the diplomatic preparations were transferred from Lisbon to Berne, Switzerland. An important consideration of this was the presence in Berne of Royall Tyler, in an important position with the American Legation. Tyler spent many years in Hungary as a commissioner of the League of Nations reconstruction loan, and he had learned to speak Hungarian fluently. He had made numerous friends in Hungary, with many of whom he had kept in touch. He knew Hungary's conditions thoroughly, and there was no doubt of his sympathies and his desire to help Hungary. Royall Tyler and Allen W. Dulles, head of the American intelligence service in Berne, had received from Washington full powers to negotiate with Hungary.

These discussions led to the sending of an American military mission to Hungary, headed by an American colonel, and an American diplomat was scheduled to accompany them. This officer was Howard K. Travers, who served as counselor in the American Legation in Budapest from 1936 to 1941. He could not leave Washington at the appointed time, however, and the mission was dispatched without him and dropped by parachute in western Hungary on March 15, 1944. When the mission arrived a proposal was laid before them that at a given moment Regent

Horthy was to go to Transylvania and proclaim Hungary's surrender. The Western Allies were begged to support this action with a parachute landing in West Hungary of 20,000 troops; they would be accompanied by the Hungarian troops turning against the Germans and a full-scale military operation would be started.

At about the same time, in the first days of March, 1944, President Roosevelt had another conversation with Archduke Otto and told him that if Hungary would give a binding assurance of her willingness to support the Allies at the decisive moment he would be willing to support Hungary's claim to the 1940 line in Northern Transylvania (he was not willing now to support Hungary's claim to all Transylvania probably because of Russian pressure), and to a reasonable and amicable settlement of her frontier with Czechoslovakia on the basis of the principle of self-determination. A Hungarian courier was en route towards Budapest with this communication on March 19, 1944, when the Germans occupied Hungary. The courier, who knew what was in the communication, destroyed it before reaching occupied Budapest.

The Germans could break the code used between Budapest and Berne. They knew all the details of the American enterprise, including the nationality of both the airplane and the mission, and the time and place of the landing. On March 16, 1944, Dietrich von Jagow, the German envoy in Budapest, was instructed to request that Regent Horthy go to meet Hitler at once. Next day, Horthy conferred with Kállay: he had to go, but he told the Premier to be extremely careful and not to obey any orders or do anything without hearing from Horthy personally. Shortly afterwards the Regent left for Klessheim, Germany. There, on March 18, Hitler thoroughly abused the old Horthy. He was insulted, accused, and threatened by Hitler, who told him that orders had already been given to the German Army to enter Hungary. He put a paper before Horthy, requesting his signature: a common communiqué agreeing to the arrival of the German forces in Hungary. Horthy refused to sign. Hitler accused him again of preparing a Leftist putsch and of making a deal with the Anglo-Saxons, and whether the Regent wanted it or not, German forces had already crossed the frontiers of Hungary.

At evening, Horthy's train left Klessheim; then it was halted somewhere in eastern Austria. Meanwhile, German troops marched toward Budapest and German parachute troops descended onto the Hungarian airfields, and when Horthy's train pulled into the capital the next day, the **coup d,état** was over. Many Hungarian Conservatives and opposition leaders were arrested. Kállay fled to the Turkish Legation, where he was offered sanctuary. A complete black-out of news and radio messages was imposed upon the country. German police closed in on all possible resistance centers and took measures for the deportation of the Hungarian Jews.

All of this changed Hungary's internal situation. The advancing Russians reached the crest of the Carpathians, and the Anglo-Americans knew that the secret air agreements with Hungary were now worthless; on April 3, 1944, the first American and British air raids on Budapest and other Hungarian centers began. Hungary lost the game. A small country, in the center of gigantic, global events can hardly make history: it suffers it.

CHAPTER XI

CONCLUSIONS

In October, 1918, as a consequence of World War I, the Austro-Hungarian Monarchy broke up. The result was a complete change in the Eastern European international structure. New national states came into being on the basis of self-determination.

Hungary's primary objective was to secure a moderate peace treaty. To achieve this, Hungary was proclaimed a "People's Republic." The Hungarian National Council elected Michael Károlyi President of the new republic. But it soon became obvious that the Allies had taken sides with the successor states against Hungary, and Károlyi reached the bitter conclusion that his country had little to expect from the victorious Western democracies. As a result, Hungary turned from the West to the East and became a Soviet Republic.

The establishment of the Hungarian Soviet Republic represented the first victory of communism beyond the borders of Russia and strengthened Bolshevik hopes. This communist projection into Hungary appeared more menacing due to the possibility of Hungary's military link-up with Russia, and the growing Bolshevik menace to all of Eastern, and even Western, Europe. Bolshevik Hungary in the heart of Europe cast a temporary pall over the Paris Peace Conference, but Western Powers definitely rejected the use of their forces against her because public opinion sharply opposed new sacrifices after a long and bloody war. The overthrow of the Soviet Hungarian regime may be traced to its own failures as well as to Rumania's military intervention.

In August, 1919, Béla Kun was expelled and a counter-revolutionary regime came into power. There came an outbreak of
anti-Semitism, largely due to the fact that nearly all the leading
figures of Béla Kun's regime, including Kun himself, were Jews.
This resulted in a good deal of propaganda against Hungary by
left radicals who lived in emigration. This propaganda reached
the United States, too. Although it was serious and caused many
problems for Hungarian politicians, it had not, except in some
academic circles, any great political success. Nevertheless Hungary
at that time was regarded by many people abroad as a dictatorship.

Indeed, post-war Hungary was not a dictatorship. After a
period of transition, Count Stephen Bethlen, premier from 1921
to 1931, carried through a complex combined policy. The peasant's
leaders were induced to abandon cooperation with the industrial workers and to accept the reintroduction of the open
franchise in the rural areas in return for a very modest land reform and promises of further reforms when conditions had become more stable. The industrial workers renounced cooperation
with the agrarian proletariat and promised to support the government's foreign policy in return for secret franchises in the larger
towns, an amnesty and the restitution to the trade unions of their
funds and their liberty of action in the purely industrial field.
Meanwhile a provisional solution had been found to the question of the crown by recognizing the monarchy as still existing
and electing Admiral Nicolas Horthy as Regent for the absent king.

Post-war Hungary was not a democracy in the Western meaning.
The word "democracy" could not be accepted as a ruling idea and a
national way of life in post-war Hungary simply because the Paris
peace treaties which reduced Hungary to one-third of her former area
were carried out allegedly under principles of democracy. It must
be definitely stated, however, that Hungary always was an Eastern
outpost of all Western ideas — political or religious, scientific or
artistic—and respect for human rights, individual liberty, and
constitutional safeguards in post-war Hungary had been far greater
than they were in many other Easternt European states of that time.

In June, 1920, the Treaty of Trianon, imposed on Hungary at the close of World War I. had in effect wiped out the historic Hungarian state, a state which for one thousand years had occupied the whole Carpathian Basin. The Treaty of Trianon was the most drastic of all the peace treaties of the period. It had been carried through in the name of the national principle, but so many concessions had been made to the strategic and economic interests of the successor states that no less than 3,200,000 Hungarians, one-third of the whole Hungarian speaking people, had been assigned to these successor states. Whether the Treaty of Trianon was just or not, whether it was carried through on the principle of self-determination or not, are questions which do not need discussion. As a matter of fact, the whole Hungarian nation was united in its conviction that the treaty was unacceptable, and the chief aspiration of Hungarian foreign policy, up to the close of World War II, was the desire for treaty revision.

On the other hand, the memories of Kun's regime bit deep into the minds of the nation, and its hatred and fear of Bolshevism equaled in intensity its desire for treaty revision. All governments after 1920 described themselves as "counter-revolutionary" and acted in that spirit towards any manifestation of international Bolshevism. On this point the whole Hungarian ruling class was united, and the Soviet Union played no part in influencing Hungary's foreign policy and her economy. This factor must be remembered, considering the later part of the story, as a lack of political realism.

But within itself the Hungarian ruling class was deeply divided, falling into two distinct camps. The differences between the two groups were primarily social and economic in origin, but they led to a strong ideological differentiation which resulted in widely differing approaches to the foreign political problem.

The first group, of which Count Bethlen had emerged as leader in 1921, included most of the large and medium landowners, the businessmen, the professional classes, and a large number of civil servants. This group described their own political tenets by the word "Conservative-Liberal". The foreign observer would have described this political tenet, quite simply, as conservatism. In this political creed, the word "liberal" meant only not anti-Semitic, while "conservative" meant a certain blindness towards social problems although the regime was not anti-social in general. Nevertheless, the regime had qualities which it would be unjust to deny. It tried to solve Hungary's problems in peaceful fashion, through cooperation with the Western democracies and with their support. It brought considerable economic and financial revival for the country. When, however, the Western democracies did not even attempt to remedy the injustices of the Paris peacet reaties, when the effects of the world's economic crisis reached Hungary and set her back very seriously on her road towards economic recontruction, Bethlen's policy could not avoid bankruptcy.

The "New Generation" of the 1930's wanted revolutionary changes in the internal as well as the international field: changes which should include land reform, restriction of the rights of capital, and a new orientation in foreign politics. They were thus the enemies of conservatism; but to oppose conservatism they would not use the program of the "left," for Michael Károlyi had made a revolution of the left, which had been followed by the dismemberment of Hungary and had led to Béla Kun's Bolshevism. Even democracy was suspect to them, as the pet ideology of these European forces which they regarded as especially bent on the destruction of Hungary. The Jewish question played a large part in determining what particular direction this group should take and thereby its program meant one form or another of Fascism.

The two groups headed by Count Stephen Bethlen and Julius Gömbös waged a bitter struggle for power. The question of which group should rule Hungary was primarily a domestic one, yet it became in time entangled with the foreign political problem. Each side naturally sympathized with those countries whose ideology was similar to its own, bade for its support, and in return offered its own support. This was always subject to national interest and each group was inclined to believe sincerely that its own friends would help Hungary towards treaty revision, and when it became clear that concessions would have to be made in any case, each preferred that these should be to its own friends. Due to this situation Hungary's policy became one of hesitations and intricate maneuverings between the West and Hitler's Germany.

Among the various reasons for this hesitation was the fear for Hungary's independence awakened by the re-establishment of a great, united German power, which, after the occupation of Austria, stood on Hungary's very frontier. Furthermore, there was a question of simple calculation. It was obvious that a conflict must soon break out between Germany and the West, and both groups wanted Hungary to be on the winning side when the war ended.

The outbreak of World War II found Hungary on the Axis side as a nonbelligerent. But the country became involved in the conflict soon, and after that there was no way out. That policy of hesitations and maneuverings, however, continued and its effect was that Hungary held out against any major German demands until the spring of 1944. The Liberal group argued that with American help the Allies were bound to win the war, and it was therefore essential for Hungary to dissociate herself from Germany; and they believed it was possible. They believed that the Western Allies regarded their alliance with Russia as a wartime necessary evil; that would not take Hungary's military operations against Russia amiss. In other words, they believed that Germany's defeat could not mean that Russia would be let into Eastern Europe. The fundamental idea of this policy was to offer the maximum resistance without endangering the nation's interests: to give the least possible moral, material, and military aid to Germany but to avoid by all means occupation by her. They tried to lead the nation on the right road "so that at the end of the war the "West" when it entered Hungary would find a nation, people, parliament, military forces, public order, and economic life so well organized that Hungary could without a jar join in a world reformed in the spirit of the Atlantic Charter".(1)

The other group argued that Hungary could never hope to outbid the Little Entente states in the competition for the favor of the West. They argued that no effort on Hungary's part to secure from the West any satisfaction for what she believed to be her just claims, or even protection against the Soviet Union, would be other than fruitless. Hungary's only course was therefore to cooperate with Germany.

Hungary's leaders certainly did make mistakes. But, in the light of later events, we can say that no matter what policy had been adopted at any particular time, the result would have been exactly the same. The leaders of the Western Powers concentrated everything on winning the war and political though had been pushed into the background. The war became the end and the West forgot why it had begun. At first all the states between Germany and Russia looked to the West. They had not thought other than to link up with the Anglo-American world. And what happened? The national regime in Poland had to defer to Russia's wishes. King Peter of Yugoslavia was dropped for Tito. Czechoslovakia turned to the Soviets. Those enormous successes of Soviet diplomacy happened at a moment when Russia was only holding her own through British and American help.

The Atlantic Charter began to take the place of Wilson's Fourteen Points, but both were ill-fated documents that eventually became the ideal, not of the authors, but of the conquered. How many times did America pay, and will pay, for these mistakes?

In spite of many accusations, Hungary had one great accomplishment during the tragic years of war: the treatment of refugees (both Jews and gentiles) and prisoners-of-war. Until the German occupation in March, 1944, of all of the Axis belligerents, Hungary alone fulfilled to the last letter the Geneva Convention

---

1 Kállay, **Hungarian Premier**, p. 369.

concerning prisoners-of war. In this respect Hungary often acted far more bravely and humanely than the neutral countries. Several thousand French escaped war prisoners were allowed complete freedom; British and American prisoners-of-war were courteously and humanely treated in Hungary. An evidence of their freedom of movement is that on March 19, 1944, when the Germans occupied Budapest, they collected most of the British and American prisoners-of-war at the horse races in Budapest.(2) Hungary did not discriminate among people seeking asylum, and Jews and non-Jews alike were admitted if they requested admission into the country. It is also a remarkable fact that the only Polish high school operating at that time was in Hungary.

Another question which needs to be answered is the relation between Hungary and the United States during the peaceful years between the two wars. This relationship was not at all without significance. Those men who represented the United States in Hungary: Major General Harry Hill Bandholtz; Jeremiah Smith, Commissioner General of the League of Nations; Ambassador John Flournoy Montgomery; and many others, represented the best type of their countrymen in Hungary—the upright, fair-minded, and humane Americans. Their works resulted in friendly political relations, and close economic connections between Hungary and the United States, and deepened the cultural relations for the benefit of both countries. In this work, the Hungarian-Americans also had a share.

---

2 On the same day that the Germans occupied Hungary, the Hungarian minister in Lisbon sent the following telegram to Budapest:

"Lisbon, March 19, 1944. Letters from American prisoners-of-war of the air force were read at the United States embassy here in the presence of highranking officers of the American air force, who happened to be passing through. These letters made the best impression. The ambassador cabled their names to Washington with the comment that a nation which treats prisoners of war in such a manner deserves the greatest consideration."

Kállay, **Hungarian Premier**, p. 344.

APPENDIX I

TREATY OF PEACE WITH HUNGARY

A TREATY BETWEEN THE UNITED STATES AND HUNGARY
SIGNED AUGUST 29, 1921, TO ESTABLSH SECURELY
FRIENDLY RELATIONS BETWEEN TWO NATIONS
THE UNITED STATES OF AMERICA
AND HUNGARY

Considering that the United States, acting in conjunction with its co-beligerents, entered into an Armistice with Austria-Hungary on November 3, 1918, in order that a Treaty of Peace might be concluded:

Considering that the former Austro-Hungarian Monarchy ceased to exist and was replaced in Hungary by a national Hungarian Government;

Considering that the Treaty of Trianon to which Hungary is a party was signed on June 4, 1920, and came into force according to the terms of its Article 364, but has not been ratified by the United States;

Considering that the Congress of the United States passed a Joint Resolution, approved by the President July 2, 1921, which reads in part as follows:

"**Resolved by the Senate and House of Representatives of the United States of America in Congress assembled,***"

"That the state of war declared to exist between the Imperial and Royal Austro-Hungarian Government and the United States of America by the joint resolution of Congress approved December 7, 1917, is hereby declared at an end.

"SEC. 4. That in making this declaration, and as a part of it, there are expressly reserved to the United States of America and its nationals any and all rights, privileges, indemnities, reparations, or advantages, together with the right to enforce the same, to which it or they have become entitled under the terms of the armistice signed November 3, 1918, or any extensions or modifications thereof; or which were acquired by or are in the possession of the United States of America by reason of its participation in the war or to which its nationals have thereby become rightfully entitled; or which, under the Treaty of Saint Germain-en-Laye or the Treaty of Trianon, have been stipulated for its or their benefit; or to which it is entitled as one of the principal Allied and Associated powers; or to which it is entitled by virtue of any Act or Acts of Congress: or otherwise.

"SEC. 5. All property of the Imperial German Government, or its successor or successors, and of all German nationals which was, on April 6, 1917, in or has since that date come into the possession or under control of, or has been the subject of a demand by the United States of America or any of its officers, agents, or employees, from any source or by any agency whatsoever, and all property of the Imperial and Royal Austro-Hungarian Government, or its successor or successors, and of all Austro-Hungarian nationals which was on December 7, 1917, in or has since that date come into the possession or under control of, or has been the subject of a demand by the United States of America or any of its officers, agents, or employees, from any source or by any agency whatsoever, shall be retained by the United States of America and no disposition thereof made, except as shall have been heretofore or specifically hereafter shall be provided by law until such time as the Imperial German Government and the Imperial and Royal Austro-Hungarian Government, or their successor or successors, shall have respectively made suitable provision for the satisfaction of all claims against said Governments respectively, of all persons, wheresoever domiciled, who owe permanent allegiance to the United States of America and who have suffered, through the acts of the Imperial German Government, or its agents, or the Imperial and Royal Austro-Hungarian Government, or its agents, since July 31, 1914, loss, damage, or injury to their persons or property, directly or indirectly, whether through the ownership of shares of stock in German, Austro-Hungarian, American, or other corporations, or in consequence of hostilities or of any operations of war, or otherwise, and also shall have granted to persons owing permanent allegiance to the United States of America most-favored-nation treatment, whether the same be national or otherwise, in all matters affecting residence business, profession, trade, navigation, commerce and industrial property rights, and until the Imperial German Government and the Imperial and Royal Austro-Hungarian Government, or their successor or successors, shall have respectively confirmed to the United States of America all fines, forfeitures, penalties, and seizures imposed or made by the United States of America during the war, whether in respect to the property of the Imperial German Government or German nationals or the Imperial and Royal Austro-Hungarian Government or Austro-Hungarian nationals, and shall have waived any and all pecuniary claims against the United States of America".

Being desirous of establishing securely friendly relations between the two nations;

Have for that purpose appointed their plenipotentiaries:

The President of the United States of America, U. GRANT-SMITH, Commissioner of the United States to Hungary; and Hungary, COUNT NICHOLAS BANFFY, Royal Hungarian Minister for Foreign Affairs;

Who, having communicated their full powers, found to be in good and due form, have agreed as follows:

ARTICLE I

Hungary undertakes to accord to the United States, and the United States shall have and enjoy, all the rights, privileges, indemnities, reparations or advantages specified in the aforesaid Joint Resolution of the Congress of the United States of July 2, 1921, including all the rights and advantages stipulated for the benefit of the United States in the Treaty of Trianon which the United States shall fully enjoy notwithstanding the fact that such Treaty has not been ratified by the United States. The United States, in availing itself of the rights and advantages stipulated in the provisions of that Treaty, will do so in a manner consistent with the rights accorded to Hungary under such provisions.

ARTICLE II

With a view to defining more particularly the obligations of Hungary under the foregoing Article with respect to certain provisions in the Treaty of Trianon, it is understood and agreed between the High Contracting Parties:

(1) That the rights and advantages stipulated in that Treaty for the benefit of the United States, which it is intended the United States shall have and enjoy, are those defined in Parts V, VI, VIII, IX, X, XI, XII and XIV.

(2) That the United States shall not be bound by the provisions of Part I of that Treaty, nor by any provisions of that Treaty including those mentioned in paragraph (1) of this Article, which relate to the Covenant of the League of Nations, nor shall the United States be bound by any action taken by the League of Nations, or by the Council or by the Assembly thereof, unless the United States shall expressly give its assent to such action.

(3) That the United States assumes no obligations under or with respect to the provisions of Part II, Part III, Part IV and Part XIII of that Treaty.

(4) That, while the United States is privileged to participate in the Reparation Commission, according to the terms of Part VIII of that Treaty, and in any other commission established under the Treaty or under any agreement supplemental thereto, the United States is not bound to participate in any such commissions unless it shall elect to do so.

(5) That the periods of time to which reference is made in Article 364 of the Treaty of Trianon shall run, with respect to any act or election on the part of the United States, from the date of the coming into force of the present Treaty.

ARTICLE III

The present Treaty shall be ratified in accordance with the constitutional forms of the High Contracting Parties and shall take effect immediately on the exchange of ratifications which shall take place as soon as possible at Budapest.

In witness whereof, the respective plenipotentiaries have signed this Treaty and have hereunto affixed their seals.

Done in duplicate in Budapest, this twenty-ninth day of August, 1921.

(SEAL.)   U. GRANT-SMITH,
          Commissioner of the United States to Hungary.
(SEAL.)   COUNT NICHOLAS BANFFY,
          Royal Hungarian Minister for Foreign Affairs.

LETTER FROM PRESIDENT FRANKLIN D. ROOSEVELT
TO REVEREND EDMUND VASVÁRY

THE WHITE HOUSE
WASHINGTON

March 15, 1939

My dear Mr. Vasvary:

I am glad to learn that The Hungarian Reformed Federation of America is planning to hold commemorative services on June fourth next in connection with the seventy-fifth aniversary of the battle of Piedmont, Virginia where Major General Julius H. Stahel exemplified such bravery that he later received the Congressional Medal of Honor. Men of Hungarian blood — many of them exiles from their fatherland — rendered valiant service to the cause of the Union. Their deeds of self-sacrifice and bravery deserve to be held in everlasting remembrance.

Very sincerely yours,
Franklin D. Roosevelt

Reverend Edmund Vasvary,
The Hungarian Reformed Federation of America,
1726 Pennsylvania Avenue, N. W.,
Washington, D. C.

259

BIBLIOGRAPHY

Primary Sources

Documents

Ádám, M., Juhász, Gy. and Kerekes, L. eds. Magyarország és a Második Világháború, Titkos Diplomáciai Okmányok a Háború Előzményeihez és Történetéhez (Hungary and the Second World War, Secret Diplomatic Documents on the Origins and History of the War). 3d ed. Budapest: Kossuth, 1966.

Bodula, Ida. The Hungarian Material of the Library of Congress. Microfilmed MS of the Mid-European Studies Center, No.131, 1951. Library of Congress. Washington, D.C.

Department of State. Papers Relating to the Foreign Relations of the United States. The Paris Peace Conference, 1919. 13 vols. Washington, D.C.: Government Printing Office, 1942-1947.

Diplomáciai Iratok Magyarország Külpolitikájához, 1919-1945. (Diplomatic Documents on Hungary's Foreign Policy, 1919-1945). Budapest: State Publishing, 1962.

Edward H. House Papers. In the Sterling Memorial Library of Yale University.

House of Commons. Documents on British Foreign Policy 1919-1939. 1st ser., vol. 2. London: H.M. Stationery Office, 1952.

The Hungarian Question in the British Parliament. Speeches, Questions and Answers in the House of Lords and in the House of Commons. London: Grant Richards Pub., 1933.

League of Nations. Danubian Studies I. Hungary. Chronology of political and economic events in the Danubian Basin, 1918-1936. Hungary. Paris: International Institute of Intellectual Cooperation, League of Nations, 1938.

The National Archives. Papers of the Department of State Relating to Internal Affairs of Hungary. File No. 864/1-864.911/16. Washington, D. C.

— Papers of the Department of State Relating to External Affairs of Hungary. File No. 711.64/1-711.6442A/110. Washington, D. C.

— Records of the Department of State Relating to Internal Affairs of Austro-Hungary and Hungary, 1912-1929. Microscopy No. 708. Washington, D. C.

— Records of the Department of State Relating to External Affairs of Hungary, 1919-1929. Microscopy No. 709. Washington, D. C.

Nemzetközi Szerződések, 1918-1945 (International Treaties 1918-1945). Budapest: State Publishing, 1966.

Papers and Documents Relating to the Foreign Relations of Hungary, 1919-1920. Budapest: Royal Hungarian Ministry for Foreign Affairs, 1939.

Szinai, M., and Szücs, L., eds. Horthy Miklós Titkos Iratai (The Confidential Papers of Miklós Horthy). Budapest: Kossuth, 1963.

United States. Department of State. America's Interests in Hungarian Struggle for Independence. Documents and State Papers. Vol. I, No. 5. Washington: Government Publishing, 1948.

United States Treaties, 1921-1923 (Harding). Treaty of Peace between the United States and Hungary. New York: American Association of International Conciliation, 1922. (January, 1922, No. 170.)

William C. Bulitt Papers. In the Sterling Memorial Library of Yale University.

Woodrow Wilson Papers. In the Library of Congress.

Contemporary Journals

Hungarian Newspapers

Az Est (The Evening). Budapest, daily.
Az Ujság (The News). Budapest, daily.
Magyar Nemzet (The Hungarian Nation). Budapest, daily.
Magyarország (Hungary). Budapest, daily.
Népszava (People's Voice). Budapest, daily.
Pester Lloyd. Budapest, daily in German.
Politikai Hiradó (Political Information). Budapest, daily.
Uj Nemzedék (New Generation). Budapest, daily.

Hungarian Newspapers in America

Amerikai Magyar Népszava (American Hungarian People's Voice). New York, daily.
Az Ember (The Man). New York, weekly.
Chicago Hungarian Tribune. Chicago, daily.
Otthon (Home). Chicago, daily.
Saint Louis és Vidéke (Saint Louis and District). St. Louis, daily.
Szabadság (Freedom). Cleveland, daily

American and Foreign Papers

Arbeiter Zeitung. Vienna, daily.
Bulletin Périodique de la Presse Hongriose, 1919. Paris.
Daily Mail. London.
Echo de Paris. Paris.
Izvestiia. Moscow.
Kommunisticheskii International. Moscow, daily.
Le Figaro. Paris, daily.
Le Temps. Paris, daily.
The Milwaukee Journal. Milwaukee, daily.
The Morning Post. London.
New York Herald.
The New York Times.

Pravda. Moscow, daily.
The Times (London).

Periodicals

American Political Science Review. Quarterly, published by the American Political Science Association. Menasha, Wisconsin.
The Annals of the American Academy of Political Science. Bimonthly. Philadelphia.
Eastern Review. Quarterly (in English, French, and German). Vienna.
The Eastern Quarterly. Published by the Institute for Eastern Affairs. London.
East European Accessions List. Monthly publication of the Library of Congress. Washington.
Foreign Affairs. Quarterly, published by Council on Foreign Relations. New York.
Foreign Policy Bulletin and Headline Series. Bimonthly, published by the Foreign Policy Association. New York.
The Hungarian Quarterly. Published by the Society of the Hungarian Quarterly. Budapest.
Journal of Central European Affairs. Quarterly, published by the University of Colorado.
Journal of **International Affairs.** Published twice a year, Columbia University.
Magyar Nemzeti Bibliográfia (Hungarian National Bibliography). Monthly, published by the National Széchenyi Library. Budapest.
Monthly List of Selected Articles. Published by United Nations Library. Geneva.
The Official Journal of the League of Nations. Monthly, published by the League of Nations. Geneva.
The Quarterly Journal of the Library of Congress. Published by the Library of Congress. Washington.
Political Science Quarterly. Published by Columbia University. New York.

The Review of Politics. Quarterly, published by the University of Notre Dame, Indiana.

Slavonic and East European Review. Published twice a year by the University of London.

Századok (Centuries). Bimonthly, published by the Society of Hungarian Historians. Budapest.

Diaries, Letters, Memoirs, and Speeches

Bandholtz, Harry Hill. **An Undiplomatic Diary.** Edited by Fritz-Konrad Kruger. New York: Columbia University Press, 1933.

Benes, E. **Memoirs of Dr. Eduard Benes.** London: Allen and Unwin, 1954.

Böhm, Wilhelm. **Im Kreuzfeuer Zweier Revolution.** Munich: Verlag für Kulturpolitik, 1924.

Eckhardt, T. **Regicide at Marseille: The Recollections of Tibor Eckhardt.** New York: American Hungarian Library, 1964.

Gafencu, G. **The Last Days of Europe.** New Haven: Yale University Press, 1948.

Hodza, M. **Federation in Central Europe, Reflections and Reminiscenses.** London: Jarrolds, 1942.

Horthy, Admiral N. **Memoirs.** New York: Speller, 1957.

Hory, András. **A Kulisszák Mögöt** (Behind the Scenes). Vienna: Published by the author, 1965.

— . **Még egy barázdát sem** (Not One Furrow). Vienna: Publishsed by the author, 1967.

Kállay, Nicholas. **Hungarian Premier: A Personal Account of a Nation's Struggle in the Second World War.** New York: Columbia University Press, 1954.

Kamenev, L. B. **Collected Works of V. I. Lenin.** Leningrad: Under the imprint of the Lenin Institute, 1924.

Károlyi, Michael. **Gegen Eine Ganze Welt.** Munich: Verlag für Kulturpolitik, 1924.

— . **Memoirs: Faith without Illusion.** New York: E.P. Dutton, 1957.

Kun, Béla. **Kun Béla a Magyar Tanácsköztársaságról** (Kun's Speeches, Articles, and Official Statements, 1918-1919). Budapest: State Publishing, 1958.

— . **La Republiqe hongroise ûes conseils.** Budapest: Editions Corvine, 1962.

Lansing, Robert L. **The Peace Negotiations.** Boston: Houghton Mifflin, 1921.

Montgomery, John F. **Hungary, the Unwilling Satellite.** New York Devin-Adair, 1947.

Nicolson, Harold. **Peace Making 1919.** New York: Grosset and Dunlap, 1965.

Palmer, Frederick. **Bliss, Peacemaker: The Life and Letters of General Tasker Howard Bliss.** New York: Dodd and Mead, 1934.

Pospelov, P.P., and eight others. **Vladimir Ilyich Lenin. Biografia.** Moscow: State Publishing, 1960.

Seymour, Charles. **The Intimate Papers of Colonel House.** 4 vols. Boston: Hougton, Mifflin, 1926-1928.

Secondary Sources

Doctoral Dissertations

Eckert, Frank. "The Rise and Fall of Béla Kun Regime in 1919." New York, 1965.

Pastor, Peter. "The Hungarian Revolution of 1918 and the Allies: A Study of International Relations." New York University, 1969.

Stercho, P. G. "Carpatho-Ukraine in International Affairs, 1938-1939." Indiana University, 1959.

Tökés, Rudolf L. "The Communist Party of Hungary: Its Origins and Role in the Revolutions of 1918-1919." Columbia, 1965.

Studies

Benes, Eduard. "Czechoslovakia Plans for Peace." **Foreign Affairs,** XXIII, No. 1 (1944), 26-37.

— . "The Organization of Postwar Europe." **Foreign Affairs,** XX. No. 2 (1942), 226-42.

Bethlen, Stephen, Count. "Hungary in the New Europe." **Foreign Affairs**, III, No. 1 (1925), 445-58.

Borsody, Stephen. "Modern Hungarian Historiography." **The Journal of Modern History**, XXIX, No. 3 (1952), 298-405.

Brown, Ph. M. "Foreign Relations of the Budapest Soviets in 1919: A Personal Narrative." **Hungarian Quarterly**, III, No. 1 (1937), 59-69.

Burks, Richard V. "Two Teleki Letters." **Journal of Central European Affairs**, VII, No. 1 (1947), 68-80.

Cattel, A. "Soviet Russia and the Hungarian Revolution of 1918-1919." Unpublished M. A. thesis, Columbia University, 1948.

Cattel, David T. "The Hungarian Revolution of 1919 and the Reorganization of the Comintern in 1920." **Journal of Central European Affairs**, XI, No. 1 (1951), 27-38.

Deák, István. "Budapest and the Hungarian Revolution of 1918-1919." **The Slavonic and East European Review**, XLVI, No. 106 (1968), 129-40.

Gál, Stephen. "Kossuth, America and the Danubian Confederation." **Hungarian Quarterly**, VI, No. 3 (1940), 417-29.

Hopper, Bruce. "The War for Eastern Europe." **Foreign Affairs**, XX. No. 1 (1941), 18-29.

Jánossy, Denis. "Kossuth and the Presidential Election, 1852." **Hungarian Quarterly**, VII, No. 2 (1941), 105-11.

Jászi, Oscar. "Dismembered Hungary and Peace in Central Europe." **Foreign Affairs**, II, No. 2 (1923), 270-81.

— . "Feudal Agrarianism in Hungary." **Foreign Affairs**, XVI, No. 4 (1938), 714-18.

— . "Kossuth and the Treaty of Trianon." **Foreign Affairs**, XII, No. 1 (1933), 86-97.

— . "Neglected Aspect of the Danugian Drama." **The Slavonic and East European Review**, XIV, No. 28 (1934), 492-506.

Katona, George M. "Hungary in the German Orbit." **Foreign Affairs**, XVII, No. 3 (1939), 599-610.

Kerek, Mihály. "Agricultural Land-reform in Hungary." **Hungarian Quarterly**, VI, No. 3 (1940), 395-417.

Kiss, Desider. "The Jews of Eastern Europe." **Foreign Affairs,** XV, No. 2 (1937), 330-39.

Krisman, Bogdan. "The Belgrade Armistice of November 1918." **The Slavonic and East European Review,** XLVIII, No. 110 (1970), 67-87.

Low, Alfred D. "The First Austrian Republic and Soviet Hungary". **Journal of Central Europan Affairs,** XX, No. 2 (1960) 174-203.

— . "The Soviet Hungarian Republic and the Paris Peace Conference." **Transactions of the American Philosophical Society,** N.S. LIII, No. 10 (1963), 1-91.

Móricz, Miklós. "Landless Agricultural Workers in Hungary." **International Labour Review,** XVII, No. 10 (1933), 518-30.

Mosely, Philip E. "Transylvania Partitioned." **Foreign Affairs,** XIX, No. 1 (1940), 237-44.

Nicolson, Harold. "Peacemaking in Paris: Success, Failure or Farce." **Foreign Affairs,** XXV, No. 1 (1947), 190-203.

Otto of Austria. "Danubian Reconstruction." **Foreign Affairs,** XX, No. 2 (1942), 243-52.

Paikert, G. C. "Hungarian Foreign Policy in Intercultural Relations, 1919-1944." **The American Slavic and East European Review,** XI, No. 1 (1942), 42-65.

— . "Hungary's National Minority Policies, 1920-1945." **The American Slavic and East European Review,** XII, No. 2 (1953), 201-18.

Pastor, Peter. "The Vix Mission in Hungary, 1918-1919: A Reexamination." **Slavic Review,** XXIX, No. 3 (1970), 481-98.

Pelényi, J. "The Secret Plan for a Hungarian Government in the West at the Outbreak of World War II ." **Journal of Modern History,** XXXVI, No. 1 (1964), 170-78.

Pethő, T. "Contradictory Trends in Policies of the Horthy Era." **New Hungarian Quarterly,** IV, No. 12 (1963), 115-31.

— . "Hungary in the Second World War." **New Hungarian Quarterly,** I, No. 3 (1960), 193-201.

Puskás, A.I. "Adatok Horthy Magyarország Külpolitikájához a Második Világháború Éveiben" (Data to Horthyite Hungary's Foreign Policy in the Years of the Second World War). Századok (Centuries), LXXXV, No. 1 (951), 83-115.

Temperley, Harold. "How the Hungarian Frontiers Were Drawn." Foreign Affairs, VI, No. 3 (1928), 432-47.

Vincent, S. "Carpatho-Ukraine in the International Bargaining of 1918-1938." The Ukranian Quarterly, VI, No. 3 (1954), 235-46.

Books

Angell. Sir Norman. The Peace Treaty and the Economic Chaos of Europe. London: Swarthmore Press, 1919.

Apponyi, Count Albert. Lectures in the U. S. on the Peace Problems and on the Constitutional Growth of Hungary. Budapest: Corvina, 1921.

Ashmead-Bartlett, Ellis. The Tragedy of Central Europe. London: Thornton Butterworth, 1923.

Basch, A. The Danube Basin and the German Economic Sphere. New York: Columbia University Press, 1943.

Bethlen, Count Stephen. The Treaty of Trianon and the European Peace. New York: Berkó, 1934.

Birinyi, Louis. The Tragedy of Hungary. Cleveland: Szabadság Publishing, 1924.

Bizony, Ladislaus. 133 Tage ungarischer Bolschewismus: Die Herrschaft Béla Kuns und Tibor Szamuelys. Leipzig and Vienna: Waldheim Eberle, 1920.

Borsody, S. The Triumph of Tyranny. London: Cape, 1960.

Buday, László. Megcsonkitott Magyarország (Dismembered Hungary). Budapest: Pantheon Irodalmi Részvénytarsaság, 1921.

A Companion to Hungarian Studies. Budapest: Society of the Hungarian Quarterly, 1943.

Czakó, István, How the Hungarian Problem Was Created. Budapest: Danubia, Ltd., 1934.

Csonka, Emil. **Habsburg Otto.** München: Uj Európa, 1972.

Deák, Francis. **Hungary at the Paris Peace Conference.** New York: Columbia University Press, 1942.

Donald, Sir Robert. **The Tragedy of Trianon: Hungary's Appeal to Humanity.** London: Thornton Butterworth, 1928.

Dreisziger, Nándor A. F. **Hungary's Way to World War II.** Toronto: Hungarian Helicon Society, 1968.

Gál, István. **Hungary and the Anglo-Saxon World.** Budapest: Officina, 1944.

Gower, Sir Robert. **The Hungarian Minorities in the Succession States.** London: G. Richards, 1937.

Halácsy, Dezső. **A Világ Magyarságáért** (For the Hungarians of the World). Budapest: Atheneum, 1944.

Herczeg, Géza. **Béla Kun: Eine historische Grimasse.** Berlin. Verlag für Kulturpolitik, 1928.

Hoptner, J. S. **Yugoslavia in Crisis, 1934-1941.** New York: Columbia University Press, 1963.

Horváth Jenő. **The Hungarian Question.** Budapest. Sárkány Printing Co., 1938.

Jánossy, Denis. **The Kossuth Emigration in America.** Budapest: Hungarian Historical Society, 1940.

Juhász, Gy. **A Teleki-kormány külpolitikája, 1939-1941** (The Foreign Policy of the Teleki Government, 1939-1941). Budapest: Akadémiai Kiadó, 1964.

Kaas, Baron Albert, and Lazarovics, Redor. **Bolshevism in Hungary: The Béla Kun Period.** London. G. Richards, 1931.

Kende, Géza. **Hungarians in America.** 2 vols. Cleveland. Szabadság, 1926.

Kertész, Stephen D. **Diplomacy in a Whirlpool.** Notre Dame: University of Notre Dame Press, 1953.

Kornis, Julius. **Education in Hungary.** New York: Berkó, 1932.

— . **Hungary and European Civilization.** Budapest: Akadémiai Kiadó. 1938.

Kovrig, Béla. **Hungarian Social Policies 1920-1945.** New York: Committee for Culture and Education of the Hungarian National Council, 1954.

League of Nations. **European Conference on Rural Life: Hungary.** Geneva: Published by the League of Nations, 1939.

Lengyel, Emil. **Americans from Hungary.** Philadelphia: J. B. Lippincott and Co., 1948.

Lukács, J. A. **The Great Powers and Eastern Europe.** New York: American Book Company, 1953.

Macartney, C. A. **Hungary: A Short History.** Chicago: Aldine, 1962.

— . **Hungary and Her Successors.** New York: Oxford University Press, 1937.

— . **October Fifteenth. A History of Modern Hungary, 1929-1945.** 2 vols. Edinburgh: Edinburgh University Press, 1961.

— . **Problems of the Danube Basin.** Cambridge: University Press, 1942.

— . and Maxwell, H. H. **Five Years of European Chaos.** London: Chapman and Hall, 1923.

— . and Palmer, A. W. **Independent Eastern Europe.** New York: Macmillan, 1962.

Mamatey, Victor S. **The United States and East Central Europe: A Study in Wilsonian Diplomacy and Propaganda.** Princeton, N.J.: Princeton University Press, 1957.

Nagy, Iván. **Hungarians of the Five Hemispheres.** Budapest: Corvina, 1935.

Nemény, Wilhelm. **133 Tage Bolschewistenherrschaft.** Berlin: Kulturliga, 1920.

Nyiri, Jules. **Ce que fut la Révolution d'octobre 1918 en Hongrie.** Paris: André Dalpeuch, 1926.

Opocensky, J. **Eduard Benes: Essays and Reflection.** London: Paul, 1945.

Piványi, Eugene. **Hungarian American Connections.** Budapest: No publisher, 1927.

Rutter, O. **Regent of Hungary.** London: Rich and Cowan, 1939.

Sangeorgi, G. M. **L'Ungheria dalla republica di Károlyi alla reganza di Horthy.** Bologna: Editione, 1934.

Seton-Watson, H. **Eastern Europe Between the Wars, 1919-1941.** Hamden: Archon, 1962.

Shepherd, B. Gordon. **The Last Habsburg.** London: Weidenfeld and Nicolson, 1968.

Sinor, D. **History of Hungary.** London: Allen and Unwin, 1959.

Standard Oil Company (New Jersey) and Oil Production in Hungary by MAORT 1931-1948. New York: Published by Standard, 1949.

Szadeczky, Lajos. **Revision of the Peace; Opinions of English, American, French, Italian, Polish and Swedish Writers and Politicians on the Paris Peace Treaties.** Budapest: Hornyánszky, 1926·

Szalay, J. **Igazságok Középeurópa Körül** (Truths about Central Europe). Paris: Collection Danubia, 1960.

Szántó, Béla. **Klassenkampfe und die Dictatur des Proletariats in Ungarn.** Vienne: Neue Erde, 1920.

Szatmári, E. **Im Roten Budapest.** Berlin: Kulturliga, 1919.

Szász, Zsombor. **The Minorities in Rumanian Transylvania.** London: G. Richards, 1927.

Szelpál, Árpád. **Les 133 jours de Béla Kun.** Paris: Fayard, 1959.

Teleki, Count Paul. **The Evolution of Hungary and Its Place in European History.** New York: Berkó, 1923.

Temperley, H. W. V., ed. **A History of the Peace Conference of Paris.** 6 vols. London: Frowdy, Hodder and Stoughton, 1920-1924.

Thompson, Charles T. **Peace Conference Day by Day.** New York: Columbia University Press, 1920.

Thompson, John M. **Russia, Bolshevism, and the Versailles Peace.** New Jersey: Princeton University Press, 1966.

Tyler, Royall. **Reports, Financial Position of Hungary.** Geneva: League of Nations, 1933.

Varjassy, Louis. **Révolution, Bolshevisme, Réaction: Histoire de l' occupation francaise en Hongrie, 1918-1919.** Paris: Jouve, 1934.

Vasváry, Edmund. **Lincoln's Hungarian Heroes.** Washington: Published by the Hungarian Reformed Federation of America, 1939.

Wickersham, George. **Opinion Regarding the Rights of Hungary and of Certain Hungarian Nationals under the Treaty of Trianon.** New York: Macmillan, 1928.